THE CRAF

THE CRAFT OF THE NOVEL

Colin Wilson

ASHGROVE PRESS, BATH

Published in Great Britain by
ASHGROVE PRESS LIMITED
4 Brassmill Centre, Brassmill Lane,
Bath, Avon, BA1 3JN

and distributed in the USA by
Avery Publishing Group Inc.
120 Old Broadway
Garden City Park
New York 11040.
Originally published by Victor Gollancz Ltd 1975

This edition 1990

ISBN 1 – 85398 – 006 – 4

Printed and bound by Billings,
Worcester

For Roald Dahl
that splendid craftsman

CONTENTS

drama and Brechtian drama. The solution for the novel?
Wells's amphibians. The novel and human evolution.

THE CRAFT OF THE NOVEL

ONE

The Craft of Creation

IN THE SPRING of 1974, I was engaged in teaching a creative writing course at Rutgers University in Camden, New Jersey. It was a new departure for me. Eight years earlier, I had made an attempt to teach creative writing at a college in Virginia, and come to the conclusion that it cannot be taught. Not only that: but that it *shouldn't* be taught. I felt that the basic principle of creativity is survival of the fittest. Creative writing is uphill work; the weak ones drop out; the strong ones persist and slowly become good writers. Encouraging would-be writers is like putting fertiliser on a garden full of weeds. My boss—in Virginia—agreed; at any rate, he allowed me to teach a course on Shaw instead. But at Rutgers, there was no way out. I was supposed to be teaching a course on existentialism, and when I arrived, I discovered it had been changed to creative writing. The dozen or so students were already enrolled. I had to go ahead.

I found them to be unexpectedly impressive. Technically, they were all excellent—immeasurably better than any comparable group of young English writers. They expressed themselves well and easily; the writing was nearly all of professional standard. I discovered that most of them had, in fact, taken a creative writing course before—some of them, two. It was as I began to look at it all more closely that I began to see what was wrong. They had been taught how to write like James Joyce, Ernest Hemingway, William Faulkner, Virginia Woolf. But they hadn't been taught *what to say*. Most of them had been given the standard advice to 'write about something you know about'. So, naturally, they wrote about themselves. Some of the 'stories' they handed in were straight autobiography, almost confessional. Others described some episode they had experienced at first hand—a friend who died in a car accident, a man who committed suicide after taking drugs, and so on. They wrote colloquially, casually, as if they were talking in a bar. But it all reminded me of a comment Faulkner made when asked his opinion of Mailer's generation: 'They write good, but they got nothin' to say.'

Had these students of mine really nothing to say? They were a picked group—the class had deliberately been kept small—all graduates, all intelligent and articulate. One of them had been a racing driver, another a drug pedlar, another an athlete—he was fascinated by the phenomenon of 'second wind'. When we talked over a jug of beer in the local bar, they had plenty to say for themselves. So obviously, they had 'something to say'. The trouble was, they didn't know what. They made me think of the comment of Shaw's evangelist: 'The kingdom of God is within you, and it would take a damn big pill to get it out.'

I saw I was confronted with an interesting problem. They had been taught creative writing, but not creative thinking. In the *Meno*, Socrates argues that each human soul already contains the knowledge of all things; it is merely a question of 'getting it out'. He demonstrates what he means by posing a question in geometry to an illiterate slave boy; the boy solves it by reasoning it out, aided only by questions from Socrates. All this leads Socrates to suggest that a teacher is not someone who *gives* knowledge; he is a kind of midwife who helps it to be born.

The question I asked myself was this: would it be possible to teach a creative writing course that would teach the students *what* to write? When a writer sits staring at a sheet of empty paper, it is not that he has nothing to say. The problem is usually the opposite. He has so much inside him that wants to get out that he dreams of an autobiographical novel the size of *War and Peace*. But it is all packed tight inside him, and there is only one narrow entrance for it to get out from: the tip of his pen. He may begin by imitating some other writer—Hemingway, Joyce, Salinger—not because he feels he has no voice of his own, but because he feels that any kind of a beginning might get the flow started. And after days or weeks of effort, the flow still hasn't started—or it is only a pathetic trickle. He begins to understand what Hemingway meant when he said that writing looks easy, but is actually the hardest work in the world.

The problem with such a writer is that he is not capable of being his own Socrates: of asking himself the right questions. It seemed to me that the problem, if I wanted to teach that basic trick of creation, was to teach him to ask himself the right questions, and then give some indication of how to go about finding the answer.

I say 'trick' because creation is not some ineffable mystery. It is basically the knack of solving problems. The writer sets himself a problem—of necessity, something that interests him personally—and attempts to get it on to paper. He may not aim at actually solving it—although that is the ideal—but merely *stating it clearly*. That is already more than halfway to a solution. But in order to state it clearly, he also has to solve a number of purely technical (or 'artistic') problems: where to begin, what to put in, what to leave out, and so on. Most creative writing courses devote a great deal of time to these technical problems. But that leaves the *real* problem, the problem at the heart of the novel, untouched. And the creative process must begin with this other kind of problem.

Let me give some examples of the problems in novels. Proust's *Remembrance of Things Past* is an obvious one. Somewhere near the beginning of volume one, the hero dips a small cake in tea, and bites it. He immediately experiences a tremendous feeling of delight. The taste has brought back his childhood—suddenly made it *real*. Which means that the past still lives in us, perfectly preserved, and that if we knew the trick, we could re-live it as if it were still happening today. But how can we gain access to these hidden treasures? Proust's solution is to try to conjure up the past, to re-create it, by writing about it in detail. The result is, of course, a great novel. Yet it fails to solve the problem. Brooding on the past may enable us to recall it in detail, but it does not re-create those sudden moments when it *becomes real.* In recent years, experimental psychology has solved Proust's problem. Dr Wilder Penfield, of McGill University, discovered that if certain spots in the temporal cortex of the brain were touched with a probe carrying a mild electric current, it would cause distant memories to 'play back' in the utmost detail, enabling the patient to re-live them. If Proust had known that, he might have opted for brain surgery instead of writing, and we would lack a great novel. Proust's attempt is interesting because it is an example of a problem that cannot be solved through the writing of fiction.

Consider a different type of problem. In *Roderick Hudson*, one of his earliest novels, Henry James writes about a young and talented sculptor, who is too poor to follow an artistic career. Rowland Mallet, a wealthy young New Englander, is paying a visit to his cousin when he sees one of Hudson's statuettes. It so impresses him that he offers to take Hudson back to Rome, and supply him with a studio and an allowance, so that he can follow his vocation. Suddenly, Roderick Hudson is free to work out the enormous potentialities he feels inside him, his belief that life offers an infinite number of possibilities to someone with imagination and genius.

The question James is posing to himself is at once personal and impersonal. He is 'identifying' with Roderick Hudson, and asking how such a person would go about the process of self-realisation. And he was also, by implication, asking about the possibilities of his own life. For James was in roughly the same fortunate position as his own Rowland Mallet; he was affluent enough to go to Europe and lead the kind of life he wanted to lead. He was young, imaginative, intelligent. What should *he* do with his life? Or, to put it in terms of his novel, what interesting possibilities could be made to develop from Mallet's act of generosity?

James, like Proust, failed to solve his problem. Artistically speaking, the book does not live up to its early promise. It begins well, then the life begins to drain away. Roderick becomes wildly infatuated with a pretty girl, neglects his fiancée, disappoints his benefactor, and ends by falling over a cliff. It all seems quite logical; there are no actual absurdities; but it is limited—at times, almost dull. What had happened to all those possibilities?

The answer is interesting. In those early pages, you can feel how much James is enjoying it; the writing has the quality of a pleasant daydream. And anyone who has ever written a novel —or even tried—will recognise this feeling. It is a sense of freedom, as if you were swimming in a warm sea. And yet not *complete* freedom. Like the sea, this element has its own rules, and if you want to dive or turn a backward somersault, you have to do it in a certain way. You feel the freedom most strongly in the early pages; then, as you go on, you become aware of the rules and laws. (And this is the point where most beginners lose heart and give up; the experienced writer, if he feels trapped, heaves a sigh and starts all over again.)

What happens, to be precise about this, is that once you have created a character, and involved him in a definite situation, you have limited his possibilities. Roderick Hudson might possibly design another St Peter's, fight a duel, swim the Tiber. But he will not commit rape or arson or murder, because James didn't make him that sort of character. As to Rowland Mallet, it is unlikely that he will do anything but stand in the wings and look wistful; *his* possibilities are distinctly limited even on page one. The novel has a definite set of inner rules and laws, and you become aware of these, as you become aware of the laws of gravity, by trying to move around under their influence.

A few years later, James made another attempt at the same theme—the idea of a young person 'facing life' (or, as James put it, 'affronting destiny'), possessed by a sense of boundless possibilities. This time he drew a deeper breath, set his scene more carefully, and brought more foresight to bear; the result is that *The Portrait of a Lady* is a far better novel than *Roderick Hudson*. But James still fails to answer the question of what a young person 'facing life' ought to do to realise all those possibilities. His heroine marries the wrong man, but decides at the end of the book that since she has made her bed, she had better lie in it. Once again, you become aware of what might be termed 'the law of diminishing possibilities' in the novel.

It is true that there *are* a few novels that do not begin from any single 'problem'. *War and Peace* offers a panorama of Russia during the Napoleonic war; *Ulysses* attempts to convey a cross-section of life in Dublin in one day; Dos Passos's *U.S.A.* tries to do the same for the whole United States during the early twentieth century. (James was apt to refer to this type of novel as a 'fluid pudding'.) These are the exceptions. Go to the heart of most novels, and you will find a question mark. This applies also, of course, to stories, which are simply novels on a smaller scale.

The first thing that struck me about most of the stories handed in by my students was that they had no particular shape, asked no particular question. A girl described going for a drive, getting into the wrong queue at the gas station (it was during the petrol shortage) and being sworn at by another driver. A man described how he had got married, and then had several love affairs, but the story reached no particular conclusion. Both admitted that they had written straight autobiography. It was odd how many of the students seemed to feel that all they had to do was simply to describe some event—autobiographical or otherwise—in a tight, economical style. Out of the first dozen or so stories submitted, only one seemed to have the germ of an idea. It was not, in fact, a story so much as a statement. It was called 'The Guitar', and the writer explained that he loved playing the guitar, and had the ambition of 'doing for the guitar what Melville did for the whale in *Moby Dick*'. But after this oddly unpromising beginning, he went on to contrast guitar playing—which was obviously the most important thing in his life—with all the other 'necessary' activities that struck him as meaningless: the dreary lectures he had to sit through, his boring part-time job. . . . And he was *saying* something, about his sense of inner-meaning, and about the failure of American urban civilisation to offer meaning to its young people. He described attending an audition, and all the showbiz talk, and his feeling that this was not what *his* guitar playing was all about. And he spoke of watching an old instrument-maker lovingly shaping a guitar, in deep, silent absorption. . . . It was all rough, and rather badly written; but he was the only one in the class who had started from that basic position—from 'the problem', the existential problem. He was trying to state what he *wanted*, and what he *didn't want*. And this gave his story the real forward movement of genuine creativity.

The story gave me the starting point I needed. At the next session, I went through all the stories, outlining their 'plots' (if that is the word) and reading parts aloud. It was a lengthy exercise, but not unrewarding; for what it brought out was that, with the exception of 'The Guitar', what they all lacked was a sense of what the writer wanted out of life, what he wanted to *become*. There was no attempt to project a vision or a wish. Shakespeare said art was holding a mirror up to nature; but it would be more accurate to say that it is a looking glass in which you see your own face. And why do you want to see your own face? For this interesting reason: that until you do, *you do not know who you are*. A story or a novel is the writer's attempt to create a clear *self-image*.

At which point, I cited that basic parable of the creative process, the short story *The Looking Glass* by Machado de Assis.

Five men, at a late-night party, are arguing about the nature of the soul. One of them expresses the startling opinion that man has not one soul, but two. One of them is inside, looking out. The other is outside, looking in. This 'external soul' is *anything you care for deeply*. In the case of Shylock, it was gold; in the case of Caesar, power; in the case of Heathcliff in *Wuthering Heights*, it was Cathy. (Heathcliff even says: 'I cannot live without my life; I cannot live without my soul.') In short, the 'outer soul' is some external factor which gives a sense of purpose, and therefore of identity.

The man who has advanced these views goes on to illustrate them with a story from his past. The son of poor peasants, living in a remote village of Brazil, he had been made a second lieutenant in the national guard at the age of twenty-five. Since there was intense competition for commissions, half the village was delighted, the other half full of envy. One of his aunts seemed dazzled with admiration. She kept pressing him to come and stay on her remote farm, and when he finally came, instructed all the servants that he was to be addressed as 'Senhor Lieutenant'. She even had an enormous mirror placed in his bedroom, so he could stand and admire himself. . . .

Then, one day, she was called away to the bedside of her sick daughter; the lieutenant was left in charge of the farm. Suddenly deprived of his daily ration of admiration, he began to feel oppressed. At this point, the slaves all took the opportunity to desert, and he was left totally alone. The sense of imprisonment deepened. After a week of solitude, he was beginning to feel desperate, close to insanity. And one day, glancing into the looking glass, he observed that his image seemed to be blurred, insubstantial. . . . He is possessed by fear of losing his reason. And then—he has an idea. He puts on his lieutenant's uniform. Instantly, his image in the mirror becomes solid and real. Every day, from then on, he puts on the uniform for a few hours and contemplates himself in the mirror. In this way, he concludes, he succeeded in retaining his mental balance until his aunt returned.

What Machado is pointing out is that human identity depends largely upon other people. We see ourselves reflected in the mirror of their eyes. It is true that we have a certain power to resist other people's opinion of us. If they regard us with contempt, it does not necessarily make us feel contemptible. But that is only when we have established an inner-feeling of identity. Such a sense of identity has to be created, either through the opinion of other people, or by inner-effort. Schubert's career as a composer was undoubtedly aided by the admiration of a circle of 'Schubertians'. On the other hand, Einstein created the special theory of relativity single-handed, while working as a clerk in a patent office; in this case, his sense of identity came from his development of his powers as a scientist.

Now when a young aspiring-writer settles down with a sheaf of paper and a pen, the question that confronts him is not simply 'What shall I write?', but 'Who am I? What do I want to become?' His *purpose* in writing is bound up with his sense of identity. If he has no clear sense of identity, or if his self-image is blurred, like that of Machado's hero, he may still be able to observe and describe the world around him accurately. But he will be incapable of creating anything large. His stories are spineless jellies, without that inner vertebrae of purpose.

The early novels of Bernard Shaw offer a fascinating insight into this process of creating a self-image. When Shaw came to London, at the age of nineteen, he was an abnormally shy young Dubliner, with no definite sense of what he intended to do with his life. A fellow-clerk had remarked casually that every young chap thinks he is going to be a great man, which led Shaw to recognise that he *had* always assumed he would be a great man. And since writing came to him as naturally as breathing—and since his cousin, Mrs Hoey, was a successful novelist—it seemed a sensible idea to try to achieve eminence through writing. Accordingly, after two years of living off his mother, Shaw began a novel tentatively entitled *Immaturity*. It is, as one might expect from a first novel, to some extent auto-biographical. The young hero, with the commonplace name of Robert Smith, arrives in London, takes a room, and unpacks his bag. There is no mistaking Shaw's enjoyment as he de-scribes every item in the young man's shabby case. There is a ring at the front doorbell. Smith goes to answer it; a pretty young Scots girl thanks him, and Smith, who had been think-ing of finding a more comfortable lodging, suddenly changes his mind. . . . It sounds as if Shaw intends a romance to de-velop. In fact, he doesn't quite know what he intends, Smith only teaching the Scots girl French. As the novel begins to sag, he introduces more characters, subsidiary heroes and heroines. Although I re-read it only two or three years ago, I could not recall the plot without taking the book down from my shelves. Smith himself—the man who should be the hero—is little more than an onlooker, watching the other characters fall in love and get married. Even the title of the book is misleading. You might be forgiven for assuming that a novel called *Imma-turity* would be an exercise in wry humour, like those early novels of Aldous Huxley, with the hero blushing and tripping over things and making a fool of himself. But Smith has a strong sense of his own value. He never makes a fool of himself. But he does nothing.

Shaw's problem was that he had no clear self-image. He had a certain recognition that he was stronger, more intelligent and clear-sighted than most people; but he had no idea of what to *do* with these qualities.

A period of working for the Bell Telephone Company gave him an idea. It struck him that engineers have some of the qualities he admired: a quiet efficiency, lack of self-conscious-ness. So for the hero of his second novel, *The Irrational Knot*, he took an engineer, an inventor. Edward Conolly is more-or-less working class. At a concert in a church hall (the Victorians were always having concerts in church halls) he meets Marion Lind, an upper-class young lady. She finds his quiet self-possession attractive, and accepts when he proposes to her. But she is a romantic; she longs for strong emotions, and after a while, her husband's level-headedness and efficiency begin to bore her. She runs off with a more romantic admirer—who deserts her, leaving her penniless. Her husband goes to fetch her back from New York, and the reader expects a grand reconciliation scene. But Shaw is too realistic not to see the consequences of their relationship. They decide to stay apart. The novel ends.

Shaw's basic problem now appears quite clearly. He wants to create his own type of hero—based, obviously, upon himself. The trouble is that since he doesn't know what he wants to do or where he wants to go, his own qualities appear to him to be negative. Robert Smith's qualities—of balance, level-headed-ness, ability to see things objectively—could only be demon-strated in contrast to the violent, emotional behaviour of the other characters. Conolly is slightly more positive—being an inventive genius—but his qualities are still not those that provide a novelist with exciting action.

Shaw had one of the most important qualities for literary greatness: persistence. Having failed twice, he tried again. His scientific genius had been unconvincing; he would try an artistic genius. The hero of *Love Among the Artists* is based on Beethoven. His music is derided as unplayable; he ignores the attacks and carries on. Inevitably, there comes a point in the novel where one of his works—it is a piano concerto—is presented, and is triumphantly successful. Logically, it ought to happen at the end. Shaw makes it happen in the middle. This leaves him with the problem of what to do for the remaining hundred or so pages. There are many subsidiary characters, of course—as in all his novels—and their loves and quarrels are used to pad out the final chapters. By that time, it is obvious that Shaw is trapped in the old dilemma. If his hero is a man of genius, a man driven by a sense of inner purpose, then love and intrigue and all the other romantic involvements that make up the average novel are irrelevant to his story. In that case, what can you make him *do*?

For the time being, Shaw acknowledged defeat. In his fourth venture into the field of the novel, he decided to abandon his attempt to create the Shavian hero. *Cashel Byron's Profession* is about a pugilist. Son of an egotistical actress, he runs away to Australia and becomes a prize-fighter; on his return to England, he falls in love with a wealthy heiress, a Shavian heroine who knows her own mind. Their romance is unconventional, but it ends conventionally in a happy marriage. This book came close to making Shaw a successful novelist. But in terms of the problem he was trying to solve, it is a step backward.

At the age of twenty-six, Shaw attended a socialist meeting. He read Karl Marx, joined the Fabian Society, and became a formidable debater. In July 1883, he started his fifth novel, *The Heartless Man*, finally published as *An Unsocial Socialist*. This time he knew exactly where he was going. More important, he knew what he wanted to become. Therefore, his task was simply to create a hero who would be a projection of himself. The basic theme was the same as in the early novels: that a man driven by a deep sense of inner purpose is relatively indifferent to personal happiness. His hero, Sidney Trefusis, is a passionately convinced socialist; he is also rich, intelligent and highly articulate. Therefore, unlike the heroes of the first three novels, he actually has something to *do*, even if it is only to talk. Shaw also devises an absurd plot—it is one of the lightest of the novels —to enable Trefusis to demonstrate his indifference to personal happiness. Before the novel opens, Trefusis has married a beautiful girl; but he finds that marital bliss bores him. 'Love cannot keep possession of me; all my strongest powers rise up against it and cannot endure it.' So he runs away from her, disguises himself as a working man, and gets a job as a gardener in a girls' finishing school. Naturally, the girls are intrigued by the gardener who has some of the mannerisms of a gentleman. When his wife turns up on speech day—she is a relative of one of the students—he is unmasked, but persuades her to return to London. The rest of the plot hardly matters; the book bounces along on a level of light-hearted absurdity. But what Shaw has done is to convert the Shavian hero from a passive, negative character into a man with whom the reader can 'identify'. Half the girls in the school fall in love with Trefusis; he flirts with them, but no romance develops—how could it when the whole point of the novel is that Trefusis has more important things to do than fall in love? What is clear is that Shaw has finally stumbled on the trick of uniting apparently irreconcilable opposites, romanticism and anti-romanticism.

Yet oddly enough, he had *still* not assimilated the hard-learned lesson. For when, a few years later, he made one more attempt to write a novel, he made all the mistakes of the earlier novels. It was to be about a young doctor named Kincaid, who moves into a wealthy country area to join a practice. His part-ner, Dr Maddick, is a weakling who flatters his rich patients—Shaw always needed a weakling to bring out the virtues of the hero. Maddick's wife is pretty, romantic and dissatisfied, and is obviously ready to have a love affair with Kincaid. If Shaw had stopped to think about it, he would have realised that a doctor makes as unsatisfactory a hero as an engineer or com-poser. His women patients may all be in love with him, but if he is not the type to go in for seduction, what can he *do* except stand around with his arms folded on his chest, looking strong and silent? After fifty pages or so, Shaw recognised that he had landed himself in a *cul de sac*, and the fragment was published after his death as *An Unfinished Novel*. It was his last attempt at a novel. But the lesson had finally broken through. An effective hero should spring from the writer's own self-image. He should reflect the writer's own striving, his own sense of purpose and identity. Above all, identity. In *An Unsocial Socialist*, he had

not merely 'discovered' himself; he had *created* himself. Or, to
be more precise, socialism had provided him with an 'external
soul', a force of conviction. (Later, there were others—his
belief in the superman and the life-force.) He turned the lesson
to good account in the plays he began to write a few years later;
his anti-romantic heroes—Tanner in *Man and Superman*,
Higgins in *Pygmalion*—were highly articulate men of strong
conviction. You cannot write a really effective play—or a novel
—about someone who doesn't know what he wants.

Again, an interesting illustration comes to hand. Nathanael
West is undoubtedly one of the 'significant' American writers
of the 'thirties—comparable, say, to Hemingway, Scott Fitzgerald and Faulkner. Yet by comparison, he is relatively unknown. Why? The answer lies in his two major novels, *Miss
Lonelyhearts* and *The Day of the Locust*. Miss Lonelyhearts is, in
fact, a young New York journalist whose job is to write answers
to letters from readers with problems. The job ought to be a
joke; in fact, he is sickened by the tragedies that pile up on his
desk. His features editor, Shrike, is an exhibitionistic cynic who
jeers at Lonelyhearts for taking life so seriously. The book is a
series of vignettes, in the manner of *The Waste Land*, all empha-
sising the stupidity and futility and meaninglessness of life.
Lonelyhearts is basically religious, but Shrike has made him
ashamed of it. 'He was thinking of how Shrike had accelerated
his sickness by teaching him to handle his one escape, Christ,
with a thick glove of words.'
    The novel undoubtedly achieves its main purpose—to convey
a sense of tragedy, of protest about life. Like Dostoevsky's Ivan
Karamazov, Miss Lonelyhearts feels like 'giving God back his
entrance ticket'. The trouble is that a major work of literature
cannot be produced wholly out of a sense of meaninglessness
and hopelessness—a point to which I shall have to return later.
The writer must have some idea of what he wants, as well as
what he doesn't want. West is so sickened by life that *everything*
nauseates him. The same unresolved problem vitiates *The Day
of the Locust*, a novel about Hollywood down-and-outs. The
boring scenes are boring, the futile scenes are futile, the sickening

scenes are sickening, but there is no positive pole to counter-balance all this negativity. West's problem was closely related to that of Shaw in those early novels—total lack of an 'external soul', a self-image. He recognised this, and tried to remedy it in his next novel. It was to be about a journalist who hires a young girl to try to penetrate a 'friendship club' run by a group of dissipated rich people. His only interest is in the 'story' he hopes to dig out. Then she disappears, and suddenly he ex-periences an urgent sense of involvement, a sense of the values he has always ignored. . . . But West never completed the novel. He died in a car crash—caused by his own carelessness—at the age of thirty-seven. His biographer Jay Martin remarks: 'West drove badly chiefly because he was quickly bored by the mech-anical routine of driving'—just as Miss Lonelyhearts was bored by the mechanical routine of living. We could say, then, that his death, like his books, was the outcome of his lack of a self-image. Miss Lonelyhearts is as negative and passive as Robert Smith in Shaw's *Immaturity*. Unlike Shaw, West never had time to develop a self-image. And so his work, for all its honesty and technical brilliance, remains largely unread.

It was in *Back to Methuselah* that Shaw finally stated the role of the self-image in all art. 'Art is the magic mirror you make to reflect invisible dreams in visible pictures. You use a glass mirror to see your face; you use works of art to see your soul.' That is to say, a novel is basically a kind of dream-mirror in which the novelist tries to reflect his essential self. Shaw's artist-spokesman concludes: 'You can create nothing but yourself.'

In practical terms, then, the first question to be answered by every would-be writer is not so much 'Who am I?' as 'Whom do I wish to become?' That is, if he had the power to transform himself by magic, as the fairy godmother transforms Cinder-ella, what identity could he choose? Julius Caesar, Leonardo, Columbus, Shakespeare, Henry Irving, Jack Dempsey, Charlie Chaplin? It sounds like a party game; in fact, it is the necessary first step towards creation.

There are, of course, a thousand different ways of utilising the self-image. In *An Unsocial Socialist*, Shaw used it in the most direct way, projecting an idealised version of himself. Frederick Rolfe, a paranoid, maladjusted homosexual, asked himself: 'What would I like to become?', and answered: 'The Pope.' The result, a minor masterpiece: his novel *Hadrian the Seventh*. In *War and Peace*, Tolstoy splits his self-image into two, and distributes it between Pierre and Prince Andrew—characters who are diametrically opposed. In *Crime and Punishment*, the murderer Raskolnikov is plainly an aspect of his creator, Dostoevsky, but this obviously does not mean that Dostoevsky ever contemplated murder, or wanted to be a murderer. Finally, when an author has achieved a clear self-image, he may prefer to keep it carefully *out* of his work. Flaubert's image is nowhere present in *Madame Bovary*; but *Madame Bovary* could only have been written by a man who had committed himself to literary creation as a monk takes a vow of celibacy. It could not have been created by a man without a powerful self-image.

The students obviously found the idea of the self-image fascinating but confusing. One of them asked: 'How can you have a self-image if you have no sense of purpose? I mean, you get up in the morning because you know you've got to go to school. And you go to school because you know you need a degree for a good job, and you're living in a competitive society. But that's not *your* purpose. It's been imposed from outside.' It was a good point, and I could see from the nods of the others that they all knew exactly what he meant. I had to try and point out that everybody has *some* purpose, even if it is submerged by boredom and habit. Everybody wants something. You only have to face the prospect of immediate death to realise that you have an extremely strong attachment to life. In the face of crisis, the submerged purpose rises like the Loch Ness monster. The problem is to get it to the surface. And this is as much a part of the task of creation as the actual writing. In fact, you may use the writing to help you to do it.

He still wasn't happy. 'I'd like to be a writer, but I can't believe that novels are important. If I take part in an anti-war march, it might possibly have some practical effect. But if you write a story, you know it's just imagination. No novel ever made any difference to the world. . . .'

That seemed to me to be one of the greatest misconceptions of all. The novel is not yet two and a half centuries old. But in that time, it has altered the consciousness of the civilised world. We say that Darwin and Marx and Freud have changed the face of western culture. But the influence of the novel has been greater than all three put together.

So in order that no writer should underestimate the importance of his trade, let us leave further discussion of the mechanics of creation until we have looked at the strange story of the novel.

TWO

The Mind-Moulders

ON THE MORNING of 6 November 1740, bookstalls in St Paul's Churchyard, Paternoster Row, and Little Britain displayed for sale a two-volume novel entitled *Pamela, Or Virtue Rewarded*. Anyone who opened the book casually would have seen nothing to indicate that he was holding one of the most revolutionary works of the age. The style was unexceptionable: at once formal and inelegant:

'Dear Father and Mother,
    I have had great trouble, and some comfort, to acquaint you with. The trouble is that my good lady has died of the illness I mentioned to you, and left us all much grieved for the loss of her; she was a dear good lady, and kind to all us her servants . . . Well, but God's will must be done!'
    [However] . . . I shall not be obliged to return back to be a clog upon my dear parents! For my master said, 'I will take care of you all, my good maidens. And for you, Pamela' (and took me by the hand; yes, he took my hand in front of them all), 'for my dear mother's sake, I will be a friend to you, and you shall take care of my linen.' God bless him! . . .

But the young master's intentions become clear, to the reader at least, in the postscript:

I have been scared out of my senses; for just now, as I was folding up this letter in my late lady's dressing room, in comes my young master! How I was frightened!

Apparently he has insisted on reading the letter, then paid her compliments that have left her blushing and trembling. . . .

Londoners had never read anything like it. Of course there had been novels before *Pamela*, including *Don Quixote*, *Robinson Crusoe*, and the risqué concoctions of Mrs Aphra Behn. But most of these were picaresque tales, 'true narrations' of the lives of criminals and vagabonds, often little more than travel books. *Pamela* described everyday events in everyday language. Everybody who read that first letter had an urgent desire to know whether she gets seduced. And the author, in spite of his high moral tone, showed no reluctance in supplying the details of Mr B.'s attempts to ravish Pamela. In Letter XXV, she describes how she has just got undressed when Mr B. leaps out of a cupboard and throws her on the bed. On this occasion, the presence of the housekeeper saves her. The wicked squire then sends her to a country house—under the pretence of sending her home—and places her in charge of a procuress. Next time he tries to rape her, the procuress holds her hands; but he is deterred when she has a kind of fit. For the readers of the eighteenth century, the impact of the sexual realism must have been like a kick in the solar plexus—not unlike that of the James Bond novels two centuries later.

The author of *Pamela* had stumbled on one of the great perennial plots of melodrama. But who *was* the author? No name appeared on the title-page. After a few weeks, London gossip began to mention the name of a fifty-year-old printer named Samuel Richardson. He seemed an unlikely candidate. Apprenticed to the trade at the age of seventeen, Richardson had married the boss's daughter, set up as a master printer, and become a fairly wealthy man. His friends knew he scribbled, in an amateurish way; but it was hard to believe that he possessed the kind of sustained creative power to write a work as original as *Pamela*.

What had happened, in fact, was that Richardson had been approached by a publisher who wanted him to write a Teach Yourself book on the art of correspondence—to include demands to creditors, letters of condolence, and so on. As he wrote, Richardson suddenly found himself swept away by a flood of inventiveness. He composed letters from deserted

women to their unfaithful lovers, letters from anxious fathers
to daughters living in the big city. . . . And at this point, he
recalled a story he had heard in his youth, of a virtuous servant
girl who had resisted all her master's attempts at seduction, and
ended by becoming his wife. Possibly Richardson may have
started to tell this story in the *Familiar Letters*, before it struck
him that it would be a waste of good material. He began to
write *Pamela* on 10 November 1739. It poured out at a rate of
three or four thousand words a day, and as the heap of manuscript deepened, and his involvement in the story increased, it
became clear that this was going to be a very long novel indeed.
By 10 January 1740, he had completed it—two hundred
thousand words, twice the length of the average modern novel,
—in a mere two months. When it appeared in November, it
made Richardson one of the most successful writers in England
—and incidentally, the first 'best-seller'.

In 1741, the *Pamela* craze swept across England to the Continent. To his surprise and embarrassment, the retiring
Richardson found himself hailed as a great moral reformer and
unique literary genius. A few ladies had doubts about the
realism of the attempted rape scenes, but the general view
seemed to be that they were justified by the lofty moral purpose.
By some curious artistic instinct, Richardson had produced
exactly the right combination of realistic sex and moralising.

Inevitably, the praise was followed by attacks. There were
many of Richardson's less fortunate fellow-authors who felt
he was having it both ways. It was all very well for clergymen
to praise *Pamela* from the pulpit and compare it to the Bible.
But it wasn't Pamela's virtue that was rewarded; it was her
refusal to sell her virginity for anything less than marriage.
Surely that wasn't virtue so much as commercial astuteness?
The point was driven home, rather unkindly, in a parody
called *Shamela* (probably by Henry Fielding) which purported
to reveal that Pamela was actually a lady of loose morals, and
that Mr B. had been the victim of a plot to entrap him into
marriage. (Fielding's later parody, *Joseph Andrews*, was altogether gentler, and became a classic in its own right; this time
it is Pamela's brother Joseph who defends his virtue against the

assaults of the nymphomaniac Lady Booby.) London's *literati* were obsessed by *Pamela*; producing books called *Anti-Pamela* became a minor industry in the early 1740s.

All the attacks, satires and parodies only increased the book's popularity. Richardson went on to write a sequel, in which Pamela discovers that her husband is being unfaithful, but ends by forgiving him. It sold as well as its predecessor, demonstrating that it was not entirely the sex that appealed to the public. And the critics continued to be enthusiastic. Doctor Johnson declared that Richardson had 'enlarged the knowledge of human nature', while Diderot said that *Pamela* made him feel as if he had actually lived through the experiences described in it—a comment that, more than any other, explains Richardson's popularity.

From the perspective of the twentieth century, we can see that even Richardson's greatest admirers failed to grasp the extraordinary nature of his achievement. Dr Johnson had the warmest regard for Richardson, but if anyone had told him the retired printer was one of the greatest innovators in literary history, he would have dismissed it with one of his bear-like growls. ('Your feeling does you more credit than your intelligence, sir.') Today, we can see that what made Richardson so remarkable was not that he enlarged our knowledge of human nature—he didn't—but that he *freed the human imagination*.

Nowadays, when we can switch on a colour television and be transported to Samarkand—or even the moon—it is almost impossible to imagine what it was like to be born three or four centuries ago. The words 'Shakespeare's England' or 'Johnson's London' evoke a colourful picture of sailing ships on the Thames and crowded taverns and coffee houses. In fact, the chief characteristic of life at that period must have been its sheer dullness. We can gain some idea of it from some of those Russian novels of the nineteenth century, with their small villages and shabby towns in which nothing ever seems to happen; *this* is closer to the truth of Shakespeare's England. There were theatres, of course, but only in the major cities. There were books—even novels—but only the rich could afford them; and, in any case, most people could not read. The majority of people lived and died without ever seeing beyond the same daily routine that their parents and grandparents had known. It was as if they were born in a yard with high walls, and they never saw over the walls.

Standards of education slowly improved; more people learned to read. But still, there was nothing much *to* read. This explains the immense success of Addison and Steele's *Spectator*, which began to appear—daily—in 1711. It was not a newspaper in our sense; it rambled cheerfully from subject to subject. But it *was* a breakthrough in communication; one single voice was speaking to several thousand Englishmen at the same time, as they drank their coffee or mulled ale. And the most unexpectedly popular of those *Spectator* articles were those dealing with the absent-minded old knight Sir Roger de Coverley. They were in a low key; they talked about his everyday life, his relations with his servants and tenants. His creators intended him to be an example of the kind of amiable old Tory landowner they approved of—a convenient starting point for discussions about morality and social duty. To everyone's surprise, he became the most popular character in the *Spectator*; readers could not get enough of him. Addison and Steele had stumbled on a discovery that is known to every television producer: that people enjoy reading about everyday events, because they can 'identify' with the characters involved. In effect, Addison and Steele invented the modern novel.

Most critics would give that credit to Defoe, whose *Robinson Crusoe* appeared eight years later, in 1719. But *Robinson Crusoe* really belongs to that earlier picaresque tradition of *Lazarillo de Tormes* and *Don Quixote*. Besides, Defoe was a reporter rather than an inventor—Crusoe was based on Alexander Selkirk, an actual castaway whose life story was purchased by Defoe for a few crowns. But the popularity of *Crusoe* certainly demonstrates that the reading public was ready for the advent of the novel. If it had not been immediately pirated by other publishers, it would have made Defoe a rich man.

Literature had never been so much in demand. There was a new audience of female readers, middle-class women with time on their hands. In that age of cheap domestics, the wives of country gentlemen had little to do but embroider cushion covers and read whatever happened to be available. Volumes of sermons sold out on publication day. There was a wide demand for newspapers, and for journals like the *Spectator* and Johnson's *Rambler*. There were also novels, with titles like *The Royal Slave, Ornatus and Artesia, The Jamaica Lady*, and they were about far-away places and far-fetched events. By present-day standards, most of them were little more than long short-stories. Few had any literary merit; they were mostly Grub Street productions, churned out by hacks for money. Still, they were eagerly snatched up by a public that was developing an increasing appetite for journeys of the imagination.

And at this point, the retired printer, with his passion for psychological analysis, wandered on to the scene. *Pamela* was the book everyone had been waiting for. It satisfied a deep, urgent demand that had been building up for decades. It differed from early novels as much as cinema differs from the theatre. The reader could become *totally involved* in it, like entering another world, living someone else's life. We must try to make an imaginative effort to grasp what this meant. Imagine the daughter of a country clergymen, on a wet after-noon, with nothing much to do but stare at the rain. She opens *Pamela*—and it is as if she has walked out of her own home into Mr B.'s country house. For the next few hours, she *is* Pamela. She is moved to tears by the indignities and shocked by the attempts at rape. At certain points she lays down the book and drifts into a daydream, wondering how she would react to being kissed by Mr B. . . . In two hours, she lives through more experience than in two years of daily routine. *Pamela* may be long, but for her it is not long enough; she would like it to go on forever. She has made the discovery that 'living' is not necessarily a matter of physical experience, that the imagina-tion is also capable of voyages. Today, this sounds utterly banal; in 1740, it was as startling as discovering you could fly by flapping your arms. Richardson had taught the European mind to daydream.

*

Perhaps the oddest part of the story is that historians do not seem to have noticed the revolutionary significance of *Pamela*. They recognise it as a literary landmark, of course. They also observe that there was an immense gulf—psychological and cultural—between the age of Swift and the age of Dickens. But they are inclined to set it down to social causes—wars, upheavals, the Industrial Revolution. A glance at the history books shows this to be untrue; there was nothing very revolutionary happening in Europe around 1740. As to the Industrial Revolution and the French Revolution, they came fifty years later, when the imaginative revolution had already transformed Europe. They were the consequences, not the cause.

No, it was Richardson's *Pamela* that brought about the great change. To grasp what happened, you only have to turn to Pepys's *Diary*, written a hundred years earlier. Pepys is always describing what he *does*—a trip on the river, a visit to the theatre—but never what he thinks or feels. It doesn't strike him that a sheet of paper is a medium for *talking to yourself*. If you then turn to almost any diary written in the century after Richardson, you will find it by contrast full of reflections and meditations. For that, Richardson was chiefly responsible. He was the first to treat prose as a medium for expressing thoughts and feelings—what his contemporaries called 'sentiments'—rather than actions. His novels were immensely long, but they are never boring, because Richardson himself was never bored by them. The ideas and reflections flow out in a slow, broad, majestic stream like the largo of a symphony. Johnson said that anyone who read Richardson for the story would hang himself, and it is true there is very little external action. The drama takes place *inside* the characters. In effect, he had taught his contemporaries that the written word can be used as a vehicle for inner voyages. Eighty years later, the mystical painter Caspar David Friedrich expressed the essence of the discovery when he said: 'Shut the living eye; then you begin to see with the spiritual eye.'

The literary history of the next few decades was so rich that, if this were a chronological account of the novel, I would feel obliged to devote several chapters to it. For while *Pamela* was the first novel to make an impact on a 'mass audience', it was by no means the last. And, by an interesting coincidence, the first circulating library was established in London in the same year *Pamela* was published. This was important because, at three shillings a volume, *Pamela* was too expensive for most people (at a time when the average labourer earned ten shillings a week). Everyone could afford the few pence per volume charged by the library. So the means of circulating *Pamela* to the widest possible audience was now at hand. Within twenty years, every small town in England had a library, and England had become, in the words of Doctor Johnson, 'a nation of readers'. It meant that a novelist with a 'message'—like Richardson—had an enormous ready-made audience. The novelist could achieve the kind of impact that would have been envied by Savonarola. He was in a position to alter the manners —and moral attitudes—of nations. Not since Luther had nailed his ninety-five theses to the church door in Wittenberg had the written word exercised so much influence.

Inevitably, the public clamoured for more novels like *Pamela*. The hacks of Fleet Street would have been happy to oblige, if they had had any idea of what made *Pamela* so successful. Fielding's *Tom Jones* was immensely popular; so were Smollett's *Roderick Random* and *Peregrine Pickle*; so was Sterne's *Tristram Shandy*. But while Fielding preached as unashamedly as Richardson (in the introductory chapters to each book of *Tom Jones*), and Sterne adopted his leisurely pace and psychological realism, none of them could reproduce that peculiar quality of obsession that made *Pamela* such compulsive reading. Only Richardson himself understood the secret, as he proved in his masterpiece *Clarissa Harlowe* (1748). *Clarissa* is more than twice as long as *Pamela*—making it one of the longest novels in literary history. There is almost no action. It concerns a virtuous middle-class girl who is lured to a brothel by a self-centred rake, who lays siege to her virtue, and finally drugs her and rapes her. Clarissa dies of shame and humiliation, and her seducer is killed in a duel. This slender plot is dragged out for half a million words. The formula should have guaranteed failure. In fact, its success surpassed even that of *Pamela*. Why? V. S. Pritchett expressed it concisely when he called *Clarissa* 'a novel about the world seen through a keyhole'. 'Prurient and obsessed by sex, the prim Richardson creeps on tiptoe nearer and nearer, inch by inch . . .; he beckons us on, pausing to make every kind of pious protestation, and then nearer and nearer he creeps again, delaying, arguing with us in whispers, working us up until we catch the obsession too. . . . Nothing short of the rape of Clarissa Harlowe by a man determined on destroying her can satisfy Richardson's phenomenal daydream with its infinite delays.'

Oddly enough, there *was* one other writer who grasped the reasons for Richardson's success, even before the publication of *Clarissa*. John Cleland was a poverty-stricken bohemian who had spent most of his forty years in debtor's jails. In 1745, he embarked on his own tale of an innocent country girl pursued by lustful males. The chief difference between *Fanny Hill* and *Clarissa* is that Cleland includes detailed descriptions of sexual intercourse. He had written the first pornographic novel. Since he sold it outright for twenty pounds, he derived no benefit from the twenty thousand pounds it went on to make for its publisher; but the government was sufficiently alarmed by it to offer Cleland a pension on condition he wrote no more dirty books. His name is seldom mentioned in histories of literature; yet he was, in his way, as interesting a revolutionary as Richardson. For he had turned the novel to a new use: to serve as a substitute for the physical presence of a naked member of the opposite sex. Disgusting or not, it was a kind of breakthrough for the human imagination.

Still, you only have to compare *Fanny Hill* with *Clarissa* to grasp the essence of Richardson's greatness. It is the *seriousness* of *Clarissa* that impresses; it has some of the same realistic, tragic yet exalted quality that is found in the novels of Dostoevsky. Like all great art, it taught people to take themselves, and their lives, more seriously. This was the element in Richardson that Smollett, Sterne, even Fielding, could not reproduce. 'Experience hunger' is fundamental in all human beings, because we need experience to mature. (The stories of

Chekhov are about the agony of people to whom nothing *ever happens*.) Books *can* provide a substitute-experience—in fact, a wider range of experience than is possible in reality—but if it is to provide the spiritual vitamin necessary for growth, a novel must involve the reader's deepest emotions. *Tom Jones* and *Tristram Shandy* are great novels, but no one could claim they give the reader the feeling of having lived through the events they describe. Only Richardson seemed to have that secret. At least, in England. . . .

In the year *Pamela* appeared, a young Swiss vagabond had just moved to Paris and taken a mistress. At twenty-nine, Jean Jacques Rousseau was unknown, and seemed likely to remain so. His problem was his inability to apply himself to anything, complicated by a tendency to self-pity. In every way, he was apparently the opposite of the industrious Richardson. He had been apprenticed to a lawyer, then to an engraver, and had abandoned both occupations. He had also been a servant.

His problem was one that has become increasingly common. He was too intelligent for the circumstances he was born into. Son of a watch-maker, he had lost his mother in childhood and his father's idea of education was to spend whole nights reading aloud historical novels to the child. His favourite novelist was the author of immense, tedious historical novels called La Calprenède. They lacked plausibility and realism, but they developed Rousseau's capacity to daydream—the capacity that then proceeded to make his life almost impossible. They fed his imagination and destroyed his ability to cope with the real world. The result is that, from the point of view of integrity and consistency, Rousseau is among the least admirable of men of genius. In his autobiography he tells candidly how he stole a scarf and accused a housemaid of the theft, so she was dismissed. When his mistress bore him children, he deposited them without hesitation on the doorstep of the Foundlings Home.

He was almost forty before his luck began to turn. In 1749, his friend Diderot was imprisoned at Vincennes, for publishing a work of atheistic tendencies called *Letter on the Blind*. One hot

summer afternoon, on his way to visit him, Rousseau saw in a
newspaper the announcement that the academy of Dijon was
offering a prize for the best essay on the question of whether art
and science had improved mankind. 'All at once, I felt myself
dazzled by a thousand sparkling lights. . . . I felt my head
whirling in a giddiness like that of intoxication.' He had to sink
down under a tree, overwhelmed by the flood of ideas; in half
an hour or so he had sketched out the *Discourse on Sciences and
Arts* that was to win the prize and make him famous.

Rousseau's controversial thesis was that science and art
have not improved human manners; only made man more
corrupt and vicious. Primitive man, he said, must have been
innocent, self-sufficient and happy. Then came Society, the
idea of private property, and all the machinery of tyranny and
injustice used by the strong to repress the weak.

Understandably, his contemporaries assumed he was recom-
mending that man should go 'back to nature' and become a
'noble savage'. (Voltaire wrote sarcastically to him: 'Come and
have a drink of my cow's milk with me. If you want to eat grass
you can do it here.') But the simplification caught the essence
of what he was saying. His work was an explosion of yearning.
His imagination created an ideal world, peopled with dignified,
independent, benevolent human beings.

With this intense perception of this difference between the
ideal and the real, Rousseau was just the man to give expression
to the deepest instinctive cravings of his age.

Rousseau moved to Mortmorency, in Switzerland, and fell
in love with a countess; she preferred to remain faithful to a
current lover, so Rousseau sublimated his desires in a novel:
Julie, or the New Héloise. It appeared in 1760, twenty years after
Pamela.

If *Pamela* was a volcanic eruption, *Julie* was an earthquake.
Probably no other novel has had a greater influence on the
intellectual history of Europe. (It is ironic that it is now un-
obtainable in England, and available only in a 'shortened'
edition in America.) It brought Rousseau unimaginable
celebrity. Libraries hired it out *by the hour.* One contemporary
records that women would kiss a scrap of paper on which

Rousseau had written, and pay any price for the glass from which he had drunk. The philosopher Kant, by whom his fellow-townsmen regulated their watches, only once forgot to take his afternoon walk, and that was when he was absorbed in *The New Héloise*.

Richardson died in 1761, just before the novel appeared in English. This was perhaps just as well; he would have ex-perienced deep misgivings about the genie he had let out of the bottle. The highly moral Richardson would undoubtedly have regarded *Julie* as a shocking and disgusting book. For, like *Pamela* and *Clarissa*, it is about seduction; the difference is that the heroine does not try to escape her fate; she embraces it with pleasure.

The plot of *La Nouvelle Héloise* is, as Rousseau pointed out, even simpler than that of *Pamela*. Baron D'Etange hires a good-looking young tutor, Saint-Preux, for his daughter Julie and her cousin Claire. As the novel opens, Saint-Preux writes to Julie confessing he is in love with her. (Rousseau follows Richardson in writing the novel in the form of letters.) After some hesitation, she admits she feels the same. Saint-Preux goes away to place himself beyond temptation. But the Baron is so pleased with his daughter's progress that he recalls him. And one night, Julie admits Saint-Preux to her bedroom, and they become lovers.

This, of course, was the episode that made *Julie* the most successful and controversial novel of the century. Rousseau's moral tone is as exalted as Richardson's, but he argues that if a man and woman are truly in love, they have a right to con-summate it in defiance of social conventions. This made *Julie* more shocking than *Clarissa*—because, for some reason, the idea of a young girl surrendering her virginity without being married has always been infinitely titillating, to male and female readers alike. In fact, the appeal of *Julie* was so enor-mous that it ran through seventy editions in France before 1800. (Rousseau seized the opportunity to insert long essays on his educational and social theories.)

Julie is redeemed by a moral ending. The Baron refuses to allow Saint-Preux and his daughter to marry. Saint-Preux goes off on a round-the-world voyage with Anson, and Julie marries her father's choice, De Wolmar. When Saint-Preux returns, he visits their home—on the husband's invitation—but although they are still in love, they decide not to betray De Wolmar. Julie dies as the result of an accident, and Saint-Preux, now ennobled by self-sacrifice, becomes the tutor of her children. . . .

Female readers were even more moved by Julie's death than by Clarissa's. And, what is more surprising, young men learned to cry too. *Julie* released a Niagara of tears. This was not simply on account of Saint-Preux's bereavement. It was because Rousseau had done something that, up to that time, was unique in literature. He had induced a *mood* of tremendous sadness and longing. It was the romantic mood: distant trumpets, silver mists, fading sunsets that tempt the soul to leave this dim vast vale of tears. . . . Rousseau was a composer as well as a novelist, and the last pages of the novel have an effect like music.

But, more important, there was also the hint of a whispered question. Is man a god? Why, if not, is he capable of these strange ecstasies, this soaring, bird-like sense of freedom? Is man a victim of some practical joke of the gods? Is he deliberately tormented by glimpses of freedom he can never attain? This is where Rousseau is superior to Richardson (as, with characteristic lack of modesty, he himself pointed out). Clarissa's tragedy remains personal; Rousseau seemed to be asking questions about the whole universe, the life of man, the meaning of existence. It is true that he did not *state* these questions openly; but he set the mood. The reader who closed *Julie* felt as if he was returning from an immense distance. Rousseau was teaching him to ask questions that had so far been asked only by a few philosophers. Richardson taught Europe to dream, but Rousseau taught it to think.

It now only remained for someone to state Rousseau's question in so many words. This happened in the country that we now regard as the original home of romanticism: Germany. Two poets of genius were responsible.

At the age of twenty-three, Johann Wolfgang Goethe fell violently and hopelessly in love; and, like Rousseau, he poured his miseries into a novel. The name of its hero deliberately rhymed with his own; he called it *The Sorrows of Young Werther*.

Werther is a painter, staying in a small German town. When he meets Charlotte, he falls in love at first sight, and his love takes on the character of a disease, a fever, an obsession. Goethe had brought something new to literature. Saint-Preux and Julie had been in love, but they soon avowed it and spent the night together, like any other normal pair of eighteenth-century lovers. By comparison, Werther's passion for Charlotte has a morbid, almost religious intensity. Lotte is not just a woman; she is a symbol of all man's longings, the 'eternal womanly'. So when she marries another man, it is more than just a personal loss for Werther; it is like a mocking whisper that all man's highest ideals are unattainable. In desperation, Werther finally declares his love; Lotte flees, and he shoots himself. Hearing of his death, she collapses, reinforcing the reader's suspicion that she was in love with him all along.

Goethe was not only asking whether life is essentially tragic; he was also expressing the feeling that *man does not need society*. Saint-Preux was, on the whole, a normal, sociable human being; Werther is a Man on His Own, an Outsider. 'I am completely alone, and find life so enjoyable, in this spot which was created for souls like mine. I am so happy, so absorbed in the sensation of a tranquil existence. . . .' Trees and mountains mean more to him than human beings. Forty years earlier, Alexander Pope had said that the proper study of mankind is man. Rousseau and Goethe had created a new conception of man as a being who stands alone, outside society, a kind of god in exile. They were saying that the proper study of mankind is the Infinite.

It might seem that, after *The New Héloise* and *Werther*, it would be impossible for anyone ever again to achieve that same stunning emotional impact on the public. It *was* achieved, however, seven years after the publication of *Werther*, this time by a play. The author was Friedrich von Schiller, who had started it when he was eighteen. Understandably, *The Robbers* now strikes us as crude, melodramatic and absurd. In its own day, it was regarded by many people as one of the most dangerous books ever written. Nietzsche quotes an old German military man as saying: 'If God had known Schiller would write *The Robbers* he wouldn't have created the world.'

Like *Julie* and *Werther*, it was a product of deep frustration. Schiller was the son of an army surgeon, and at an early age he was signed over into the service of his father's employer, the Duke of Württemburg. The Duke decreed that Schiller should be a doctor. Schiller had no interest in medicine, but he had a devouring passion for literature. The Duke disapproved, and ordered him not to write. At the age of twenty, Schiller became a doctor, and also borrowed the money to publish *The Robbers* at his own expense. (It was, of course, anonymous.) Two years later, it was presented at a Mannheim theatre; Schiller sneaked off to attend the first night. A large audience, crowded with intelligentsia from surrounding cities, received it with rapture. Listening to the applause from his obscure corner of the theatre, it dawned on Schiller that he had become famous.

The Duke ordered Schiller's arrest. (This was more serious than it sounds; a writer named Schubart had been arrested for satirising the Duke, and had been held in a dungeon for ten years without trial.) Schiller fled, and became a salaried dramatist at Mannheim, then a professor of history at Jena, and a close friend of Goethe. Overwork undermined his health, and he died of tuberculosis at the age of forty-five, reinforcing the romantic feeling that geniuses die young because they are too good for this earth.

The Robbers is a violent and exaggerated drama of protest against tyranny; not human tyranny, but against life itself, against man's lack of spiritual freedom, against God. It is a story of two brothers, Franz and Karl Moor, one a devious schemer, the other an impetuous idealist. They are also in love with the same girl. Franz somehow persuades their father to disinherit Karl. When Karl hears the news, his rage is tremendous; he calls upon his fellow-students to join him and become a band of robbers. They will murder, rape, pillage, throw off all the false restraints of society. Man is born for total freedom,

Karl declaims. 'Am I to squeeze my body into stays and strait-lace my will in the nets of the law? What might have risen to an eagle's flight has been reduced to a snail's crawl by law. Never yet has law created a great man; it is freedom that creates giants and heroes.'

Whereupon, Karl and his robbers become the scourge of the countryside, expressing their freedom in the form of murder, robbery and rape (they violate a whole nunnery)—but always with the highest of motives. The incredible complications of the plot and its absurd ending do not concern us here. Franz is burned to death, the father goes mad, Karl murders his beloved —at her own request—then gives himself up.

From the twentieth-century point of view, *The Robbers* was the greatest influence of all. Its mad dialectic of freedom inspired generations of visionaries, dreamers and revolutionaries. 'Never yet had law created a great man; it is freedom that creates giants and heroes.' Therefore the laws of an unjust society deserve to be broken, and criminal violence is justified. We no longer cry over the death of Julie or Werther, but two centuries after *The Robbers*, a baffled Los Angeles jury would hear Karl Moor's arguments from Charles Manson, who had ordered his followers to make war on the 'pigs' (bourgeoisie). And they have been echoed by every kind of political activist, from the Russian anarchists of the 1890s to the Symbionese Liberation Army that kidnapped Patricia Hearst.

It seems incredible that *Pamela* and *The Robbers* were written a mere forty years apart. They seem to be separated by a gulf of centuries. Less than ten years later came the French Revolution, for which Rousseau and Schiller are about equally responsible. The age of order—and authority—was over; the modern age had arrived. It had all started a mere fifty years earlier, in the midst of the age of Dr Johnson, when *Pamela* appeared on the London bookstalls. Four writers had influenced the course of history more than the torture chambers of the Inquisition or the armies of Frederick the Great.

Schiller was right; the novel—and to a lesser extent, the play—

represented a new dimension in human freedom. The novel's range was wider than the play's; it could create imaginary landscapes and whole historical epochs. It could turn frustrated vicars' daughters—like Jane Austen and Emily Brontë—into creators. And during the nineteenth century, its empire expanded faster than that of Alexander the Great or Julius Caesar. Gothic novelists explored new realms of fear with stories of demons, werewolves and vampires. Scott invented a kind of time-machine that could transport his readers to the Holy Land with Richard the Lion Heart or the battlefields of France with Quentin Durward. Balzac created whole cities with their cobbled streets and dark houses. Dickens was so fascinated by his power to make a generation laugh or cry that he finally killed himself with the strain of public readings. (And he was, incidentally, the father of a new genre, when Inspector Bucket of *Bleak House* introduces himself as a 'detective officer', the first time the word had been used.) Dostoevsky brought the novel back to its metaphysical concern with human freedom, and once again expressed the feeling that, for all his suffering, man may be more god-like than he realises. And, as the century drew to a close, H. G. Wells transported his readers to the moon, and showed the earth invaded by monsters from Mars. It seemed there were no limits to the human imagination; using this vehicle of the novel, it could explore all space and time.

But perhaps its greatest achievement was to free man *from himself*, to open up new possibilities of evolution. There is a scene in Dickens's *Christmas Carol* where the Ghost of Christmas Past shows Scrooge a vision of himself as a schoolboy, sitting in a schoolroom when all his friends have gone to their homes for the holiday. But he is not unhappy; he is reading the *Arabian Nights*, and his mind is in Baghdad with Ali Baba. *A Christmas Carol* is not one of Dickens's more ambitious works, but it is one of his most interesting. Scrooge has become negative through miserliness; he is locked in the most inescapable of prisons: habit. By making him aware of the multiplicity of the reality that surrounds him, the spirits have presented him with the secret of self-transformation. It was a secret that eluded

Schiller; Karl Moor talked of freedom but he never found it. Through his glimpses of other times, other places, Scrooge has become more free, more god-like. Not much, perhaps, but a step in the right direction. The arch-sentimentalist Dickens had succeeded where the arch-rebel Schiller had failed. He understood that freedom is a condition that permits us to evolve.

I have tried to show that the rise of the novel was closely associated with the question of human freedom and evolution. Most critics seem to be agreed that, since the beginning of the twentieth century, the novel has been in decline. James, Bennett, Galsworthy, Huxley, Lawrence, have added nothing new, while experimentalists like Proust, Joyce and Beckett seem to demonstrate that there is not much new to add. This seems to suggest a poor prospect for anyone thinking of becoming a novelist in the future. On the other hand, no one seems to have explained exactly *why* the novel has reached some kind of limit. This is something we must look into more closely in the next chapter.

THREE

Decline and Fall

Clarissa Harlowe WAS not Richardson's last novel. The eagerly awaited *Sir Charles Grandison* appeared (in seven volumes) in 1754–57, but was generally felt to be inferior to its predecessors. It was; but from our point of view, it is in some ways even more interesting. *Grandison* is 'the story of a truly virtuous man'. The hero may have been inspired by Addison's Sir Roger de Coverley—a country gentleman who spends his time looking after his estates and 'doing good for others'. One of Richardson's friends, Lady Bradshaigh, 'bounced off her chair' when Richardson told her that two women were in love with Grandison, and he was in love with them both; but she need not have worried. Grandison is pursued by a number of ladies, but his conduct is always unexceptionable, and he ends by marrying a girl he saved from rape at the hands of a jealous suitor.

Perhaps the most interesting thing about the novel is that Grandison is obviously an idealised self-portrait. Richardson was not only the inventor of the novel; he was also the first to use it to project a 'self-image'. It would be another six years before Rousseau thought of creating Saint-Preux.

However, the self-image concept had its own inherent dangers. They can already be seen in *Werther*. The first thing the reader notices about *Werther* is that it is intensely personal; the next, that it is very short. There is an obvious connection between the two. *Werther* is only incidentally a story. It is primarily about the hero's 'soul'. It is about *his* feelings, *his* thoughts, *his* insights. That is to say, if you think of the novelist as a kind of camera-man, Richardson was pointing his camera at the outside world. Goethe was treating the hero's heart as a mirror,

and pointing the camera at that, recording whatever is reflected in it. This gives the novel a new kind of unity and intensity; but the world reflected in a small mirror soon gets
monotonous.

The problem becomes clear in the remarkable novel *Obermann* by Etienne de Senancour, a young dilettante with a gift
for painting, who wandered through Switzerland for some
years before he wrote his novel. It appeared in 1804, and
caused little stir, although it became what we would now call
an 'underground classic', and influenced many greater writers,
including Balzac. Obermann is a self-portrait of his creator, a
gloomy young poet who stays in hotels and boarding houses,
and commits his 'reveries' to paper. He has been unhappily in
love, but she was married. Now, although he finds the Swiss
scenery magnificent and mysterious, his chief problem is boredom—*ennui*, which became known as *'le mal d'Obermann'*. He
notes the paradox that although the rain depresses him, he feels
the sunlight to be 'useless'. He spends too much of his life in a
lukewarm state, experiencing no desire, no feeling. Scenery
stirs him deeply, giving him a sudden sense of hidden meaning
—then the *ennui* is back.

This is a long novel (written, as usual, in the form of letters),
but it has no plot. Senancour's intention is to express his frustration, and the sudden flashes of meaning. He sits with his
camera focused on the heart for days at a time. But nothing is
reflected there; only drifting clouds. . . .

In short, as the novel became more personal, more subjective,
it lost its clear *forward* movement.

W. B. Yeats expressed this fundamental problem in a three-
line poem:

> Shakespearian fish swam the sea, far away from land;
> Romantic fish swam in nets, coming to the hand;
> What are all those fish that lie gasping on the strand?

That is to say: Shakespearian art is objective; the creator is like
a fisherman who goes far out to sea to catch his fish. The

romantic stays nearer home, on the shore, and by comparison, his fish are not the free-roaming monsters of the deep, but smaller creatures constricted by nets. And this tendency to subjectivism, 'personalism', has finally led to fish that cannot swim at all: to plotless novels all about the hero's feelings. . . .

Still, in those early days of the nineteenth century, nobody even suspected such a problem. The realm of the imagination was the promised land, a great virgin continent like Africa. All the novelist had to do was explore it.

And foremost in this field of exploration were the Germans. Perhaps the most influential novel of the age was Goethe's successor to *Young Werther*, *Wilhelm Meister's Apprenticeship* (1795–6), to which he later added *Wilhelm Meister's Travels*. In spite of appearances, this immense, sprawling novel is not a return to the old picaresque romance. It is the story of the hero's education *by life*. Wilhelm is the son of a businessman, and he is expected to take over his father's business; instead, he joins a troop of wandering actors. The implication: that it is more important to learn to live than to learn to make a living. Now in his forties, Goethe was rather ashamed of the feverish romanticism of *Werther*, and the adventures of Wilhelm Meister take place in an obviously real world. But younger novelists saw no reason to confine themselves to the real world; what is the imagination for if not to improve on reality? It was this tendency that led Madame de Stael to remark sarcastically that if the English are lords of the sea, and the French lords of the land, the Germans are lords of the air.

By far the most popular novelist among Goethe's contemporaries was Jean Paul Friedrich Richter, known simply as Jean Paul. Today he is almost forgotten, even in Germany. To his contemporaries, he was a universal genius who ranked with Shakespeare. Novels like *Hesperus* and *Titan* are as eccentric as *Tristram Shandy*: humorous, sentimental, tragic, sublime, clownish—wholly unpredictable. His characters wander through an enchanted landscape. He is fond of writing about country schoolmasters who lead peaceful, idyllic, uneventful lives. The basic feeling in all his novels is that man *ought* to be happy; he was born for happiness, and if he looks far enough, he will find it. The hero of *Titan* is a prince in search of his kingdom. On the other hand, the hero of *Flower, Fruit and Thorn Pieces* (Jean Paul loved baffling titles) is a dreamy country lawyer who is unhappy with his practical wife. Then he meets a true soul-mate, and in order to escape his wife, pretends to be dead and allows an empty coffin to be buried. Jean Paul and his fellow-romantics believed firmly in the existence of soul-mates and living happily ever after.

The novels of the German romantics—Tieck, Novalis, Musaeus, Hoffmann, Eichendorff—are full of idyllic landscapes: green rolling hills, tiny villages, peaceful rivers, castles rising from the midst of trees. . . . But as the century wore on, it became increasingly clear that these dream-landscapes had no real existence. The tales of E. T. A. Hoffmann—now best known through Offenbach's opera—take place almost entirely in a world of fantasy. Hoffmann himself was a misfit who drank himself to death. A large number of the romantics were alcoholics or (like de Quincey and Coleridge) opium addicts. Suicide, insanity and early death from tuberculosis became commonplace. Slowly, the romantics reached the sad conclusion that the real world and the ideal are irreconcilable. The 'promised land' began to seem like a mirage.

Meanwhile, in France, the novel had been following a totally different course. The influence of Rousseau and Goethe had been great; but France had another tradition: of psychological realism. As early as 1678, Madame de la Fayette's *Princesse de Clèves* had portrayed a 'triangle' situation in which everyone behaves with rigid propriety because of their sense of moral obligation. A century later, in 1782, came a novel that shocked Paris and brought a different kind of realism. *Les Liaisons Dangereuses* was written by an artillery officer, Choderlos de Laclos. In an almost clinical manner, it dealt with the theme of seduction as a pastime. The seducer, Valmont, is an aristocratic blackguard; his accomplice, Mme de Merteuil is, if anything, worse. Her creator likened her to 'the most insatiable of the Roman empresses'. Both are hunters, for whom sexual intrigue is the most interesting form of sport. The novel describes, in what seems gloating detail, how Valmont seduces two virtuous women, driving one to her death and the other to a nunnery. Laclos was apparently amazed by the scandal caused by his novel. Some critics feel this was because he had 'taken the lid off' French society. This is unlikely. The real reason was that, in an age of romanticism, he had dared to create a tradition of cynical realism.

In 1807, when the Germans were devouring novels of exalted love affairs, a young Frenchman, Benjamin Constant, was being completely honest about the egotistic nature of his own sexual drives. The hero of *Adolphe* falls in love with the mistress of a German count—largely because she belongs to someone else. He falls in love out of desire for a love affair; when she rejects his advances, hurt pride makes him re-double his efforts. When they become lovers, he finds she bores him. Nevertheless, they run away together. The bond becomes wearisome, and when she finds out that he intends to leave her, she dies of a broken heart. Like Laclos, Constant is concerned to tell the exact truth about the least admirable aspects of human nature.

Of course, a novel like *Adolphe* does not *disprove* the sentiments of Jean Paul or Hoffmann. They are simply concerned with different aspects of human nature—one with sexual egoism, the other with idealistic aspirations. The trouble is that realism seems so much more solid and durable than romanticism—particularly to people who dislike ridicule, as most of us do. As romanticism declined into a sad twilight of defeat, realism (or naturalism, as it came to be called) gained strength, and slowly became the dominant tradition in the history of the novel.

In 1829, a writer who had published sensational romances under the name of Horace de Saint-Aubin decided to bring out a novel under his own name: Honoré de Balzac. (In fact, he was not entitled to the 'de', but he added it because he felt a man of genius *ought* to be an aristocrat.) *Les Chouans (The Owls)* is a realistic novel set in Brittany at the time of the French Revolution, and it is the first volume of the *Comédie Humaine*, which would run to ninety-one novels and stories by the time of his death twenty years later. Balzac is regarded by many as the greatest novelist of all time. What makes his works so unique is their feeling of total reality. However melodramatic the story, he tells it with such passionate concern for detail that he has you believing it is factual reportage. He seems to get equal pleasure from describing a printing press, a farm, a provincial drawing-room or the Paris stock exchange. A dictionary of Balzac's characters runs to two volumes, and their lives and destinies are worked out over forty novels. No novelist has ever made such a determined attempt to create a whole world.

Still, in spite of appearances, Balzac was no naturalist—a word that came into use after his death—or even a realist. The aim of naturalism is to show life 'as it is', like a photograph. Balzac wasn't interested in life as the average person sees it—only in life as *he* saw it: that is, as something strange, immensely complex—and above all, *heroic*. He wanted to prove that the creator is a kind of Prometheus, a god-like demiurge who towers above his creations, conjuring whole worlds and epochs into existence. This is why Balzac included no self-portraits in his novels—not even Rastignac, the ambitious young provincial who shakes his fist at Paris and utters the tremendous words, 'It's between the two of us now'. *All* Balzac's work is his attempt to create a self-image, to convince the world that he was a creator, and creators are a kind of god.

When you begin to read Balzac, the impact of the realism is overwhelming. But after a few volumes, you begin to notice inconsistencies. People in real life often gamble and win. They choose the right person and make a happy marriage. They strive for something and achieve it. They often trust without being betrayed, and repay kindness with gratitude. In Balzac, such things seldom happen. If gamblers win, it is only so that they can be more completely destroyed. If a father or a mother love unselfishly, it is only so that their children can rob them. Idealists are seldom strong enough to survive, and the few who succeed—like the writer Daniel D'Arthez—are only peripheral characters. In Balzac's dark world, the best guarantee of success is calculating egoism.

In short, the *Comédie Humaine* is permeated with an atmosphere of pessimism which is obviously an expression of the
artist's temperament. There was a certain self-destructive
tendency in Balzac; he was obsessed by social position and
sexual conquest; he was wildly extravagant, buying gold-
headed canes and expensive furniture. His novels never
achieved the enormous sales of Dumas or Hugo, so he drove
himself, writing all night, until he died of overwork. Again, we
see the paradox that destroyed romanticism—and started the
novel on the long, slow path of decline: the belief that man is a
god, allied to a self-destructive pessimism. Literature, like
nature, operates on the principle of survival of the fittest, and
a pessimist is not ideally equipped to survive.

Balzac was still alive on 6 March 1848, when a young nymphomaniac, Delphine Delamare, took a fatal dose of arsenic. But
he did not live long enough to see the tremendous consequences
of her act.

Delphine was the daughter of a farmer who lived near
Rouen. At the age of seventeen, she met a young doctor named
Delamare—a widower—and accepted his proposal of marriage.
Soon she was bored out of her mind with existence as the wife
of a country doctor—a rather mediocre doctor at that. She
dreamed of an exciting, romantic existence in cities. She began
to spend heavily on clothes. Then she committed her first
adultery, with a neighbour. She was pretty and shapely, and
when the men of the district realised she was an easy conquest,
they were around like dogs after a bitch on heat. She had a
series of lovers—probably running to dozens—but none of
them stayed long. Nine years of this left her emotionally bankrupt; and her husband, without knowing it, was on the verge
of financial bankruptcy. Wracked by self-pity, she took the
arsenic, and died within hours. She was twenty-seven. Her
husband, who adored her, was shattered by her death. When
he discovered the extent of her debts, and the details of her
love-life, he was more shattered than ever. He committed
suicide, leaving their small daughter in the care of his mother.

Three years after Delphine's death—and a year after Balzac's

—a young poet named Louis Bouilhet called on a doctor's widow, a Madame Flaubert, at Ry, near Rouen; there he met Delphine's mother-in-law. When the sad old lady had gone, Madame Flaubert told Bouilhet the story. Some months later, Bouilhet was spending an afternoon with Madame Flaubert's son, Gustave, in his garden, and Flaubert was complaining that he felt artistically barren. Bouilhet asked: 'Why not write the story of Delphine Delamare?'

It was the kind of thing that Flaubert would not normally have dreamed of undertaking. He liked writing of historical and allegorical subjects. But he was thoroughly dissatisfied with himself and his work, and he saw the merit of the self-discipline that such a work would entail. He carefully researched his subject; then slowly, painfully ('What a heavy oar the pen is,' he remarked), he produced *Madame Bovary* over the next five years. The original manuscript is nearly two thousand pages long; with a final effort of ruthless self-discipline, Flaubert reduced it to less than five hundred.

The book appeared as a serial in 1856. Flaubert was astounded by the scandal. Dozens of the magazine's subscribers cancelled it. Critics said the book was a slur on French womanhood, and doubted whether such nymphomaniacs existed, even though Emma Bovary only has two lovers. There were demands that the government should suppress the book. Flaubert and two of the publishers were arrested and put on trial for disseminating a pornographic and anti-religious work, but the judge dismissed the case as 'not proven'.

Madame Bovary is a masterpiece; of that there can be no doubt. At the same time, the enraged moralists were by no means wrong. Flaubert's photographic realism is impressive; but what he is using it to convey is not only depressing, but in a certain sense, *untrue*. *Madame Bovary* may not be a libel on French womanhood, but it *is* a libel on human nature.

At which point, it is necessary to state a general principle about art. No doubt Flaubert would have protested that his work cannot be a libel on anything, because it is just a straightforward presentation of reality, like a photograph. 'I aim only at being a good photographer, and it is a matter of indifference to me whether I point my camera at a fine sunset or a man dying of leprosy. . . .' But this is special pleading. Even a photographer selects his subject, according to what interests him. But there is another objection. When a man is on trial, he is given a defending as well as prosecuting counsel, to ensure fairness. If a novelist focuses his camera on such a small area that we see only the worst side of human nature, then he is, in effect, acting as the prosecuting counsel, and taking care to leave out the defence. In *Madame Bovary*, Charles Bovary is the victim; and as we watch Emma's increasing degradation, the egoism or weakness of her lovers, it is as if Flaubert is carefully and clinically hitting Charles with a bludgeon. It becomes slightly sickening. His insistence that he is merely aiming at artistic verisimilitude only makes it worse. Somehow, we do not mind Balzac's implication that the creator is a Promethean superman; but there is something oddly nasty in Flaubert's insistence that he is cool and detached, when he is actually involved in a kind of sadism.

All this leads to the statement of another general principle. Most talk about 'artistic detachment' is disingenuous. No writer can depict the whole world—even if, like Balzac, he makes a creditable attempt. All he can do is offer 'typical samples', like a grocer allowing you to taste a piece of cheese. But as he holds out the cheese to you on the end of his knife, he is clearly implying that this sample tastes exactly the same as the rest of the cheese on the counter. The same goes for the novelist; as he hands you his 'slice of life', there is a tacit understanding that, as far as he knows, this tastes very much like any other slice he could offer you.

This is what the critic Matthew Arnold meant when he said that literature is a 'criticism of life'. (He was speaking of poetry, in fact, but it applies to all literature.) It is handed to the reader with the implication: This is what life is like.

No doubt Flaubert was being honest according to his own lights. He was a good-natured giant of a man who loved food, friendship and women. But he lacked Balzac's self-confidence and breadth of vision. Underlying his gospel of artistic integrity, there were basic misgivings about the real value or importance of art. This may spring from the paradox that human beings only value what they have had to fight for, and the wealthy Flaubert encountered no obstacles when he decided to become a writer. So on the whole, *Madame Bovary* may be taken as a fairly accurate representation of his ideas about human beings and human existence. He felt that men are basically weak and selfish—especially artists—and that women are inclined to be blinded by their emotions.

But *Madame Bovary* became the Bible of a younger generation of writers—Zola, the Goncourt brothers, Maupassant, Daudet, Huysmans. The 'documentary method' seemed the perfect antidote to romanticism (and they were all basically romantics). You ensured maximum artistic impact by writing about adultery, debauchery and human misery, at the same time presenting it so 'realistically' that anyone who objected could be dismissed as having missed the whole point. The Goncourt brothers launched the creed of naturalism with a novel, *Germanie Lacerteux*, about a servant who destroys herself with drink and debauchery. She had actually been a servant of the Goncourt brothers (and they had been so unobservant that they hadn't even noticed her double life), so they were able to argue that this was a genuine 'documentary'. In 1880, five 'naturalistic' writers combined to produce a volume of short stories, *Les Soirées de Médan*—Médan being the home of the leader of the group, Emile Zola. It included a story called *Boule-de-Suif*, which made its author, Guy de Maupassant, famous. Maupassant and Zola were undoubtedly the two most talented of this group of naturalists. Both were obsessed by sex —Zola because his marriage was unsatisfying, Maupassant because he was sexually insatiable anyway. As with Samuel Richardson, the sexual obsession governs the subject of most of their novels and stories. Maupassant's stories are full of girls who get seduced and then abandoned, while Zola's novels contain an abnormally high proportion of adultery, incest and rape. Huysmans' *Là Bas* is about devil-worship, culminating in a black Mass in which the priest sodomises the altar-boys. Inevitably, critics accused them of pornography, and Zola's English publisher was thrown into gaol. A denunciatory work called *Degeneration* (1895) by Dr Max Nordau, seemed to voice the moral indignation of readers all over the world, and was translated into dozens of languages.

But critics who accused the naturalists of pornography were missing the point. Pornography, as we have seen, is merely intended as an aid to auto-eroticism, and the intentions of Maupassant and Zola were not to help the reader towards an orgasm. They wanted to expand the field of the novel, to be allowed to describe any part of life that interested them. This is legitimate enough. The real criticism of them arises from the principle I stated a few pages ago: the principle of the 'typical sample'. When Zola shows the village idiot engaged in incest with his sister, or a farmer's wife holding down a servant girl while her husband rapes her, he is implying that this is typical of 'the human condition', like Romeo's love for Juliet, or Othello's jealousy of Desdemona. Zola would deny that it is supposed to be 'typical'; he would reply that it 'merely happens' in certain parts of rural France. But if we examine Zola's work, from the early *Thérèse Raquin* (a remarkable study in murder and adultery) to the late *Truth*, we shall find that he always seems to be a prosecution witness against life, and never tries to present the defence. It is true that he believes in social justice, and it is this concern with human suffering that makes *Germinal* his masterpiece. But his overall view of human existence is still that it is tragic and futile. Like Flaubert, he claims to be an impartial observer of human existence, while he presents only one side of the case. Max Nordau should have attacked him on logical and artistic, not moral grounds. He wanted to be allowed to describe 'the whole of life', presumably for the benefit of the novel, and for art in general. Yet although he did so fearlessly, enduring bitter attacks (and becoming a best-seller in the process), his work *loses* strength and conviction instead of gaining it. Obviously, something has gone wrong with the calculation somewhere.

And because Maupassant is a better artist than Zola, his work enables us to see precisely what went wrong. That early story *Boule-de-Suif* (revealing how badly 'respectable' people can treat a good-natured prostitute) and the early novel *A*

Woman's Life, seem to be full of genuine compassion for suffering. The heroine of *A Woman's Life (Une Vie)* has to endure a mean and unfaithful husband and an ungrateful son. Yet at the end, as her son's baby is handed to her, a servant remarks: 'Life is never as good or as bad as people think it is.' Maupassant seems to be making a real effort to encompass as much of life as possible, to present the defence as well as prosecution. But having achieved secure success, he ceases to make this effort, and begins to express more of his own natural responses to existence. Since his major interest was sex (he had lived in a brothel for a time, and contracted syphilis), seduction naturally plays an important part in his work. His next novel, *Bel Ami*, is a kind of wish-fulfilment fantasy, in which a handsome but empty-headed journalist rises to the top of his profession by good luck and his attractiveness to women. He has no scruples, seducing the wives of friends, and sleeping with the proprietor's daughter as cheerfully as with the mother. This is no disapproving portrait of a scoundrel; you sense that he takes the attitude that women are man's natural prey—because of their tendency to be blinded by emotion—and that if they get betrayed, that is their own look-out.

In the next novel, *Mont-Oriol*—perhaps his best—this becomes very clear. The novel is about the pursuit and seduction of a young married woman by a friend of her brother's; then, when she is pregnant, he loses interest in her. With the birth of her child, she fortunately loses interest in him too. On one level, the novel is a detached, clinical piece of observation in the emotional difference between the sexes, and Maupassant could have claimed without absurdity that it was a scientific document. But it is also apparent that Maupassant is enjoying the seduction-fantasy, and feels a touch of sadistic pleasure in man's sexual 'superiority' to woman. So the novel lacks true detachment, and you feel that it has brought Maupassant no deeper insights. (For after all, a novel is not simply intended to give pleasure to the reader; it is also a device for enabling the writer to 'digest' his experience.)

The remaining novels reveal Maupassant's total disintegration: a disintegration not due so much to syphilis as to loss of artistic direction. *Pierre and Jean* need not detain us—a novel about the rivalry between two brothers and the effect on one of them of realising he is the son of his mother's lover. *Notre Cœur* is another study in sexual slavery—but this time from the opposite angle: the slavery of a man to a woman. The 'hero' is an artistic dilettante who attends the *salon* of a beautiful widow and, in spite of his resistance, falls in love with her. They become lovers, but it is she who tires of him. He consoles himself by seducing a servant girl, who adores him and lives with him as his mistress. But she realises he is not in love with her; and in fact, as soon as the widow beckons, he rushes back to her. This is how the novel ends—with the prospect of the hero's permanent enslavement, the servant girl's permanent misery. . . . Well, that's life, Maupassant seems to be saying. . . .

The last novel, *As Strong as Death*, is a disaster. A successful painter has been having a love affair with a married countess for many years. Then, one day, he realises he is in love with her daughter. The novel might have been interesting if Maupassant had showed them becoming lovers; instead, the painter spends sleepless nights and goes through moral torments until he is killed in a street accident.

Not long after finishing it, Maupassant died insane.

We can now see what went wrong with Maupassant's career as a writer. He was always a cynic and a 'realist', focusing his camera on a very small area of human life; yet the early stories and novels have the glitter and sparkle of an Impressionist painting. 'Things are never as bad as the pessimists believe. . . .' In spite of cruelty, in spite of human egoism and weakness, life is infinitely fascinating. He seems to be moving towards some kind of mystical affirmation. Then he becomes self-indulgent, and allows himself to wallow in the details of seductions; a touch of sadism creeps in. But now his counter-weight has gone—now he has become wholly preoccupied with cruelty, weakness and egoism—he doesn't know what to *do* with the hero once the bedroom scene is over. So in *Mont-Oriol*, the lovers drift apart without too much pain. In *Notre Cœur*, they remain entangled and ensnared, but basically unhappy. And

in *As Strong as Death*, he cannot even bring himself to write the
bedroom scene, because he can now see no solution.

What has gone wrong? After *A Woman's Life*, he ceased to
try to solve *the problem* that was implicit in his whole attitude
towards human existence. And a novel derives its power from
the novelist's struggle with the problem. Once this struggle has
ceased, he begins to die as an artist. We can see that the motive
that led him to write *As Strong as Death* was a kind of feeble
curiosity: what would it be like to become the lover of your
mistress's—and perhaps your own—daughter? But before the
fantasy is half-developed, he has lost interest.

And now it is possible to see, in very precise terms, why the
novel went into decline. It began by offering a new dimension
in human freedom. The problem of freedom is stated clearly
even in Richardson, when Lovelace declares that the only
thing he cares about is 'my own imperial will and pleasure'.
It sounds through all the major works of romanticism, from
The New Héloise to the second part of Goethe's *Faust*. But the
problem of freedom also raises the problem of what we intend
to *do* with it. Faust summons the devil to help him gain freedom; but all he does when he has it is to seduce a peasant girl.
This was the problem the romantics were unable to solve, and
they turned away in despair. The 'realists' now took over, and
their work had a power and conviction that made it look as if
they were going to succeed where the romantics had failed.
In one form or another, realism went on to conquer the world
of literature. But by the year 1900, it had already turned bitter
and sour. What is the point of holding a mirror up to nature,
if the nature you reflect is chaotic and meaningless?

In England, the decline of the novel was less obvious. This was
because English novelists were less experimental and ambitious
than their European counterparts; so their failure was less
apparent. A Scottish writer of genius, David Lindsay, once
made a convenient division of novels into those that describe
the world, and those that try to explain it. With rare exceptions, English novelists have belonged to the class of 'de-

scribers'. They have always been fascinated by the surface of life, by its sheer multiplicity. An English painter, William Frith, produced a huge canvas called 'Derby Day', full of hundreds of people and horses; it could serve as a symbol of the English novel in the Victorian age: Jane Austen, the Brontës, Dickens, Thackeray, Trollope, George Eliot, Meredith, Gissing, George Moore, Thomas Hardy. . . . If their novels are considered as a single panorama, it is the most detailed description of an epoch in time that has ever been created. Beside it, even Balzac's *Comédie Humaine* seems narrow and limited. But if we look at this list of names, we also observe the signs of slow decline. Jane Austen's colours are bright and serene, Dickens's are often sombre; Thomas Hardy's are thunderously gloomy. The vitality seems to be draining away. By the late 1920s, it seemed clear that the novelists who continued to write in the Victorian tradition—Arnold Bennett, H. G. Wells, John Galsworthy—had nothing much more to say. For a while, the work of younger experimental novelists— James Joyce, Aldous Huxley, D. H. Lawrence—seemed to suggest that the novel had recovered some of its old vitality. But by 1940, it was plain the hope was premature; Lawrence was dead, Joyce was entangled in the linguistic web of *Finnegan's Wake*, and Huxley was repeating himself. No one doubted that the novel, as a literary form, had reached the end of its tether.

By way of a postscript to this chapter, it is worth looking briefly at the history of the Russian novel; for even compared to the French or English novel, its rise and fall were spectacular. Because of political repression, the Russians were late-comers to the literary scene. It would hardly be an exaggeration to say that Russian literature sprang into being with Pushkin's *Eugene Onegin* in 1833. This novel in verse is a full-blown romantic work, heavily influenced by Byron, about a bored young aristocrat who, like Obermann, doesn't know what to do with himself. A young girl, Tatiana, falls in love with him, but he rejects her; some years later, he sees her again and falls in love with her; this time, she rejects him. The Russians had already caught the European mood of romantic despair. Pushkin had been dead five years—killed in a duel—when the first great Russian novel, Gogol's *Dead Souls*, appeared in 1842. This is a fundamentally Dickensian work, satirising the sloth and mediocrity of Russian provincials. It also set a fashion—of minute examinations of provincial boredom and futility. In Goncharov's *Oblomov*, the idealistic young nobleman cannot bring himself to act in any way; he sinks into sloth and becomes a kind of vegetable. Schedrin's *The Golovlyov Family* shows the other side of the coin: the decline of a family of utterly material-istic landowners who think only of money.

The golden age of Russian literature began around 1850 with the advent of Tolstoy and Dostoevsky: arguably the two greatest novelists in world literature. Both are emphatically 'explainers' rather than 'describers'. In fact, Tolstoy was the first novelist to ask in so many words: 'Who am I?' 'Why am I here?' 'What is the purpose of human existence?' And his heroes—Peter Bezhukov and Prince Andrew in *War and Peace*, and Levin in *Anna Karenina*, ask themselves these questions. Tolstoy's solutions were oddly close to Rousseau's: a return to simplicity, a preoccupation with peasant life, with elementary education, with New Testament fundamentalism. But his work has precisely the kind of breadth that the French novelists lacked. *Anna Karenina* has basically the same subject as *Madame Bovary*, and the adulterous heroine also ends by killing herself; but it has none of the stifling, slightly cruel atmosphere of that novel. A kind of breeze seems to blow through Tolstoy's books. But his concern with the 'solution' to the problem of human existence led him to become increasingly obsessed with morals towards the end of his life, and the vitality has drained out of *Resurrection*, a novel about a repentant rake and the girl he has betrayed.

Dostoevsky was even more of an obsessive than Tolstoy. The problems of human destiny, of freedom, of good and evil, have never been presented so clearly as in his novels. *Crime and Punishment* is a variation on the theme of Schiller's *Robbers*: has man a right to commit crimes in the name of moral freedom? Unfortunately, Dostoevsky himself was a guilt-laden neurotic, a disadvantage for a man who writes about the problem of freedom. It means that his heroes have a compulsion to purge themselves through suffering; so, for example, *The Brothers Karamazov* ends with the paradox of an innocent man prepared to undergo life imprisonment because he feels guilty for hating his thoroughly detestable father. Dostoevsky came closer than any other novelist to understanding the basic question of human freedom; but his masochism inclines him to regard suffering as the final answer.

After Dostoevsky, Russian novelists continued to be pre-occupied with these problems of the meaning of human existence; but, lacking his almost insane, obsessive quality, their solutions tend to be negative. There was Chekhov, whose stories and plays show decent, honest people trapped in bore-dom and a sense of helplessness. There was Leonid Andreyev, a savagely pessimistic writer whose brilliant stories set out to demonstrate that human life is meaningless and 'absurd' (in the sense that the existentialists later used that word). There was Dmitri Merezhkovsky, a kind of religious mystic who was obsessed by the contradictions and antinomies of human existence—spirit and nature, Christ and Antichrist, illusion and reality, and whose historical novels on Julian the Apostate, Leonardo da Vinci and Peter the Great deserve to be more widely read; but he remained trapped in his antinomies and reached no solution. For a while, it looked as if Michael Artsybashev might become a great force in Russian literature; his first novel *Sanine* (1907) swept Russia with its gospel of healthy sensualism and Nietzschean freedom from morality. As its hero stands over the grave of a friend who has com-mitted suicide, he comments cheerfully: 'One fool less in the world.' But Artsybashev found it impossible to develop beyond this point. Like Maupassant, he became increasingly pre-occupied with sexual problems: the capacity of men and women to make one another miserable. Although he died in 1927, his last novel, *The Breaking Point*, had been published as long ago as 1912; it is about a depressing provincial town, and most of the characters commit suicide. Artsybashev is, perhaps, one of the most interesting cases of moral and literary bank-ruptcy in the history of literature.

Significantly, Andreyev and Artsybashev detested the Revolution and everything it stood for. With the coming of the Soviet regime, Russian novelists ceased to be 'explainers' and became 'describers'. The model for the new generation was Maxim Gorky, a fine short-story writer whose major interest had always been social revolution. Gorky has some of the same faults—and virtues—as the American Jack London; he writes of the open air, of labourers and tramps and prostitutes. But because of his political convictions, his work is often one-sided, and takes its place in the history of socialism rather than of literature. And this, on the whole, is true of the majority of Soviet novelists: Alexey Tolstoy, Michael Sholokov, Leonid Leonov, Ilya Ehrenberg. (Recent revelations by the exiled novelist Alexander Solzhenitsyn suggest that Sholokov's *Quiet Flows the Don*, usually regarded as the greatest novel of the Soviet period, was mostly written by another novelist, Fyodor Kryukov, who died of typhus in 1920.) One notable exception, a short novel called *Envy*, by Yuri Olesha, proved to be its author's only major work; the Soviet authorities discouraged Olesha from writing more novels. It re-states the problem that had bothered Russian writers since *Oblomov*: the idealist's natural distaste for the 'real world'. The hero is picked out of the gutter by a Party official and given a home; but although his benefactor is kindly, he loathes everything he stands for. Since he feels himself to be worthless, the hero construes this feeling simply as envy. The Communist Party took the same simplistic view, which explains Olesha's original success. Then, slowly, the implications of the story began to dawn on them: the hero's feeling that, even if he *is* a futile dreamer, the healthy world of socialist labour is still no answer to his basic needs. The authorities discouraged Olesha before he went further into this dangerous problem.

The same doubts—about the role of the individual in a totalitarian state—were expressed by Pasternak in *Doctor Zhivago*, and by Solzhenitsyn in *The First Circle*, and both writers suffered the same displeasure as Olesha. Yet neither work is particularly revolutionary, either from the point of view of literature or ideas. Both merely assert that the problems of human existence are more fundamental than problems of 'social justice'. Neither Pasternak nor Solzenitsyn denies that social justice is an urgent necessity; they simply insist that the problem of individual destiny is ultimately more important. In doing so, they are simply re-stating something that Rousseau, Goethe and Schiller took for granted. So in two centuries of development, the position of the novel could be summarised: This is where we came in. . . .

FOUR

As For Living . . .

'As for living, our servants can do that for us,' said the
hero of *Axel*, a famous 'decadent' play of the 1890s. Did he
mean that he wanted to die? On the contrary. He meant that
there is an intenser, more interesting form of existence than
that provided by everyday experience. He was merely re-
stating Richardson's discovery: that the imagination—operat-
ing through literature—can provide a form of *substitute experience.* And the strange thing about this substitute experience is
that it is, in many ways, preferable to the real thing. If I am
hungry, daydreaming about food will not fill my stomach;
it will only make me hungrier. Yet if I am frustrated and
bored, and I set the imagination to work, the daydream can
provide the same inner satisfaction as actual experience. A
frustrated vicar's daughter elaborated a daydream in which
she had a love affair with a handsome gypsy. Her novel does
not strike us as the daydream of an inexperienced spinster.
It has *its own* reality, and it has a quality of intensity that
surpasses everyday experience. The feelings evoked in us by
'everyday reality' are fairly limited. Emily Brontë had created
the means of evoking a whole new range of feelings. In a
sense, she had created a new reality.

And what is the secret of creating substitute-realities? The
self-image. *That* was the essence of Richardson's discovery. In
Gulliver's Travels and *Robinson Crusoe*, Swift and Defoe were
merely telling stories, without real involvement. Richardson
taught the writer the trick of using the novel as a mirror to see
his own face.

At which point, it is necessary to make an important quali-

fication. This does *not* mean that the novelist's aim is to create
an autobiographical self-portrait. That is easy enough, and
not particularly valuable. The true aim is to project an image
of *what he wants*. And sometimes, what he wants is not at all
obvious. For example, what would you say Richardson
wanted, to judge by *Pamela* and *Clarissa*? To see the downfall
of vice and the triumph of virtue? No; we can see—if his contemporaries couldn't—that Richardson had a powerful obsession with rape and seduction. Does that mean, then, that
he wanted to see the triumph of vice and the downfall of virtue? No, it is not as simple as that either. Through Lovelace
and Mr B., he was giving rein to a certain *aspect* of himself—an
aspect that certainly found no expression in his otherwise
respectable life.

In philosophy, there is a useful concept called the 'thought-
experiment'. I can ask myself, for example, what the world
would be like if all the books in it were destroyed, or if men and
women were obliged to look exactly alike. I cannot actually
perform these experiments; but I can use my imagination to
give me an idea of what the world would be like if something
of the sort really happened. You could say that Richardson
performed the thought-experiment of raping Clarissa, and
studying the consequences. The conclusion he reached was
that such an act would be disastrous for the rapist as well as
the victim. You may reply that he might have reached that
conclusion without writing *Clarissa*, but that would not be
true. By performing the thought-experiment in such detail, he
gave his conclusions an authenticity they would otherwise
have lacked. Moreover, it is fairly certain that Richardson
would not have created *Sir Charles Grandison* if he had not first
lived vicariously through the experiences of Lovelace and
Mr B. Originally he intended Grandison to be another rake;
but he changed his mind, started all over again, and produced
his portrait of 'a truly virtuous man'. One of the chief advan-
tages of thought-experiments is that they are reversible.

Sometimes, a novelist may go through with a thought-
experiment which, even at the halfway stage, is obviously
going to be a failure. This is what happened to Maupassant

in those later novels. On the other hand, some thought-experiments are successful beyond all expectation. Dickens intended *Pickwick Papers* to be a series of comic sporting sketches. Instead, Mr Pickwick and Sam Weller took over the novel, and launched Dickens on his career as a novelist. Dickens had stumbled upon a 'law of increasing returns'. His experience illustrates that the novel could be regarded as a method for discovering the laws of the human mind through thought-experiments.

Human beings are apparently the only animals who daydream. *Why* do we daydream? What is its purpose?

It requires no intellectual effort to grasp that all 'dreaming' gives us a certain kind of freedom. Our basic human experience is a feeling of *limitation*. We are held down by a dozen invisible cords—gravity, hunger, our instincts, the craving for security.

In March 1804, a nineteen-year-old youth was suffering acutely from toothache. After three weeks of agony, he met an acquaintance who recommended opium. At that time it could be bought in any druggist's shop. On a rainy Sunday afternoon, Thomas de Quincey bought a bottle of 'tincture of opium' for a few pence, then returned to his dreary lodgings and drank some of it. 'In an hour, O heavens! what a revulsion! what a resurrection, from its lowest depths, of the inner spirit! That my pains had vanished was now a trifle in my eyes; this negative effect was swallowed up in the immensity of those positive effects which had opened before me, in the abyss of divine enjoyment thus suddenly revealed. Here was a panacea . . . for all human woes; here was the secret of happiness.'

And in her book on *Opium and the Romantic Imagination*, Alethea Hayter describes its effects:

'The first sensation from taking opium, in nearly all cases, is a relaxation of tension and anxiety, the onset of a special kind of calm enjoyment usually summarised . . . under the word euphoria . . . the condition of being borne along by a favourable breeze . . . cares, doubts, fears, tedium, inhibitions, sink away and are replaced by a serene self-assurance. . . . He is now in a state of listless complacent tranquillity. Nothing worries him, nothing moves him; he is at peace with his fellow-men because he does not care about them; their sorrows do not move him; their injuries and slights, of which he was so conscious, now rebound harmlessly off his invulnerable self-esteem.'

I cite this because it is not merely a description of the effects of opium; this is a general description of *all* states of mental freedom, although they may not necessarily involve indifference to your fellow-human beings.

All daydreams and 'thought-experiments' produce some-thing of the same effect—even if they happen to be of murder-ing someone you hate: a relief from oppression, such as an underwater swimmer feels as he surfaces and takes gulps of air.

And so, from the very beginning, the basic aim of the novel was bound up with this sense of freedom, and the problem of freedom became one of its main themes. Richardson's Lovelace talks about the satisfaction of 'his own imperial will'. Rousseau declared that 'man is born free, but is everywhere in chains', and suggested that democracy, education and a more equitable distribution of wealth would give all men the freedom that was their birthright. Schiller declared that 'only freedom creates giants'. The Marquis de Sade based all his novels on the assumption that the whole aim of life is pleasure, and that man should be free to pursue this even if it involves murder and torture. The famous Byronic hero shook his fist at heaven, and asserted his right to do whatever he liked, regardless of society. And Emily Brontë's Heathcliff is another Byronic rebel. . . .

The effects of these thought-experiments in freedom were not unlike the effects of opium. To become absorbed in a novel, or in one of those long narrative poems of Byron (which sold even better than novels) was to feel the 'relaxation of tension and anxiety, the onset of a special kind of calm enjoyment . . .' and so on. There was even a certain resemblance between the after-effects; everyone who has been reading for too long knows that feeling of listlessness, loss of contact with reality, a kind of mental dyspepsia.

There was one crucial difference. Opium achieves its effects on the central nervous system, soothing it into quiescence and leaving the mind to drift like a glider. The novel produced its effect through a kind of *widening of vision*. Our everyday consciousness is narrow, like a camera with a narrow-angle lens. It takes excellent close-up pictures, but its range is restricted. On the other hand, a professional photographer can slip a wide-angle lens into his camera, and photograph a whole panorama. And *this* describes the effect produced on consciousness by the novel. It slips a wide-angle lens into the mind. It enables us to 'pull back', as if the camera was rising into the air, suddenly revealing tracts of countryside. Of course, we always 'knew' they existed, in an abstract sense; but the narrow-angle lens of everyday consciousness prevented us from *seeing* them. Many opium-eaters have described this same effect—of hovering over mountain ranges or broad oceans—but their vision had the uncontrollable quality of a dream. The novel was, in effect, a controlled opium-trip. It was a device for producing wide-angle consciousness.

We can now see why the 'naturalistic novel' was not the revolutionary advance Flaubert and Zola believed. In *Madame Bovary*, Flaubert had actually taken a step backwards—in fact, two steps. He had switched the wide-angle lens back to the narrow-angle lens. And he had chosen for his central character an empty-headed flirt who cannot, by any stretch of the imagination, be regarded as Flaubert's self-image. (Flaubert once remarked: 'I am Madame Bovary', but it is patently untrue.) It is true that *Madame Bovary* is about 'freedom'—a suburban housewife's attempt to achieve a kind of freedom—but it is not an *exploration* of freedom; Charles and Emma are foredoomed from the beginning. And not by the novelist's tragic intention, but by his contempt.

If Flaubert and Zola had been great enough, they would have attempted to *combine* the wide- and narrow-angle lens—rather like those bi-focal spectacles that enable you to switch range in a moment.

Only one novelist instinctively grasped this truth: Tolstoy. *War and Peace* combines the wide- and narrow-angle vision. E. M. Forster says accurately that 'the sense of space until it terrifies us is exhilarating, and produces an effect like music'. He goes on: 'After one has read *War and Peace* for a bit, great chords begin to sound, and we cannot say exactly what struck them. . . . They come from the immense area of Russia over which episodes and characters have been scattered, from the sum-total of bridges and frozen rivers, forests, roads, gardens, fields. . . .' But Forster is mistaken in thinking that the sense of 'space until it terrifies' is the explanation for the 'effect like music'. If this was so, then the old picaresque novels—*Don Quixote, Gil Blas, Tom Jones*—would produce the same effect, for they cover a great deal of space, and every travel book would 'sound great chords'. Forster has failed to recognise that the novel is basically about freedom. The battle against Napoleon is one symbol of freedom; the vast areas of space covered are another. But even more interesting is the obsession of the central characters with freedom—notably Prince Andrew and Pierre. What is so remarkable about Tolstoy is that he is the first great novelist to grasp the *paradoxical* nature of freedom: what Obermann was hinting at when he said that the rain depressed him but the sunlight struck him as useless. He is fascinated by the way that actual physical freedom—the ability to go where you like and do what you want—is often boring, whereas any kind of crisis or emergency can create an intense consciousness of freedom. Pierre is a bored and rather aimless young man when he has nothing to do but amuse himself. He discovers the meaning of freedom when he is standing in front of a French firing squad, about to be shot as a spy, when life suddenly seems infinitely desirable. But even here, Tolstoy is inclined to allow his rational intellect to falsify the result. After being reprieved, Pierre becomes a prisoner of war, and is struck by the contentment of the old peasant Platon Karataev, who believes everything is the will of God, and who sleeps the dreamless sleep of the innocent. Tolstoy, like Pierre, came to believe that this Rousseau-istic 'back to nature' attitude was the answer to man's complex longing for freedom.

In spite of which, his work is full of instinctive insights into the 'absurd' nature of freedom. Gorky tells a typical story of this aspect of Tolstoy. They were walking along a street when they saw two dragoons marching towards them. Tolstoy began to grumble: 'Military idiots . . . marching like mechanical toys, not a thought in their heads. . . .' Then, as the two dragoons passed in perfect step, in their blue uniforms, Tolstoy suddenly exclaimed: 'Aren't they magnificent!' He was never a slave of his intellectual convictions; he recognised the appeal of sheer vitality as more deeply true. This is expressed in *War and Peace* in the episode of the oak tree. When Prince Andrew passes the tree on his way to see the Rostovs, it seems to be dead, as he feels his own hopes and beliefs to be dead. At the Rostov's, he overhears a conversation between two young girls as they sit at the bedroom window at night, and it touches some hidden spring of delight in him. When he passes the oak tree on his way home, it is covered with spring buds. . . .

Now Flaubert or Zola would have been incapable of this kind of 'double vision', this simultaneous response to *two* sets of values, intellectual and vital. (I have called it elsewhere 'dual value response'.) Once Emma Bovary has begun to dream of freedom and love affairs, she is like a fly with its feet stuck on fly paper; her struggles only get her more securely stuck. Zola's early novel *Thérèse Raquin* is another powerful study of a vital young girl married to a dull husband; the husband's closest friend becomes her lover, and together they plan her husband's murder. But after the crime, they are trapped; they bore one another, they suspect one another. You are aware that Zola can see no alternative to killing them off, and the novel ends with an unbelievable double-suicide. Without 'double vision', Flaubert and Zola could see no solution to the problem of the craving for freedom; and, unlike Tolstoy's oak tree, their novels expire predictably.

On the whole, and in spite of its defects, *War and Peace* remains a touchstone of greatness in the novel. No novelist ever conveyed more clearly that sense of sheer absurd vitality; the sleigh ride, the wolf hunt, Andrew's mystical glimpse on the field of Austerlitz, all reveal Tolstoy's power of 'dual value response', double-vision.

Towards the end of the book, as if impelled by some demon

of perversity, Tolstoy begins to insert long essays on his own
theory of history. And the essence of this theory is that free will
is an illusion. Historical events roll on like a river in flood;
Napoleon, Caesar, Alexander the Great, are no more than twigs
swept along by the river. He jeers at the theory that men like
Rousseau and Diderot had anything to do with the French
Revolution, and compares 'great men' to rams being fattened
for the slaughter by a shepherd; they are only 'great' because
some inscrutable fate chooses to feed their voracious egos. . . .

And so a novel whose greatness lies in the intensity of its
vision of freedom tails off into pessimism, demonstrating once
again that great creators can be extremely muddled thinkers.

The problem of the naturalistic novel was that it became a
slave not only to the 'narrow-angle lens' (i.e. to space) but also
to time. If you begin to describe someone's life carefully,
naturalistically, from day to day, the inevitable result is that
they end in the grave. You may, like Tolstoy, end the novel
with another generation rushing into the room—as their
mother did in Volume One—but that is something of a confidence trick, for the same problem still arises. Many fine
novelists have found themselves caught in this particular trap.
For example, in Romain Rolland's vast *Jean-Christophe* (originally published in ten volumes between 1904 and 1912), the
hero is a musician based on Beethoven. The first volumes are
superb—showing the childhood of the young genius, how his
father heard him playing the piano and decided to turn him
into a virtuoso, his youth in the court orchestra, his love affairs,
his flight to Paris after killing a soldier in a brawl, gradual
recognition of his talents, increasing fame. . . . But once Jean-
Christophe has been recognised, what is there left for the
novelist to do? He describes more love affairs, more friend-
ships, another flight (this time to Switzerland). You get the
feeling that Rolland would like to end the novel if only he
knew how. So finally, the heroine dies, and then Christophe
himself finally dies. The last thousand pages of the novel are a
long anti-climax.

The same problem can be seen in Sigrid Undset's Nobel

Prize-winning novel *Kristin Lavransdatter*, almost as long as *Jean-Christophe*. The basic theme is religious; the heroine is torn between religion and the world. After being almost raped, she enters a convent; but on a shopping trip, falls in love with a betrothed man, with whom she has a love affair. She finally marries him, and herself becomes a mother and mistress of an estate. And the complications begin all over again; until, at the end of the third volume, Kristin dies in a convent of the Black Death. The re-creation of fourteenth-century Norway is remarkable; but in spite of the religious theme, which gives the novel power and depth, it fails to escape the 'time trap'. In the first volume, you are fascinated by Kristin's vitality and appetite for life. The problem of her freedom—and what she intends to do with it—becomes absorbing. Before the end of the book this interest, like Kristin's freedom, has evaporated. And the novelist seems powerless to do anything about it.

Arnold Bennett's *The Old Wives' Tale* is a somewhat different case, if only because the theme is *intended* to be the destructive power of time. In a Paris restaurant, Bennett had observed a fat old lady, behaving so eccentrically that all the waitresses were laughing behind her back. It came into his head that this repulsive old creature had once been young and slim, and he planned a short story about her—giving her a sister, in order to 'go one better' than Maupassant in *Une Vie*. The result is a novel that starts with the Baines girls, aged fifteen and sixteen, and ends with their deaths half a century later. One marries a clerk and runs a small shop; the other elopes with a good-looking young man, is deserted by him, and survives the siege of Paris. Both widowed, the sisters come together again, and live on quietly into old age. The book produces a sense of sadness and waste and the general meaninglessness of human existence. So although *The Old Wives Tale* is an authentic attempt at 'wide-angle vision', it is also a kind of dead end. This may explain why, as Forster points out, it misses greatness as a novel. Significantly, Bennett was strongly influenced by the French naturalists.

*

To say that all serious literature is basically about the problem of freedom may seem too sweeping a generalisation. A less abstract way of putting it would be to say that all good writers set out to embody their own attitude to life in their work; and in order to illustrate this—to show how it would work out in actuality—they perform 'thought-experiments' with their characters. Naturally, they are inclined to cheat, for they are arguing in favour of their own view of life, and wish to make out as good a case as possible. Dickens makes his villains unnaturally villainous and his virtuous people unnaturally virtuous. Gogol is a satirist, so his characters have more than their share of human failings: dishonesty, jealousy, cupidity. Hardy felt nature to be mechanical and ruthless, so his characters have more than their share of bad luck. Charles Lever, a popular Victorian novelist, was a happy-go-lucky person, so his characters have more than their share of good luck.

And yet—and here is the interesting point—in spite of this distortion, these thought-experiments have something of the same objective value as real scientific experiments in a real laboratory. If a writer has integrity—and, by definition, all good writers have—he cannot fake the outcome of the experiment. Like a mathematical calculation, the result is inevitable. Walter Pater, the Victorian essayist, believed that the chief aim of life is to achieve a certain intensity of experience—to live with a 'hard, gem-like flame', and he wrote a novel, *Marius the Epicurean*, to illustrate his philosophy. But three-quarters of the way through the novel, Marius begins to find his 'epicureanism' unsatisfying, and ends by joining a Christian sect and losing his life as a result of a gesture of self-sacrifice. Similarly, in *Against the Grain*, Huysmans set out to show that the pursuit of sensual pleasure is the highest aim; yet the novel ends with the hero in a state of mental and physical exhaustion.

In the 1840s, the Danish philosopher Kierkegaard coined the word 'existential' to describe a type of philosophy that poses the question: 'What should we do with our lives?' He pointed out that we are all in a state of *becoming*, and that therefore logical thought is a poor guide to living. We need a deeper, more passionate kind of instinct for truth and freedom.

'Abstract thinking'—of the kind practised by Hegel—is no use. It never seems to have struck Kierkegaard that the kind of 'existential' thinking he had in mind is the type practised by all serious novelists. Yet it is true. The novel is the embodiment of what Kierkegaard meant by existential philosophy. It is an attempt to demonstrate clearly the outcome of certain attitudes to life. And even if the novelist happens to be a muddled thinker, he cannot evade the strange, inexorable laws of creation.

Let us look a little more closely at the way these laws work out in practice.

On the morning of 14 November 1916, Hector Hugh Munro was killed on the Western Front by a German sniper. He was the author of half a dozen volumes of short stories, and two novels, one of them a masterpiece. At the time of his death, he was considering ceasing to be a writer, and taking up farming in Siberia after the war.

In a memoir of her brother, his elder sister records that the first thing she remembers about him was the occasion when he plunged a hearth-brush into the nursery fire, then chased his brother round the room shouting: 'I'm God. I'm going to destroy the world.' The story catches the essence of 'Saki's' later work: the 'demonic' sense of humour. After a period of travelling around Europe—then essential to the education of all upper-class Englishmen—and a period in the Burmese police, he returned to England and began writing satirical short stories. When he began to write, in the mid-1890s, the most 'scandalous' writer on the English literary scene was Oscar Wilde. One of Munro's strongest desires was to scandalise; so it was inevitable that he began to write in the manner of Wilde. What is perhaps more surprising is that his stories and epigrams are often as good as Wilde's.

Munro was a Scot, and a member of a military family; he found the British upper classes effete, and the middle classes ridiculous. Most of the stories are about clever young men (or women) scoring off respectable and conventional people. Reginald and Clovis—heroes of early short stories—are first cousins to Wilde's Algernon Moncrieff. Here is Reginald describing an unsuccessful house party:

There's such a deadly sameness about partridges; when you've missed one, you've missed the lot—at least, that's been my experience. And they tried to rag me in the smoking-room about not being able to hit a bird at five yards, a sort of bovine ragging that suggested cows buzzing round a gad-fly and thinking they were teasing it. So I got up the next morning at early dawn—I know it was dawn, because there were lark-noises in the sky, and the grass looked as if it had been left out all night—and hunted up the most con-spicuous thing in the bird line that I could find, and measured the distance, as nearly as it would let me, and shot away all I knew. They said afterwards it was a tame bird; that's simply *silly*, because it was awfully wild at the first few shots. Afterwards it quieted down a bit, and when its legs had stopped waving farewells to the landscape, I got a gardener's boy to drag it into the hall, where everybody must see it on their way to the breakfast-room. I breakfasted upstairs my-self. I gathered afterwards that the meal was tinged with a very unchristian spirit. I suppose it's unlucky to bring pea-cock's feathers into the house; anyway, there was a blue-pencilly look in my hostess's eye when I took my departure....

That is typical Saki (Munro took his pen-name from the second edition of Fitzgerald's *Ruba'iyat*). In story after story, the same kind of thing happens; he seems to want to make the middle classes feel guilty about merely existing. At times, it is clear that the hatred of authority is almost paranoid; in *Sredni Vashtar*, the small boy's domineering female cousin has her throat torn out by a savage ferret; like Poe's *Cask of Amontillado*, the story is an almost psychotic hate-fantasy. But usually, the detestation expressed itself in barbed epigrams: 'Her frocks come from Paris, but she wears them with a strong English accent'; 'She lost everything she had, and gave the rest to God'; 'She is so fond of talking of certain pictures "growing on one" as though they were a sort of fungus'; 'Waldo is one of those people who would be enormously improved by death.'

His first novel, *The Unbearable Bassington*, appeared in 1912, when he was forty-one. He had been satirising small sections of English society for long enough; apparently he now decided to do it on a larger scale. On the back of the title-page, he has a typical 'author's note': 'This story has no moral. If it points out an evil, at any rate it suggests no remedy.' 'Morals' were something the middle classes expected, and remedies were the kind of thing offered by Bernard Shaw, a writer towards whom Munro's attitude was highly ambivalent. ('Bernard Shaw had discovered himself and gave ungrudgingly of his discovery to the world.') Munro was determined to maintain his attitude of detached superiority.

From its title, we can guess that *The Unbearable Bassington* is going to be about another of Saki's *enfants terribles*, determined to do the opposite of what 'respectable people' expect of him. But even on the first page, we can sense that the author finds himself in an unaccustomed position of moral ambiguity. He is talking about the hero's mother, Francesca Bassington, an attractive widow of slender means: '. . . she was not of the perverse band of those who make a rock-garden of their souls by dragging into them all the stony griefs and unclaimed troubles they can find lying around them. . . .'; that is to say, she is not Saki's pet detestation, a do-gooder. So presumably she is to be one of the people of whom he approves? Not that either. 'Francesca herself, if pressed in an unguarded moment to describe her soul, would probably have described her drawing room.' She is strongly attached to her social comforts—particularly to her pleasant West End house, which will have to be vacated when her niece Emmeline marries. But Francesca is hoping Emmeline will marry her son Comus—the 'unbearable Bassington'—and they will all be able to live in the house. She makes the mistake of writing to Comus, asking him to be especially nice to Emmeline's younger brother, who is a new boy at the same public school as Comus. Typically, Comus takes the first opportunity to thrash the boy, destroying his mother's hopes.

Two years later, now a young man about town, Comus is

determined not to be turned into a useful member of society.
When his uncle finds him a position as secretary to a Governor
in the West Indies, Comus persuades a friend to write a satirical
article about his future employer, which appears in a newspaper over Comus's signature; the offer of the job is withdrawn.

And so it goes on; Comus continues to be witty, perverse,
clever, immoral, decorative and determinedly useless. Elaine,
a wealthy and rather attractive girl, is in love with him; Comus
manages to alienate her so that she marries someone else.
Finally, Comus is forced to take a job in West Africa. It bores
him and he loathes it. Before leaving, he has a premonition of
his death. The last time we see him, he is sitting on a brown
African hillside, watching the ant-like activity of the blacks. 'It
was so utterly trivial to his eyes, so devoid of interest, and yet
it was so real, so serious, so implacable in its continuity.' Later,
Francesca receives a telegram informing her of his death from
malaria.

Saki has carefully pursued the implications of the values he
has been advocating in the early stories, and realised that they
are unreal. He is too honest not to face the realisation. But it
leaves him intellectually and morally bankrupt.

How would he have backed out of the *cul de sac*? The answer
is that he probably wouldn't. In any case, he was spared the
decision by the war. If he had survived, it seems possible that
the farm in Siberia might have provided the solution: rejection
of society, return to the simplicities of nature. . . . But there is
an episode in *Bassington* that suggests otherwise. During a ride
in the country, Elaine meets a man she used to know, a retired
adventurer who now runs a small farm, and describes the life
as being 'like the old chronicles of mediaeval Europe in the
days when there was a sort of ordered anarchy'. It sounds as if
Saki is stating his own basic values. 'Sitting there in the little
paddock, grown thickly with tall weeds and rank grasses, and
shadowed by the weather-beaten old grey barn, listening to
this chronicle of wonderful things, half fanciful, half very real,
she could scarcely believe that a few miles away there was a
garden party in full swing. . . .' She sees the farm as a 'magic
city', and tells the owner he is to be envied. 'Envied?' he says,

and tells her that he once read a story about a crippled crane that lived in a park: 'There was one line that I shall always remember: "It was lame, that was why it was tame".' Munro saw through Rousseau's 'Back to Nature', but he had no better suggestion.

Why is *The Unbearable Bassington* so oddly memorable, when its flavour is so negative? (It appeared in 1912, long before the post-war era of disillusionment.) I personally find that the scene that has haunted me—ever since I read the novel at the age of fourteen—is the last appearance of Comus, sitting by the muddy river, feeling that it is all so trivial and yet so real. It poses a fundamental question with startling clarity. Comus knows what he doesn't want, but has no idea of what he *does* want. Suppose a telegram now told him that he had come into a legacy and could return to his life as a man about town. Would this be what he wants? Obviously not. Boredom has produced a loss of contact with reality. But this 'reality' of Africa is no answer either. In spite of its sheer persistence, it is no realler than London. Something in man hungers for a deeper reality, hence Axel's 'As for living. . . .' But how does one gain contact with this other 'reality'?

Or—an equally interesting question from the novelist's point of view—how do we *lose* contact with it? Boredom, lack of vital striving, causes consciousness to go 'flat', like a bottle of soda-water that has been left open. But the word 'flat' affords another interesting clue. When I am in a state of 'wide-angle consciousness', I am not only *aware* of more than when in a 'narrow-angle' state. I see it all in a quite different way. And I can only compare the difference to seeing a drawing or photograph of something, and then seeing the real thing, *in three dimensions*. Or think of those red and green cellophane spectacles that children have in their Christmas stockings, with a set of blurry-looking photographs. You look at the photographs through the spectacles, and at first, it just looks a little clearer, but still a mere photograph. Then suddenly, it leaps into three dimensions.

This is what happens in those moments of sudden contact with reality: the world leaps from 2-D to 3-D. And if I experience sudden fatigue, it *flattens* just as abruptly from 3-D to 2-D.

A moment's thought reveals the reason for this. When I am happy and full of energy, I can afford to let my eyes rest on things, and really *see* them. There is a faint jerk—like switching into overdrive on your car—and the subconscious mind relaxes. And then things you are looking at seem to blossom, like those paper flowers you put into water, and turn into three-dimensional objects. On the other hand, life is complex and difficult, and for ninety-nine per cent of my time, I cannot afford to go into overdrive. To deal with this complex world, I need the visual equivalent of shorthand: I see that red, noisy object as an approaching bus, that green spot ahead as a traffic light that may change as I approach. I 'speed-read' the world. And to do this, I deliberately deprive it of its third dimension—of reality—and turn it into a series of flat symbols, which are easier to scan. When I become tired, a robot-computer in my subconscious mind switches to 2-D quite automatically, to conserve energy.

Clearly, this is why Rousseau disliked civilisation. With its complexity, it refuses to allow us to relax into 3-D consciousness. We flick the overdrive switch, but it fails to work; the inner tension remains, and the reality around us stays determinedly flat. The chief advantage of Nature is that it induces relaxation.

And there, of course, is the trouble. If often induces too much relaxation. The subconscious works best when you keep spurring it with a sense of purpose. The average farm labourer or countryman experiences no more 3-D consciousness than a harassed townsman. *That* is why Obermann found the sunlight pointless. 'Nature' is not the solution of the problem; the solution lies inside us.

All of which brings us to the heart of the matter, a problem that will recur in many forms throughout the rest of this book. We experience narrow-angle, 2-D consciousness ninety-nine per cent of the time—or, say, ninety-five. 3-D consciousness is a fairly rare occurrence. And, as Wordsworth pointed out, it tends to become rarer as we get older. Which hardly matters, provided we recognise that the world we see in wide-angle consciousness is *realler* and truer than the world we see in 'everyday consciousness'. But self-pity and fatigue can lead us to the dangerous conclusion that 'everyday consciousness' shows us the world as it 'really is', and that 3-D consciousness is somehow artificial, like de Quincey's opium visions. This is not a conscious judgment. It is a feeling of cold that creeps over the heart, the inner certainty that boredom, triviality and gloom are more lasting, and therefore more real, than the sudden flashes of absurd joy.

This is, as we can see from this analysis, untrue. The Taj Mahal and the Great Wall of China are realler and more exciting than any of their photographs. The world *is* 3-D, and our ordinary 2-D consciousness has robbed it of a dimension of reality. If we could only *grasp* this, deeply, instinctively, we would have solved one of the worst problems we are likely to encounter in the course of a lifetime.

One more point. The three-dimensional image applies, of course, to every type of experience, not just visual. If I have been starved of music, a Mozart symphony on the car radio can fill me with delight. If I am tired and dull, the same symphony reproduced in stereo through the finest loudspeakers can leave me indifferent. The truth is that in order to enjoy the symphony fully, I need to *add* a certain energy to it, just as I need to add water and milk to a cake-mix. Trying to listen to the symphony when my mind is 'flat' is like trying to eat the cake-mix straight out of the packet; it only clogs my mouth. (This is what the philosopher Husserl meant when he said that consciousness is intentional—but that is something we need not go into here.) Experience has to be 'reconstituted' like dried-egg powder. So we have at least the outline of an answer to the question: How do we re-establish contact with reality? The first necessity is to be optimistic—that is, to know that 3-D consciousness is realler and somehow more 'natural' than 2-D. This in turn allows a certain 'energy of optimism' to form in us—a kind of state of 'delighted expectation'—which is the essential ingredient in reconstituting 2-D into 3-D experience.

And now we have the concepts that enable us to understand the failure of so many novelists. Saki's Bassington is obsessed by his dislike of authority, surrounded by people who expect him to 'do' something and 'make something of himself'; so he reacts into a passive and satirical hedonism. Drifting becomes a way of life; inevitably, it causes more-or-less permanent 2-D consciousness. This was obviously a reflection of Saki's own state of mind, as we can see from the novel; the world he shows us is flat and thoroughly negative.

At least he recognised the problem instinctively, which is what gives the novel its strange vitality. Greater novelists had been—and would again be—defeated by it. For example, D. H. Lawrence, whose work shows many close parallels with that of Munro. At first sight, this seems absurd; Lawrence is an altogether more vital and complex writer than Munro. Still, the comparison holds. Lawrence is also preoccupied with the question of how civilisation causes loss of contact with reality. He also detests the middle classes and has an ambivalent attitude to the upper classes. And although we tend to think of him as a writer who was centrally concerned with the world of instinct and Nature, it is surprising how much of his work is grimly negative. Between *The White Peacock*, his first novel, and *Lady Chatterley's Lover*, his last, he explores a whole series of solutions that prove to be false or inadequate. In *The White Peacock*, the answer seems to lie in Nature and the instinctive life of the body; even so, the young farmer hero becomes a defeated drunkard. With *The Trespasser*, Lawrence began to consider the possibility that sex could be the answer. For the orgasm is a sudden surge of energy that turns 2-D into 3-D consciousness. But this raises new problems. Sex involves another person, another *personality*, and this is likely to produce a clash of wills. In *Sons and Lovers*, *The Rainbow* and *Women in Love*, he broods on this problem of the ideal relationship between a man and a woman. It proves to be more complicated than appeared at first sight—so much so that he appears to be losing his old certainty that the sexual relationship holds the solution. We also observe in these novels that Lawrence is very clear about what he dislikes: industrialism, intellectual cleverness, snobbery, domineering will-power; but, like Saki, he seems to have only the vaguest idea of what he wants. In

Aaron's Rod and *Kangaroo*, he explores the idea that the man-woman relationship needs to be supplemented by a deep and mystical man-man relationship. Lawrence is also experimenting with the idea that he himself might become a spiritual leader or messiah. In *The Plumed Serpent*, the deep world of instinct and reality is identified with the dark gods of Mexico, who return to cast out Christianity. A pendant story, *The Woman Who Rode Away*, makes the point clearer still; the American woman, trapped in her own ego and the moral deadness induced by civilisation, finds ultimate fulfilment in allowing herself to be sacrificed by Mexican Indians to their dark gods. Lawrence has taken Rousseau's 'Back to Nature' to its extreme, and unintentionally demonstrated its absurdity. In *Lady Chatterley's Lover* he returns to the notion that the solution lies in sex; and the scenes in which Constance Chatterley finds sexual fulfilment with the gamekeeper have considerable power. But then, as we want to know what happens next, the book becomes less convincing; it is difficult to believe that a life in a gamekeeper's cottage is the ultimate solution to the problems of civilisation. There is also an irritable, carping tone in the book, a bitter flavour, that seems to contradict the mystical assertions about the redeeming power of sex. Lawrence was backing himself into the same *cul de sac* as Saki in *Bassington*. And, like Saki, he died leaving the problem unsolved. His books are like a heap of jotting paper covered with notes on possible solutions—all incomplete.

But when we look more closely at Lawrence as a writer, we can see what went wrong. There can be no doubt that he is deeply concerned to make human beings recognise that their consciousness is narrow and inadequate. All his works emphasise that the world is more immense and complex than we realise; men must somehow turn away from the trivialities that waste their lives, and recognise this mystical 'otherness' of the universe. The power of his work lies in his ability to suggest this 'otherness'. His mistake is to assume that the enemy is 'consciousness'—daylight consciousness—which leads him to assume that the answer lies in some darker, more instinctive form of consciousness. The daylight consciousness he dislikes is what I have called narrow-angle consciousness; the alternative is not the unconscious world of instinct, but a wide-angle consciousness which *includes* instinct. (A moment's thought will show that when we are in a state of wide-angle consciousness, we are more closely in touch with our instincts.) Lawrence failed to grasp this distinction; that is why his work, for all its genius, remains unsatisfactory.

The conclusion of all this may be regarded as the central thesis of this book: that where the craft of the novel is concerned, a little insight into its basic aims and motives is worth a great deal of undisciplined talent.

Let us summarise some of the major conclusions so far:

1. The aim of the novel is to produce wide-angle consciousness. Everyday consciousness is narrow and limited; the novel is one of the most interesting compensations that man has so far devised.

2. The novel is substitute experience. Most of us have an appetite for a far wider range of experience than our lives afford. To some extent, the novel can provide it. It can even provide forms of experience that would have been impossible in reality.

3. The novel is a form of thought-experiment. Like the thought-experiments of the philosopher, its aim is to teach us something about the real world.

4. Ideally, the aim of the novel is not only to produce wide-angle consciousness, but also three-dimensional consciousness—something allied to the opium experience (the sense of relaxing and opening-up), but with an unimpaired sense of reality—a recognition of the enormous and fascinating complexity of the world.

5. Unsuccessful novels are thought-experiments that have failed to 'come out right', like a calculation that has gone wrong, or a laboratory experiment in which the experimenter has made some crucial error.

6. The aim of all these thought-experiments is the exploration of human freedom.

FIVE

The Formula for Success

THIS CHAPTER WILL be a short one. Its aim is simply to
reassure any would-be novelist who feels that to write an artistically successful novel is an almost impossible task. On the
contrary, it is fairly easy, and has been accomplished thousands
of times. For there is a sense in which the basic rule is simply a
law of biology. Biologically speaking, freedom is discharge of
tension. Therefore, a successful novel is one that builds up
tension, and then allows it to be discharged, like a bursting
thunderstorm. The Victorian melodrama—or early Hollywood
movie—that begins with the villain twisting his moustache as
he plans some piece of malpractice, instantly creates this tension: a certain desire, even in the most sophisticated audience,
to see the villain get his come-uppance. George Meredith, the
most 'difficult' of Victorian novelists, applies the same formula,
without shame, in the opening words of his best novel:

> There was an ominously anxious watch of eyes visible and
> invisible over the infancy of Willoughby, fifth in descent
> from Simon Patterne, of Patterne Hall, premier of this
> family, a lawyer, a man of solid acquirements and stout
> ambition, who well understood the foundation-work of a
> House, and was endowed with the power of saying No to
> those first agents of destruction, besieging relatives.

Not a memorable or striking opening sentence, you may feel.
Many of George Meredith's contemporaries had similar reser-
vations about his style. Still, that opening paragraph tells us a
great deal. It tells us that the founder of the family fortune,
Simon Patterne, was a lawyer—and therefore a member of the

middle classes—whose ambition turned him into a landed gentleman. We also gather, from his attitude to 'besieging relatives', that he was something of a Scrooge. So we are not surprised to learn that his descendant, Sir Willoughby Patterne, is also a ruthless egoist. In the same short chapter, Meredith goes on to tell how, when Sir Willoughby came into the title and money, he sent a cheque to a distant relative, whose heroism in China has been reported in the newspapers. He has also invited the officer to call on him when convenient. In due course, the officer walks up the drive, carrying his bag —a thick-set, stumpy man 'definitely *not* bearing the stamp of a gentleman'. So when the card of Lieutenant Patterne is handed to him, Sir Willoughby sends the footman back with the message 'not at home'. And the stumpy lieutenant in the melancholy hat plods off down the drive under gathering rain-clouds.

And so, before he has read more than two and a half pages, the reader already finds 'the Egoist' detestable. And this has been accomplished without any Dickensian show of sympathy for the underdog; Meredith is far too sophisticated to wear his heart on his sleeve. But he induces in the reader precisely the same effect as Dickens: an intense desire to see the villain get his come-uppance.

Meredith is too clever to keep the reader waiting long. In the following chapter, we learn that Laetitia Dale, a shy girl who lives on the estate, is in love with Sir Willoughby, and that he has given her reason to think she might become Lady Patterne. But he deserts her to get engaged to the beautiful Constantia Durham, whose thoroughbred lines have earned her the nickname 'the Racing Cutter'. We recall that, at the end of the last chapter, it was this young lady who blushed angrily when Sir Willoughby 'cut' his ungentleman-like cousin, and we receive the first hint that the egoist's path may not be as smooth as he hopes. A few pages later, she elopes with a military man. Yet if Sir Willoughby is humiliated by his rejection, he fails to show it. When Laetitia asks after Miss Durham, he replies coldly, 'There is no Miss Durham to my knowledge.' So the villain is still unscathed, and we read on eagerly, waiting for the next setback. . . .

In short, in spite of the polished style and sophisticated irony, the basic technique of *The Egoist* is as crude as that of *Sweeney Todd, The Demon Barber of Fleet Street*. Meredith knows that all his intellectual brilliance would only irritate the reader without this underlying appeal to very simple human emotions, and the basic pattern of tension and discharge of tension. In those first three or four chapters, he has already written the novel in a nutshell, and told the reader exactly what to expect. Now, having engaged our full attention, he will proceed to do the whole thing over again on a much more leisurely scale. Sir Willoughby returns from a trip abroad—presumably to lick his wounds—with his cousin Vernon, who is to become manager of the estates. Will he now marry Laetitia Dale? Of course not. He repeats his offence —raises her hopes, then gets engaged to someone else—this time, Clara Middleton, a doctor's daughter. Now we shall watch his humiliation with Constantia Durham repeated on a larger scale.

Sir Willoughby has also brought back with him young Crossjay Patterne, the son of the ungentlemanly lieutenant. Is this not a mistake? Surely Meredith is now showing the villain in a sympathetic light, as a man who has repented of his ruthless treatment of his cousin? But no; it is soon apparent that the act of charity is designed solely to make Sir Willoughby pleased with himself. His egoism has many subtle twists and turns. And the author's subtlety has the effect of flattering the reader's intelligence: this is no crude melodrama; it is scrupulously true to life. . . .

And so we watch Sir Willoughby's second fiancée experiencing the same disillusionment as the first, and the growth of affection between her and Sir Willoughby's cousin Vernon. When Sir Willoughby realises he is about to be jilted a second time, he tries to soothe his wounded vanity by asking Laetitia to marry him. Of course, she refuses. (She wouldn't refuse in real life, but in the novel her job is to administer another kick to his egoism.) He now tries to arrange a marriage between Vernon and Clara—another attempt to convince himself that when he pulls the strings, the puppets dance. But even this satisfaction is denied him when Clara tells him that she and Vernon had every intention of getting married anyway. . . . Now all that remains is for the egoist to crawl to Laetitia's feet, and beg her to marry him as a favour, even if she no longer loves him. Of course, she loves him, but she doesn't let on; merely accepts him. And so the novel ends in a grand blaze of reconciliation. There isn't a dry eye in the house. We even like Sir Willoughby.

Of course, it's preposterous. If he's as much of a bastard as Meredith represents, he isn't going to change overnight. Within six months he'll probably be bullying the poor girl and behaving as badly as ever. Looked at closely, the whole book is no more 'true to life' than Dickens's *Christmas Carol*. As far as that goes, it is just another Victorian novel full of absurd events. But we don't mind—even when we see through the trick. We enjoy allowing Meredith to manipulate our emotions. We enjoy hating Sir Willoughby and adoring Laetitia and sympathising with Vernon and Clara. And the fact that Meredith appeals to such simple emotions, while appearing to be sophisticated and intellectual, makes us feel that we're all rather brilliant. . . .

That, then, is the trick: tension and discharge of tension, producing a sensation of freedom. But it can be carried out on many levels. Most of the novels of Jane Austen, for example, are about an attractive young lady in need of a husband. The freedom her heroines dream about is a home of their own and an agreeable husband. As in the case of Meredith, her wit and sophistication prevent us from recognising that her novels are basically schoolgirl wish-fulfilment fantasies. Their fascination lies in the basic simplicity of the plot. So, for example, we have in *Persuasion* a variant of the Cinderella story, with two sisters, one beautiful, brilliant and spoilt, the other sweet, self-effacing and intelligent. The self-effacing sister, Anne, has been engaged to a Captain Wentworth at one point, but her family have forced her to break the engagement because he is not rich; so eight years later, Anne is still high and dry, while Captain Wentworth *has* actually become rich. . . . Any reader can now predict what will happen. All Jane Austen has to do is to somehow bring Anne and the Captain together again. And she does this with the instinctive skill of a born story-teller—that is to say, a lifelong daydreamer. The family move to Bath (because the father is in financial difficulties, and is forced to rent their home, Kellynch Hall). There they are in contact with a wider circle of people, and the complications can begin. Naturally, Anne soon meets Captain Wentworth again. And in order to get them together under the same roof, Jane Austen resorts to a singularly clumsy piece of contrivance; Louisa Musgrove, Anne's chief rival for Captain Wentworth, insists on jumping down a flight of steps to the beach at Lyme Regis. 'She was too precipitate by half a second, she fell on the pavement on the Lower Cobb, and was taken up lifeless! . . . the horror of that moment to all who stood around.' Louisa is taken to the home of some friends of Captain Wentworth, and the quiet and capable Anne stays on to nurse her. And so it goes on. This is not the end of the novel. Jane Austen is enjoying her romantic fantasy too much to bring it to a close. Anne becomes convinced that Captain Wentworth loves Louisa. Captain Wentworth believes that Anne is in love with her cousin, a certain Mr Elliot, who turns out to be a villain. And finally, all is sorted out, and the various couples pair off, as in a musical comedy. The whole thing is basically much ado about nothing, for if Anne had had any sense, she would have married Captain Wentworth when she was nine-teen. But then, there would have been no novel, and this would have been a pity, for *Persuasion* is a delightful piece of detailed daydreaming.

But the freedom that interests Jane Austen is obviously on a lower level than the freedom that interests a modern novelist like Jean Paul Sartre. Mathieu Delarue, the central character of his trilogy *The Roads to Freedom (Les Chemins de la Liberté)* is obsessed by other forms of freedom—moral, political and 'existential'. And when we contrast Mathieu Delarue with Anne Elliott, we see why Sartre's problems as a novelist are so much greater than Jane Austen's. Mathieu is an assistant professor, and is thoroughly dissatisfied with himself without knowing quite what he wants. He has a mistress, and she is pregnant; in any case, he is no longer in love with her. He is in love with one of his students, but she doesn't care for him; and in any case, Sartre knows that it would solve nothing even if she did. Like Comus Bassington, Mathieu knows what he doesn't want, but has no idea what he *does* want. He is repelled by the bourgeois idea of security and material success; he doesn't believe in religion; he cannot work up any strong convictions about communism, although he is attracted by it. In the first volume, *The Age of Reason*, he certainly has a problem that creates the necessary tension: he has to find money for his mistress to have an abortion, and no one will lend it to him.

Now the odd thing is that this first volume is a successful and satisfying novel, even though Mathieu comes no nearer to finding inner freedom. His mistress solves the problem of her pregnancy by marrying a homosexual. And we become absorbed in the problems of the various characters: the homosexual, a young kleptomaniac, a cabaret singer, and so on. When you reach the last page, you are perfectly willing to open the second volume, because you want to know what becomes of the characters. But about halfway through this second volume, the reader experiences the first stirring of an uncomfortable suspicion. Is it possible that Sartre *doesn't know where he is going*? A hundred pages later, there can be no doubt whatever. Astounding as it seems, we have an author who is taking us on a voyage with no idea of the destination—and with no guarantee that we will actually arrive anywhere.

How can this be? What went wrong? We can answer this question, even if Sartre cannot. He has overlooked the basic rule about tension and release of tension. He has reached the mistaken conclusion that the reason Volume One was so interesting was because it moved busily from one character to another. Now he tries to do the same thing on a larger scale, increasing the number of characters, and extending his canvas until it covers the whole of Europe in the months before Hitler's invasion of France. He believes, mistakenly, that the seriousness of his theme, and the impending disaster of the war, will keep the readers absorbed. This is not so. The reader needs a perfectly simple problem to occupy his mind, like Mathieu's search for abortion-money. Without such a problem there can be no tension, and no release of tension. He even commits the cardinal sin against tension by switching arbitrarily from episode to episode in the middle of a paragraph, so that just as you are getting interested in one set of characters, he introduces others. Yet there *are* a few highly successful episodes, which reveal quite clearly what has gone wrong. There is the story of a romantic young pacifist, Philippe, who runs away from home, and is picked up by the homosexual in Paris. The moment the meeting takes place, the reader becomes intensely curious to know what happens. And perhaps the most memorable episode in *The Reprieve (Le Sursis)* takes place on a train, when a hospital for paralytics is being evacuated, and a young man finds himself lying next to a pretty girl—both paralysed from the waist down. There comes a point where the girl has to call for the nurse because she has diarrhoea, and a chamber-pot is placed underneath her. For a few minutes he feels revolted; then gains control of himself, tells himself she is sick, and feels an upsurge of love and tenderness. *This* is an example of the breaking of new ground in the novel. But Sartre immediately switches to a scene in which politicians read Masaryk's declaration of submission to Hitler. He obviously believes that every serious reader will find the change of scene significant and moving. In fact, it is an irritating bore, and I have no doubt that everyone who has ever read the book has hastily flipped through the next dozen or so pages, looking for the next episode with the young couple. Long before the end of the third volume, the novel has disintegrated. Sartre began the fourth volume, but abandoned it. Most readers will have done so long before.

But is *The Roads to Freedom* a failure because Sartre was unable to solve the problem of how Mathieu will achieve freedom? Clearly not, since the first volume is so successful. It is a failure because Sartre forgot to observe the basic law of tension-and-discharge.

And this, we can now see, is what went wrong with vast

structures like Rolland's *Jean-Christophe* and Undset's *Kristin Lavransdatter*—even with *War and Peace*. The tension-and-discharge element in *Jean-Christophe* is completed as soon as the musician has achieved success. And if, at that point, Rolland had said 'And he lived happily ever after . . .', the reader would lay down the book feeling quite satisfied. But if Rolland intends to continue, then he needs to start all over again, building up a new tension. There is another possibility, which would have been the correct solution of the problem. At an early stage in the novel, Rolland should have envisaged some distant and magnificent objective for his hero—perhaps something like the achievement of Wagner's creation of Bayreuth, or some tremendous, visionary Ninth Symphony that will alter the destiny of the world. And then, with enough hints of this tremendous climax, the novel could have gone on for five thousand pages—provided Rolland had also maintained a series of tension-and-discharge episodes within that structure. A novel that ends simply with the death of its hero is basically misconceived.

Of course, it hardly makes sense to say that *Persuasion* is a more 'successful' novel than *Jean-Christophe*, unless you add that Romain Rolland was aiming altogether higher than Jane Austen. Rolland was trying to write about the tremendous urge to freedom that dominated Beethoven, not about a middle-class girl's desire for a husband. Once again, we are back with David Lindsay's distinction between novels that describe the world and novels that try to explain it. Or, more simply, between 'high flyers' and 'low flyers'. Jane Austen, Charlotte Brontë and Anthony Trollope are fine novelists; but they are low flyers. Rolland, Sartre, D. H. Lawrence, Dostoevsky, and Lindsay himself, were high flyers. It is much easier to write a successful 'low-flying' novel than a successful 'high-flying' novel. I could name a dozen low-flying 'successful' novels with hardly a pause for breath, beginning with *Pamela*, *Pride and Prejudice* and *Jane Eyre*, and including Wells's *History of Mr Polly*, Arnold Bennett's *The Card*, Kingsley Amis's *Lucky Jim* and John Braine's *Room at the Top*. All these end with satisfactory 'achievement' on various levels. But it would take me a very long time to work out a list of a dozen successful 'high flyers', and I might have to end by conceding defeat. Dostoevsky and Lawrence are obviously high flyers, but few of their novels leave the reader with that sense of quiet fulfilment—as if after a good meal—that we get from *The Egoist* and *Persuasion*. And this is obviously because a totally 'successful' novel ends by solving the problem it has created, and the problems raised by high flyers are too big to be solved so neatly. Most of the masterpieces of twentieth-century fiction are 'failures' in this sense: for example, Musil's *Man Without Qualities*, Lawrence's *Women in Love*, John Cowper Powys's *Glastonbury Romance*, L. H. Myers's *The Near and the Far*, even Proust's *Remembrance of Things Past*. (I shall have more to say of most of these later.)

I can think of only two twentieth-century works that could be regarded as successful 'high flyers': Romain Gary's *The Roots of Heaven*, and Hugo von Hofmannsthal's *The Difficult Man* (the latter is a play, but the rules of the drama are basically similar to those of the novel). The hero of *The Roots of Heaven* is a man who is obsessed by the slaughter of wildlife in Africa, particularly of elephants. This sounds unpromising enough; in fact, Morel's struggle to preserve the elephants becomes a symbol of the struggle of twentieth-century man to preserve himself against his own urge to self-destruction. It is one of the few twentieth-century novels that ends by inducing in the reader a tremendous surge of optimism about human beings and the human spirit.

The Difficult Man is also worth mentioning here, because it is an ambitious attempt by a great Austrian poet to project his own idea of a superman, a kind of ideal: in that sense it may be regarded as a legitimate successor to Schiller's *Robbers*. The hero, Kari Bühl, hardly seems to be the heroic type. A member of the Austrian aristocracy, all his virtues are muted, hidden beneath the surface. He is kind and considerate, highly intelligent and at the same time, deeply intuitive. Like the Chinese notion of the 'superior man', he prefers to hide his qualities; this only leads people to pursue him. The deeply intuitive nature of his intelligence leads him to distrust words; it is a torment for him to try to turn his feelings and perceptions into words, particularly in 'society'. He feels that the whole thing is bound to become a grotesque tissue of misunderstandings. The events that take place in the play seem to justify his attitude. An old friend, Count Hechingen, begs him to intervene to persuade his estranged wife to return to him. And his sister begs him to try and persuade a beautiful, aristocratic girl, Helen Altenwyl, to marry her son Stani. There is one absurd complication. Both Countess Hechingen and Helen Altenwyl are in love with Kari himself. But he allows himself to be persuaded to attend a party to talk to both women. By appealing to her sentimentality, he half-persuades Countess Hechingen to return to her husband. But Helen is a different matter; her intuitive intelligence is the equal of his own, and he ends by getting engaged to her. But it is still not clear whether he is marrying her because he loves her, or because he is too much a gentleman to reject a woman who tells him she loves him.

Summarised in this way, it hardly sounds a masterpiece. But it *is* Hofmannsthal's masterpiece, because it is his most successful projection of a self-image. The play is really about the problem of a man who is more intelligent and sensitive than the society in which he lives. He is no 'outsider', aggressively rejecting society. He is willing to live by its rules, to observe its conventions; but he tries to place a certain distance between himself and other people. He is quite prepared to live as a spiritual exile. Even the admiration he arouses in other people embarrasses him.

The greatness of the play lies in the subtlety with which it portrays the difference between Kari Bühl and the various characters for whom words hold no ambiguities. It is a masterpiece of psychological observation, a study in the various types of egoism and self-delusion. But it is also a refutation of the twentieth-century legend that an intelligent and sensitive man is bound to be ineffectual and defeated. Like *The Roots of Heaven*, it suggests that such a man should be a leader, not a misfit. His place is at the head of society, not at the bottom.

And in saying this, we have gone to the heart of the problem of the novel in the twentieth century. A novelist can only project a clear self-image if he knows fairly clearly what he wants. Richardson, Jane Austen, Charlotte and Emily Brontë, could all write satisfactory novels because what they wanted was straightforward. But the probability is that anyone who settles down to write a novel in the twentieth century has no idea of what he—or she—wants. Yet if you could prod through the layers of uncertainty, you would come upon one basic certainty. They all have a feeling that, no matter how messy and confusing their everyday lives, the 'act of creation' ought to somehow allow them to triumph over it, to gain control of it. That is to say, human beings seem to have a curious instinct that the powers of the mind are wider than we normally assume. Every serious writer has experienced this feeling: writing about a problem that worries him, and then suddenly experiencing a surge of power, and a feeling of detachment, as if he had turned into a balloon and floated clear of the problem.

All of which leads us to conclude that the writer of the twentieth century is not basically worse off than Richardson or Jane Austen; indeed, in many ways, he is better off, for our civilisation is intellectually more 'wide open'. The main necessity for the writer is to recognise that what he is trying to do is to create a mirror in which he can see his own face. Once this is understood, the problem is already half-solved. At first, the mirror may be opaque and cloudy; but as he stares, it will slowly clear, revealing that it is no ordinary mirror, but a magic mirror, designed to free the creative powers of the subconscious mind.

One more vital point. This book has so far stuck to works that are generally acknowledged to be classics or masterpieces. This creates the impression that good writing is an abstruse art confined to geniuses and professionals. This is untrue; the mirror-principle works as well for amateurs as for professionals, and many important works of art have been produced by beginners. David Lindsay's *Voyage to Arcturus* is an example; Bill Hopkins's *Divine and the Decay* is another. No admirer of Bernard Shaw would be without his early novels, although they are all amateurish.

Not all such works are fortunate enough to attract critical attention. A case in point is *The Chinese Room* by Vivian Connell, a novel that achieved a certain *succés de scandale* when it appeared in 1943, but which has never gained the recognition it deserves. It explores the same problems as D. H. Lawrence—the way that civilisation separates human beings from their basic impulses—and does so with remarkable success.

Nicholas Bude, still a fairly young man, is the head of a bank that he inherited from his father. Banking does not suit him. He feels stifled, devitalised. When he goes into a flower shop to order flowers for his wife, he keeps his hands in his pockets. They are big, workman's hands, and he is ashamed of them.

Back at home, he learns that the lodge-keeper's daughter has committed suicide, and that she has been writing letters to herself. A new doctor, Saluby, is paying a call, and they discuss the girl's death. Saluby suggests that Nicholas should try writing letters to himself, as a kind of psychological experiment, and Nicholas agrees.

Saluby can see at a glance that Nicholas's wife, Muriel, is unhappy and frustrated. When Nicholas goes out for a walk, he proceeds to seduce her. They have an affair, but she finds his clinical, intellectual approach to sex unbearable.

At the bank, Nicholas now begins to receive anonymous letters that read: 'There is a will to death in your hands. Whose death?' We also discover that he is having an affair with his beautiful secretary, Miss Coleman. But this also seems to be a thoroughly unsatisfying relationship. Every Monday, they indulge in a cold, violent lovemaking in her flat; she never allows him to kiss her. He always leaves her money in an envelope, which she donates to charity. He later discovers that she has a deformity of the foot—a hoof instead of a toe—and that it is shame about this that causes her frigidity.

So far, the novel has a stifling, airless quality. These people are all trapped: Nicholas in his job, his wife in her middle-class background, Miss Coleman in her shame about her deformity, Saluby in his intellectualism. Then things begin to change. One afternoon, in the small town where she meets Saluby to commit adultery, Muriel encounters his partner, a huge, red-bearded Scot. She gives herself to him on impulse; they make love by the river bank, and the experience leaves her with a sense of being sexually awake for the first time.

Meanwhile, Nicholas is becoming increasingly depressed by the anonymous letters; they confirm a secret fear that his frustrations will finally lead him to murder. One day, in the act of lovemaking, he almost strangles Miss Coleman. When he notices that the letters are written on bank notepaper, he begins to suspect everyone around him. The tension builds up like a thunderstorm.

Then, in a single episode, it discharges itself. On a rainy Saturday morning, bored and frustrated, Nicholas orders his chauffeur to drive him to a nearby inn for lunch. They pass an old labourer digging a ditch to carry away a flood, and Nicholas orders the chauffeur to stop. He watches with fascination as the man slices into the wet clay. Then, as the labourer struggles with a tree root, Nicholas jumps into the ditch—in his Savile Row suit—and takes the root into his huge hands. He experiences a deep sense of satisfaction. He tells the chauffeur to take the old man for lunch; then he settles down to digging the drain. It is a long, hard job, and the author takes six pages to describe it. At the end of the day, his hands are blistered, and he is exhausted—but deeply satisfied. He has re-established contact with reality.

There follows a sexual reconciliation with his wife in which both achieve total release. After this, the author proceeds to tie up the various loose-ends of the novel. The author of the anonymous letters turns out to be Saluby, who was motivated by desire for revenge (his family used to own the bank). But these details hardly seem important. The climax of the novel is the ditch-digging scene, which achieves such intensity that it leaves the reader lethargic, almost indifferent to what follows.

It is, perhaps, one of the most memorable scenes in modern fiction. Ever since the nineteenth century, many novelists have written about the stifling sense of unreality and futility induced by civilisation. Only a few of the greatest—among them, Tolstoy and Dostoevsky—have been able to suggest the human spirit's indestructible capacity for freedom.

It may seem ironic that, technically speaking, *The Chinese Room* is not a well-made novel. The opening chapters lack tension. The scene in which Saluby persuades Nicholas to write letters to himself seems contrived. The seduction of Muriel by Saluby lacks credibility. The final chapters are perfunctory. In spite of this, the book is a compelling and powerful piece of work—and an interesting proof that, when a novelist knows what he wants to say, the technique will take care of itself.

SIX

The Varieties of Wish-Fulfilment

IN THE YEAR 1909, a young Englishman living in New York received one of the most exciting letters of his life. It was from a Mr Fred J. Rymer, of the London publisher's Sampson Low, and it was an acceptance of his first novel.

Jeffrey Farnol was born near Birmingham, and was intended for the engineering trade; in his teens his parents apprenticed him to a brass foundry. Then they relented and allowed him to study art. He married an American girl, went to New York, and became a scene painter at the Astor Theatre. Farnol did not like America, where everybody seemed to be in a hurry; he dreamed of the green lanes of his home in Warwickshire, in the old days of stage coaches. He had been trying to write since he was nineteen. His first novel, a sentimental romance called *Chronicles of the Imp*, was rejected by every publisher who saw it. His second, a bulky work entitled *The Broad Highway*, was the story of a young scholar who leaves home to wander the roads of Regency England. Farnol submitted it to a New York publisher; it was promptly rejected, without a letter of explanation. The same happened with a second. The third publisher condescended to explain that it was 'too English'. An actor offered to show the book to a Boston publisher; but forgot the manuscript at the bottom of his trunk, and returned some months later with it still there, untouched. Farnol, who was tired of sparse meals—his wife had returned to stay with her parents in New Jersey—decided that a writing career was not for him, and sent the manuscript to his wife, with the suggestion that she read it and burn it. Instead, she decided to send it to a friend in London, a magazine editor. There were more lengthy delays while the bulky manuscript crossed the

Atlantic. Fortunately, the friend, Shirley Jevons, instantly recognised its quality.

"'And to my nephew, Maurice Vibart, I bequeath the sum of twenty thousand pounds in the fervent hope that it may help him to the devil within the year, or as soon after as may be.'"

A book that begins like that may not be serious literature, but it is clearly going to be readable. Sampson Low acquired the rights, and offered the book to Little, Brown in Boston—the firm the actor had intended to show it to, but forgotten. They also accepted it. *The Broad Highway* appeared in 1910, and proved that the American publishers who had rejected it did not know their own business. Americans loved it as much as the English did. In no time at all, *The Broad Highway* had sold half a million copies, and Jeffrey Farnol was a rich man.

The story sounds like a wish-fulfilment fantasy—which is precisely what *The Broad Highway* was. In the introduction, its hero explains:

> As I sat of an early summer morning in the shade of a tree, eating fried bacon with a tinker, the thought came to me that I might some day write a book of my own: a book that should treat of the roads and by-roads, of trees, and wind in lonely places, of rapid brooks and lazy streams, of the glory of dawn, the glow of evening, and the purple solitude of night; a book of wayside inns and sequestered taverns, a book of country things and ways and people. . . .

The hero is not, of course, the Maurice Vibart who is expected to go to the devil, but his cousin Peter; and the will adds that whichever of the two men can marry Lady Sophia Sefton shall receive the remainder of the vast fortune. Whereupon Peter takes the ten guineas left him in his uncle's will, and strolls out on to the broad highway. And within a fairly brief period, he has been robbed by a highwayman, been mistaken for his cousin several times, and rescued a beautiful lady who has been imprisoned by a would-be seducer. He also engages in a hammer-throwing contest with a blacksmith, and becomes his assistant, living in a nearby hut in the woods.

One night, a terrified girl bangs on the door—Farnol's books are never short of ladies in distress; she is, of course, fleeing from a would-be seducer—by an odd coincidence, the wicked Maurice Vibart. She introduces herself as Charmian Brown, but even at this early stage, the alert reader has no difficulty in guessing that she is really Lady Sophia Sefton. She stays in the hut to nurse Peter, who has been injured in a fight with his cousin. Inevitably, they fall in love. . . .

The tale is preposterous, depending on a series of coincidences. Yet, re-reading it recently after thirty years, I found it still conjured up the old magic that had filled my head with daydreams at thirteen. It was an interesting reminder that a book does not have to be plausible to be readable. A well-constructed daydream is as satisfying as a well-constructed symphony or opera; plausibility hardly enters into it.

Farnol was a specialist in daydreams. He used that basic plot of *The Broad Highway* again and again. The cynical will accuse him of catering to his public; but no one who read him in childhood can believe this. It is true that he was not naïve enough to believe that every man with no money in his pocket and no roof over his head is a carefree vagabond. But it was the dream that fascinated him, the dream of freedom and adventure. In all his novels, there is only one small episode that suggests he knew something about the reality of the male sexual urge: this is in *The Broad Highway* immediately after Peter has rescued Lady Helen Dunstan from a would-be seducer; as they fly through a wood, he experiences the temptation to kiss her. They struggle for a moment, then he crashes his clenched fist into a tree—a gesture of self-punishment. Farnol's later heroes all behave unexceptionably.

But the situation that really delights him is to place the hero and heroine in close proximity—preferably with some misunderstandings about identity—and then allow them to fall slowly in love. The state of the girl's emotions is indicated by charming blushes, drooping eyelashes and demure smiles. The situation always sends him off into such a delicious fantasy that he is capable of dragging it out for a whole book.

To read Farnol is to realise that the daydream is the true

basis of all literature. This is, in fact, something we all know instinctively, although the sophisticated are liable to lose sight of it. Naturalism, social realism, psychological analysis, linguistic experiment: these are all interesting approaches to the novel, but they are not its substance or its essence. The basic impulse behind the novel is the need to create a 'desirable' reality: that is, to project an image of the life you would like to lead, and the sort of person you would like to be. The literary objection to Farnol is not that he is a daydreamer, but that his daydreams are so naïve. No one likes to be thought naïve, so we take care to keep our daydreams to ourselves. James Thurber's story 'The Secret Life of Walter Mitty' is about an ineffectual little man who spends his days fantasising about adventure. He is Commander Mitty, the Naval Hero, Mitty the Great Surgeon, Mitty the Flying Ace, Mitty the Crack Shot. And as he waits for his wife outside a drug store, he is Mitty the Spy, facing a firing squad: 'erect and motionless, proud and disdainful, Walter Mitty the Undefeated, inscrutable to the last.' But if we smile at the contrast between Mitty's daydreams and the 'reality', we have missed the point. Because he possesses imagination, Mitty *is* The Undefeated; his daydreams *are* his reality.

This recognition leads to another insight. All Mitty's daydreams are 'tension-inducers'. He is living a slack, dull life in a backwater; all his daydreams are of instant reactions to crisis or courage in the face of disaster. Biologically speaking, he is using his imagination to prevent himself from slipping into a state of low-vitality. Man is the only creature on earth with this capacity for resisting the numbing effects of a boring environment.

The point is underlined by an episode in Romain Gary's *The Roots of Heaven*. In a German prison camp, the Germans are trying to demoralise their French prisoners by keeping them inactive. A prisoner called Robert suggests they should play a game: to imagine that there is a girl in the hut. If someone gets undressed, he has to hold up a blanket so the girl cannot see him; if someone swears, he must bow to the corner of the room and apologise. . . . In a short time, the 'girl' has raised the morale of the prisoners so much that the Germans become suspicious. The Commandant makes enquiries and finds out about their game. He decides to use psychological subtlety. He enters the hut with an escort of soldiers, tells the men that he knows they have a girl there, and that they must hand her over. He will return the following day, he says, and his soldiers will escort her to the nearest brothel for German officers. . . . Then he leaves. The men are in a state of consternation. They know that if they symbolically hand over the girl, she will have gone for good. Their imaginations have given her life; she cannot be re-created at will. The next day, the Commandant returns and demands the girl. It is Robert, as a spokesman of the others, who tells him: 'We're not going to hand her over.' And the Commandant knows he is defeated; nothing he can do can rob the men of what they have created. Robert is arrested, and everyone assumes they have seen the last of him. But he returns, thin and exhausted, but undefeated. He has learned the lesson of the imaginary girl. In solitary confinement, he has imagined vast herds of elephants tramping over endless plains, a symbol of freedom, and this has preserved his sanity. . . .

This is one of the great parables of our age. Gary has grasped the secret of the power that lies in the heart of the human mind. Reality is *not* what happens to be most real to us at the moment. It is what we perceive in our moments of greatest intensity. And the peculiar power of the imagination enables us to cling on to this vision after the intensity has vanished. The French soldiers have not merely conjured up an imaginary sexual partner; they have succeeded in re-creating something of the mystery of the 'eternal womanly', and of their deepest motives for living. The girl is no fantasy; she is a reminder of a deeper reality than the prison camp.

So it is no criticism of a novel to say it is unreal. The real question is what *depth of human need* is symbolised by the fantasy. And it may clarify this issue if we refer at this point to the 'hierarchy of needs' theory of the psychologist Abraham Maslow. Maslow pointed out that the basic need in all living creatures is for food and drink; without this we die. Human beings who have always suffered from malnutrition have no time to develop higher values. Moreover, a man who has always been hungry imagines that if he could only eat two large meals a day, he would be ecstatically happy. In fact, if he achieves an adequate diet, the next level of need emerges: for security, 'territory', a roof over his head. (The recurrent daydream of tramps and criminals is a little place in the country with a vegetable garden. . . .) If this level is satisfied, says Maslow, the next emerges: for sex and love. The level above this is the need for self-esteem: to be respected and admired by one's neighbours, to be a 'man of position'. And there is still one higher level in the hierarchy: the level of creative self-fulfilment—'self-actualisation', as Maslow calls it, the need to do something well for its own sake, even if it is only growing roses or putting ships in bottles.

We can see the operation of this 'hierarchy' in the history of literature. The basic level is absent because men do not create literature when they need food. But most of the early epics, from the *Iliad* to the Icelandic sagas, are about wars and battles: the struggle for territory. Around the fourteenth century, the troubadours projected the ideal of the 'eternal feminine', the perfect woman for whom the knight does battle, and we have Lancelot and Guinevere, Tristan and Isolde, Aucassin and Nicolette. This ideal persists for roughly five hundred years, and it is the coming of the novel that brings about the transition to the next level; when Lovelace talks about 'my own imperial will', he has brought self-esteem into literature. De Sade's strange perversions are an attempt to satisfy the craving for self-esteem by sexual indulgence—an impossibility. And the nineteenth century saw the development of novels of 'social man', novels of ambitious social climbers like Rastignac and Bel Ami. Parallel with these ran the novels of 'self-actualisation', romantic novels about man in search of the ideal. But their time had not arrived—even a century later, when Herman Hesse wrote his tales in which the hero takes to the broad highway in search of some elusive ideal of spiritual freedom.

Purely on historical grounds, then, it seems probable that

the next phase in the development of the novel will be the phase of self-actualisation. The immense popularity of the novels of Hermann Hesse in the 1960s indicates the change in attitude. The notion of self-actualisation has ceased to be vague and abstract, as it was in the time of Goethe and Hoffmann, and become increasingly concrete. The stage seems to be set for the appearance of the Balzac of 'Self-Actualisation'.

Meanwhile, we can see the 'hierarchy of values' reflected in the wish-fulfilment fantasies of the twentieth-century novelist. It is probably safe to say that the essence of any given writer can be found in his wish-fulfilment fantasies, even if he regards these as mere 'entertainments'. Arnold Bennett's *Old Wives' Tale* tells us little about his basic desires, although it demonstrates his seriousness as an 'artist'. But *The Card* reveals the essence of Bennett. Denry Machin is a boy from the slums who succeeds in everything he attempts through sheer audacity. Like Aladdin of the *Arabian Nights*, or the Brave Little Tailor of the fairy tale, he always has luck on his side. Bennett enjoys himself so much you can almost hear him chortling, and see him winking at you. In the very first chapter, Denry gains a scholarship to a good school—not by intelligence, but by cheating. Standing by the master's desk, he notices a sheet of paper with their exam marks; he has done badly. So he picks up a pencil and puts a 2 in front of a 7. 'His trick ought to have been found out—the odds were against him—but it was not found out.' And Denry soon begins to believe that he is a remarkable boy and destined for great things. And it is this belief, says Bennett, that turns an ordinary lad from the Potteries into The Card. As an office boy to the town clerk, he inserts his name into a list of invitations to the municipal ball. There he has the audacity to ask the Countess of Chell to dance with him, laying the foundation of his reputation as a card. (He does it to win a bet.) 'The envied of all, Denry walked home, thinking violently. At a stroke he had become possessed of more than he could earn from Duncalf in a month. The faces of the Countess, of Ruth Earp, and of the timid Nellie mingled in exquisite hallucinations before his tired eyes. He was inexpressibly happy. . . .' This is Arnold Bennett's version of Cinderella. Supported and sustained by the goodwill of his creator, Denry can't put a foot wrong. All his business ventures succeed. Two women are interested in him, but it is the 'timid Nellie' that he finally carries off, with typical Denry panache. She and her parents are going to Canada because they are bankrupt, and Denry goes to see them off. The sight of Nellie, miserable and helpless, on the deck of the boat is too much for him. He tells her to come ashore for a moment because he has left her present in the cab. He bundles her into the cab and orders the driver to take them to the station.

'What are you going to do with me?' she whimpered.
'Well, what do *you* think? I'm going to marry you, of course.'

Which he does—in spite of being engaged to the other girl. And his home town is so far from being shocked that Denry is elected mayor.

The book is an undisguised wish-fulfilment fantasy, and the hero is Arnold Bennett himself—for, as Aldous Huxley pointed out, Bennett *is* The Card, his thumbs hooked in the armholes of his yellow waistcoat.

Significantly, Huxley refers to him as 'dear, kind, unhappy' Arnold Bennett. Why *should* the most successful author of his time be unhappy, when the central aim of his life had been to become the most successful author of his time? The answer lies in his work. He lived for nearly a quarter of a century after writing *The Old Wives Tale*; but artistically speaking, he might as well have died immediately after. And the reason he ceased to develop was that *The Card* was the furthest he ever went in projecting a self-image. Even a more serious attempt at self-portraiture, as Edwin Clayhanger in the *Clayhanger* trilogy, made no difference. For all Edwin does is to become a successful businessman, and make an only moderately successful marriage. Bennett began his career as a novelist with an ambitious attempt at a self-image in *A Man from the North*, in which the hero, like Bennett, is a provincial who comes to seek his fortune in London. Ten years later, with *The Old Wives' Tale*, Bennett had achieved the summit of his ambition as a serious writer. He had successfully transplanted the French naturalistic novel to England. What did he now want? The answer is: in theory, greater and greater artistic success; to become the English Balzac or Flaubert. But a writer cannot develop unless he knows what he *wants*—what he wants to become. Bennett had no idea. The Card and Edwin Clayhanger were attempts to come to terms with the problem; but his imagination was incapable of reaching beyond ordinary success. At the end of *The Card*, Denry is the most popular man in Bursley (Bennett had grown up in Burslem), and when someone asks what great cause he is identified with, someone replies: 'With the great cause of cheering us all up.' Denry has reached the summit of self-esteem. And what of Edwin Clayhanger's achievement? 'To reconcile oneself to injustice was the master achievement,' says Edwin, thereby demonstrating the moral bankruptcy of his creator.

But the problem here is very clear. Bennett's personal aim was to be a great artist. Yet the self-image he projects in *The Card* reveals that he secretly regarded himself as a super-con-man. A creator's self-image should be an idealised version of himself; Bennett's is the reverse. If Bennett's aim was to be a great artist, then he should have written a serious novel about a great artist: not necessarily a writer—perhaps a painter or musician, or even an architect. (Like Clayhanger, Bennett originally wanted to be an architect.) What sheer industry and effort could achieve, Bennett achieved. But without the secret of the self-image, he was condemned to failure.

In the case of Bennett's contemporary H. G. Wells we can recognise the same problem in a slightly different form. Wells did not regard himself as an 'artist'—he rather despised artists —but as a 'world-betterer'. He believed that all mankind's problems will one day be solved by science and commonsense. His imagination had a wider range than Bennett's; he dreamed of a modern Utopia and of men like gods. But the first thing we notice about Wells's early novels and stories is that the hero is always oddly nondescript; in fact, in Wells's first novel he is known simply as The Time Traveller. There is a novel about an invisible man—one of mankind's oldest wish-fulfilment fantasies—but although the invisible man is a young scientist, and presumably ought to be able to find all kinds of interesting uses for his discovery, he only commits a pointless murder, and is killed. The Man Who Could Work Miracles—in the story of that name—also fails to make any constructive use of his powers. It is as if, in spite of his scientific creed, Wells is crippled by some basic lack of self-belief.

We begin to gain some insight into the problem from the 'realistic' novels. The first of these, The Wheels of Chance, was written immediately after The Time Machine. The wheels of the title refer to the bicycle; the hero, Mr Hoopdriver, is a draper's assistant on a cycling holiday. (Wells had been a draper's assistant.) He bumps into an attractive young lady— literally, knocking her off her bicycle. She is running away from home with a scheming young man, who has promised to help her and really wants to seduce her. Hoopdriver grasps the situation, and pretends to be a detective, hired to track down the girl. He helps her to escape, and together they have various adventures on the roads of Kent and Sussex, until it is time for him to return to work. He confesses to the girl that he is merely a draper's assistant; she implies that she will wait for him if he can 'better himself'. And Hoopdriver goes back to the shop, determined to become worthy of her.

The wish-fulfilment element here is almost as undisguised as in The Broad Highway, and the formula is basically the same— the open road, the rescue of a young girl from a would-be seducer. . . . But while Farnol's Peter Vibart is a scholar, an athlete and a gentleman, Wells describes Hoopdriver as 'a counter-jumper, a cad on castors, and a fool to boot', empha- sising his weak mouth and general indecisiveness. Hoopdriver is Wells, in many respects, but, as with the Card, it is a reduced rather than a magnified self-image.

Nine years later, Hoopdriver reappears as Kipps. Like The Card, this is a prosperity wish-fulfilment fantasy. Kipps's early history is not unlike Wells's—working-class upbringing, apprenticeship to a draper. Then Kipps is left a fortune—we learn that his father was a 'gentleman' who was not allowed to marry Kipps's mother. He marries a childhood sweetheart. Then Kipps loses most of his money when an acquaintance speculates with it. In spite of which, they have enough to live comfortably and to run a small bookshop. Then a playwright friend writes a smash hit; Kipps had bought a quarter share, so he is rich again. And all live happily ever after. Again, it is the Cinderella fairy tale. And all Wells's biographers have agreed that Kipps is, to some extent, a self-portrait. Yet once again it is a reduced self-portrait, in which Wells sees himself as an awkward, naïve little cockney.

The History of Mr Polly, which followed five years later, is the best constructed of all Wells's novels. Again, Mr Polly is a variant of Hoopdriver: the working-class childhood and the draper's shop are more or less identical. Mr Polly has no fortune to rescue him from working-class drudgery. After falling in love with a middle-class young lady in a boarding school, he marries his cousin, runs an unsuccessful business, and develops ulcers. He decides to commit suicide and burn down the house —so his wife can collect the insurance. In the excitement of the fire, he decides he prefers to live; so he 'disappears' and becomes a tramp. And this new life, Wells suggests, suits him far better than the old one—thereby demonstrating Wells's ignorance of the human need for 'territory'. Still, Polly eventually achieves even that when he becomes odd-job man at the Potwell Inn, and drives off the ferocious Uncle Jim.

It is clear that the theme of his novel is very close to Wells's own heart: 'If you don't like your life you can change it.' But what is so strange is the modesty of Wells's self-image. Of course, we could reply that Wells was writing in the comic tradition of Dickens, and that comic heroes are necessarily absurd. Which sounds plausible until we are forced to admit that Hoopdriver, Kipps and Polly are the nearest Wells ever came to self-portraiture. Other works—like *Tono-Bungay*, *The New Machiavelli* and *Mr Britling* have an autobiographical flavour; but compared to Kipps and Polly, their heroes are little more than colourless abstractions.

There is a general agreement that after 1910—the year of

Mr Polly—Wells began to go steadily downhill as a novelist. The most ambitious novel of his later years, *The World of William Clissold* (1926) is again semi-autobiographical; but Clissold is hardly a person—more of a voice expounding ideas. The ideas are always absorbing—Wells's intelligence is the most beguiling thing about him—but they seem to have little relation to Wells as a person. In the 1930s, Wells became increasingly pessimistic about the future of *homo sapiens*, as he liked to call the human race. His last novel, *You Can't Be Too Careful*, is a negative portrait of a negative man, as the title indicates; Edward Albert Tewler is mean, trivial and small-minded. Wells seems to detest him so much that it is hard to see why he writes about him. In a kind of appendix to the novel, Wells explains that *homo sapiens* does not yet exist; all we have is 'homo tewler'. 'How can there be any "gleams of nobility" in a darkened and ever-darkening world?' he asks gloomily. And in his last book, *Mind at the End of Its Tether*, he announced that our universe is about to go 'clean out of existence'; something strange and menacing has happened; life has ceased to be Nature's pet child, and is about to be extinguished. He had plunged into a total, black nihilism. A year later, he died.

Not long after Wells's death, the first 'unauthorised' biography appeared—by Vincent Brome—and revealed to the general public a fact that had always been known in literary circles: that Wells had been a lifelong Casanova. In fact, readers of some of his novels—like *Mr Britling* and *The Secret Places of the Heart*—might have inferred this, for he is fairly candid about it. In his *Journals*, Arnold Bennett mentions calling on Wells, and seeing the mantelpiece covered with photographs of his mistresses. Wells was fond of his wife; but at a fairly early stage in their relationship, she had to get used to the idea that he was incorrigibly promiscuous—in fact, that promiscuity was a basic psychological necessity of his nature.

For the literary critic, all this would be irrelevant. But for someone who wishes to understand the nature of Wells's creative processes, it brings a flood of insight. We can see from early novels—like *The Wheels of Chance*—that Wells was dangerously romantic about young ladies—particularly middle-class young ladies. As a famous author, his opportunities for contact with them were limitless, and the modest Hoopdriver realised to his astonishment that he appeared to be irresistible. Abraham Maslow's researches have established that most highly dominant individuals—women as well as men—are inclined to promiscuity; in Wells's case it was intensified by a scientific curiosity that amounted to a passion. The prophet of the future, the architect of Utopia, became known as a notorious rake.

Promiscuity always raises a problem: someone is bound to get hurt. Each new conquest involves getting rid of the old one, or at least a certain amount of deception. On most kindly and intelligent people, this exercises a certain braking effect. Besides, experience-hunger, like any other appetite, can be satiated; as a man gets older, he outgrows the old urgencies. But the most basic reason that creative people tend to outgrow promiscuity is that it spoils the self-image; sexual desire, after all, is based on desire to explore the forbidden: it is a first-cousin to the criminal urge. Besides, there is a certain incongruity in the thought of a philosopher spending his days in pursuit of the opposite sex. That Wells never outgrew it suggests some curious fault or deficiency in the self-image mechanisms. (It is interesting to compare Wells with Bernard Shaw—whose self-image mechanism was in excellent working order; Shaw also had many affairs at the period of his emergence, but he had outgrown them by the time he was forty.)

For why does a man want to possess a strange girl? Because it brings a sense of conquest, of well-being, of obstacles triumphantly surmounted. If we could send some tiny scientific observer to hide inside a man's nervous system and record the ebb and flow of his vital powers, he would recognise that human life is a conflict between two opposing sensations: the feeling of power and well-being, and the feeling of helplessness, 'contingency', being a victim of circumstance. Healthy, vital people possess a strong credit-balance of 'well-being', the sense of being in control of their own destinies; unhappy, neurotic people can never quite escape a sense of their own 'contingency'. One of the most pleasant and interesting things that can happen to a human being is that sudden upsurge of delight, what Chesterton called 'absurd good news'. But it is not just a 'feeling'; it seems to involve some curious *insight*, which might be crudely expressed: Man is more god-like than he thinks. . . .

I have elsewhere suggested the word 'promotion' for this insight, for it is closely related to what happens when someone receives promotion in the army. It takes him a day or so to get used to his new status; then he 'becomes' a sergeant or an officer; he feels that he *is* a sergeant, whereas during the first few days, the new rank felt as strange as a pair of new shoes. We can also experience promotion in a single flash of delight: the 'god-like sensation'. And, for most human beings, it happens most frequently through sex. As Hoopdriver cycles off at the end of *The Wheels of Chance*, he is experiencing a sense of 'promotion': his few days as the protector of Jessie Milton have given him a new confidence. To his colleagues at the drapery emporium he may look the same; but *inside*, a butter-fly has started to emerge from the chrysalis.

But when a butterfly has emerged, it can never turn back into a caterpillar. Unfortunately, this is not true for human beings. Boredom, illness, humiliation, defeat, all produce 'demotion'. Wells's sense of his own value was never very secure; he could never forget that he was short, fat and had a squeaky voice. He could never overcome a sense of incongruity: of being a brilliant mind in an absurd body. And, as he admits in a novel called *Secret Places of the Heart*, 'I couldn't believe that the glow and sweetness I dreamt of were not in the world somewhere.' More than any of Wells's later novels, this is an undisguised wish-fulfilment fantasy; the eminent public man, Sir Richmond Hardy, goes to see a doctor, complaining of fatigue and anxiety; the doctor not only advises him to take a holiday, but goes with him. As they drive around England, they discuss the state of the world and its problems. Then, on Stonehenge, Hardy meets a young and intelligent American girl. They fall in love; there are more long discussions as they travel around together. She is Hardy's ideal soul-mate; alert, sympathetic, able to discuss the world's problems as an equal. Then they have to part to go their separate ways. And Sir Richmond has another heart attack and dies. It is a convenient but unsatisfactory ending, revealing that Wells was incapable of carrying the thought-experiment through to a constructive conclusion. He knows that even if he allowed Sir Richmond to divorce his wife and marry the American girl, it would be no solution; in six months' time he would be looking around for another affair.

But perhaps the most interesting thing about the novel is that although Sir Richmond Hardy speaks with Wells's voice and expounds Wells's ideas, he never becomes a living human being. Like the character in *The Tales of Hoffmann*, whose reflection is stolen by a courtesan, Wells had somehow mislaid his self-image. This is the reason that his work ceased to develop.

The lesson that emerges is that although wish-fulfilment is usually regarded with disdain, it is the true foundation of all creativity. Nearly all the most successful novels of the twentieth century have contained a strong element of wish-fulfilment; this applies equally to 'best-sellers' and to consciously 'serious' works: to *Gone With the Wind* and *Rebecca* as much as to *A Farewell to Arms* and *Ulysses*. (I shall have more to say of Hemingway and Joyce in the next chapter.) Daphne du Maurier's *Rebecca* is basically a Cinderella story in the same tradition as Jane Austen, and it qualifies as the almost perfect example of the wish-fulfilment fantasy. The shy, sensitive orphan girl is rescued from her humiliating job as a lady's companion by the handsome and aristocratic widower. As the mistress of his house, she begins to fear that she is inadequate compared to her predecessor, Rebecca. But she triumphs in the end; Rebecca, it appears, was wicked and immoral, and her husband killed her (justifiably, of course). . . .

Because the wish-fulfilment element is so plain, most critics have never rated *Rebecca* particularly highly. This seems to me to be a mistake. *Jane Eyre* and *Wuthering Heights* are also wish-fulfilment fantasies, and are no less melodramatic than *Rebecca*. But tastes have changed since the time of the Brontës; 'romanticism' has given way to 'realism'. The truth is that our realism is usually a disguised form of romanticism. For example, the structure of the wish-fulfilment fantasy can be seen in two of the most successful English novels of the 1950s: Kingsley Amis's *Lucky Jim* and John Braine's *Room at the Top*. *Lucky Jim* would usually be classified as satirical comedy, while *Room at the Top* seems to be a work of social criticism with tragic overtones. In fact, the heroes of both are almost as successful as Bennett's 'Card'. Jim Dixon is the decent, bumbling, 'ordinary chap' in a world of phonies and show-offs; but although he is always saying and doing the wrong thing, he ends by snatching the girl *and* the good job from under the nose of his disagreeable rival. From its opening page, *Room at the Top* is a success fantasy; Joe Lampton has moved from his shabby home town to an altogether more prosperous northern city, and from the beginning, he has a feeling that life is about to change for the better. It does; and we follow his affair with a married woman, and his seduction of a middle-class teenager with a great deal of sympathy. Nothing goes seriously wrong, and the guilt he feels when the married woman dies in a car accident is an emotional luxury. But from its first appearance, critics seemed determined to interpret the book as an exercise in moral indignation. The film version attempted to lend weight to the moralistic interpretation by making Joe Lampton lose a fight which he actually wins in the book.

The truth is that both *Lucky Jim* and *Room at the Top* are wish-fulfilment fantasies in the romantic tradition. Both have the air of freshness and excitement that always seems to accompany successful self-image projection.

Oddly enough, both authors seem to have accepted the judgment of the critics about what they were trying to do. Amis became a writer of satirical comedies; Braine has written several more novels about material success and moral decline. Both have become more skilled, more detached, more disciplined. Yet none of the subsequent books have attempted to project a self-image with the same romantic intensity. And none of them have repeated the success of *Lucky Jim* and *Room at the Top*.

SEVEN

Experiments

BY THE MID-1930s, both Wells and Bennett were regarded as rather old fashioned. This was not due to their subject-matter so much as to their style, which was fundamentally Dickensian. The humour of Dickens depends on anti-climax; everyday subjects are described in high-flown language. Wells treats Hoopdriver as Dickens treats Pickwick. 'Let us approach the business with dispassionate explicitness. . . . Let us treat this young man's legs as a mere diagram, and indicate the points of interest with the unemotional precision of a lecturer's pointer.' The style can be very funny for a few chapters, but it palls easily. 'Then quite abruptly he sprang to his feet and gestured with an ineffectual hand.' This sort of thing actually comes *between* the reader and the object being described; it gives experience a second-hand quality.

But the real objection to it is that it tends to shrink the self-image. Even when used seriously, it carries implications of a comic vision, and the comic vision is founded on a sense of the absurdity of human pretensions.

One of the first tasks of the post-Victorian novelists was to get rid of the Victorian style and develop something more flexible: something that would say exactly what it meant and no more.

The Victorian novel was inclined to begin with portentous statement:

> In the latter days of July in the year 185–, a most important question was for ten days hourly asked in the cathedral city of Barchester, and answered every hour in various ways— Who was to be the new bishop? (Trollope)

On an autumn afternoon of 1919 a hatless man with a slight limp might have been observed ascending the gentle, broad declivity of Riceyman Steps, which lead from Kings Cross Road up to Riceyman Square, in the great metropolitan industrial district of Clerkenwell. (Bennett)

The writers want the sentences to reverberate; they could be read by a town crier shouting, 'Oyez, oyez!' On the other hand, the opening sentence of D. H. Lawrence's first novel is deliberately low-keyed:

I stood watching the shadowy fish glide through the gloom of the mill-pond.

while the opening sentences of James Joyce's *Portrait of the Artist as a Young Man* (1916) are deliberately colloquial:

Once upon a time and a very good time it was there was a moocow coming down along the road and this moocow that was down along the road met a nicens little boy named baby tuckoo. . . .

His father told him that story: his father looked at him through a glass: he had a hairy face.

Even Joyce was not quite such a pioneer as he seemed. A quarter of a century earlier, a young Norwegian, Knut Hamsun, had caused a sensation with his first novel *Hunger* (1890), describing the sensations of a poet starving in a room in Christiana. The prose was swift, lyrical, impressionistic, producing an effect like a brook in the sunlight. He followed it up with *Mysteries*, *Pan* and *Victoria*. The opening paragraphs of the latter give an idea of his style:

The miller's son was thinking as he walked. He was fourteen, big for his age, brown from the sun and wind, and bursting with ideas.

When he grew up he would work in a match factory. It would be pleasantly dangerous, and he could get sulphur on his fingers so that nobody would dare to shake hands with him. His friends would treat him with great respect because of his goulish trade.

The resemblance between Joyce and Hamsun is immediately obvious. (Joyce could read Norwegian.)

Nowadays it is difficult for us to understand the impact caused by Hamsun's style; it strikes us as ordinary and straightforward. In those days, the short, declarative sentences were a revelation. And then there was Hamsun's subject-matter. He was unashamedly writing about himself, his love life, his passion for freedom. . . . The hero of *Pan* is a retired army officer who lives in the woods to escape the corruption of civilisation. The book glows with a strange, sensual mysticism akin to the poetry of Whitman. *Victoria* is the story of a peasant youth—like Hamsun himself—who becomes a famous writer, and who is loved by the daughter of the local squire.

In short, Hamsun was a thoroughgoing romantic, another of Yeats's fish that 'swim in nets, coming to the hand': that is to say, an intensely subjective writer, obsessed with the need to describe his own soul. Like most romantics, he is inclined to be preoccupied with death and suicide, so there is an unresolved quality about his work. But his undisguised attempts to present a kind of 'superman' self-image gave his work an intensity that was to provide creative impetus for the next half-century. (He died in 1952, at the age of ninety-three.)

So when the twenty-year-old James Joyce began to write fiction, soon after the turn of the century, he had a precedent for writing almost straight autobiography: slightly romanticised autobiography, with the artist as intellectual hero. This first novel, *Stephen Hero*, ran to over a thousand manuscript pages, of which less than a half have survived; the manuscript was apparently thrown on the fire by Joyce after its twentieth rejection, but partly rescued by his mother.

Perhaps the most interesting thing about *Stephen Hero* is that it is so badly written, and so inconsequential. Here is a typical passage:

One morning Stephen arrived three quarters of an hour late and he thought it his decenter plan to wait till the French lecture should begin. As he was leaning over the banisters, waiting for the twelve o'clock bell to ring a young man began to ascend the winding-stairs slowly. At a few steps from the landing he halted and turned a square rustic face towards Stephen.

—Is this the way to the matriculation class, if you please, he asked in a brogue accenting the first syllable of Matriculation.

Stephen directed him and the two young men began to talk. The new student was named Madden and came from the county of Limerick. His manner without being exactly diffident was a little scared and he seemed grateful for Stephen's attentions. After the French lecture the two walked across the green together, and Stephen brought the newcomer into the National Library. Madden took off his hat at the turnstile and as he leaned on the counter to fill up the docket for his book Stephen remarked the peasant strength of his jaws.

The dean of the college was professor of English, Father Butt. . . .

And so we leave Madden abruptly, without any clear idea why he was introduced. The publishers who rejected the original manuscript must have thought it inconsequential drivel.

But what is so interesting is that Joyce is willing to break with all previous literary tradition and write a book that was bound to strike readers as a piece of unabashed egoism. He was simply going a great deal further than Hamsun in casting himself as the hero and rebel. (Oddly enough, no critic—as far as I know—has commented on this influence of Hamsun on Joyce.)

Joyce made no impact on the Dublin literary scene, which was dominated by Yeats, Synge and George Russell (AE). He found Ireland stiflingly provincial. In 1904, he left for Trieste, where he made a poor living as a teacher of languages, and embarked on his first volume of stories, *Dubliners*, and a re-written version of *Stephen Hero* which was to become *Portrait of the Artist as a Young Man*. *Dubliners* is a drab and depressing book whose chief aim seems to be to emphasise the mean, narrow-spirited provincialism of Dublin; it has the air of an act of revenge. But *Portrait of the Artist as a Young Man* is a different matter; here Joyce is once again telling the story of his own life, but with an intense selectivity that was absent from *Stephen Hero*.

It is interesting to compare Joyce's *Portrait* with Wells's *Kipps* or Bennett's *Man from the North*. Wells and Bennett are also autobiographical; but there is something tentative and modest about their self-portraits. Joyce is gripped by a fierce and obsessional self-belief; it is so violent that at times it seems almost manic. He dramatises his own struggles and problems as some writer of church history might have dramatised the life of a saint. It becomes clear that he is obsessed by a craving for recognition, for admiration. Long conversations with his friend Cranly are reported in detail:

—Did the idea ever occur to you, Cranly asked, that Jesus was not what he pretended to be?

—The first person to whom that idea occurred, Stephen answered, was Jesus himself.

—I mean, Cranly said, hardening in his speech, did the idea ever occur to you that he was himself a conscious hypocrite, what he called the jews of his time, a whited sepulchre? Or, to put it more plainly, that he was a black-guard?

—That idea never occurred to me, Stephen answered. But I am curious to know are you trying to make a convert of me or a pervert of yourself?

He turned towards his friend's face and saw there a raw smile which some force of will strove to make finely signi-ficant.

The aim is to emphasise Stephen's brilliance, his discipline, his wit. It gives the impression of one of those conversations you repeat back to yourself after some humiliation, imagining all the devastating things you could have said. Stephen is never at a loss for a word; he is always epigrammatic ('are you trying to make a convert of me or a pervert of yourself?'). The observation about Cranly's smile, 'which some force of will strove to make finely significant', reveals Joyce's insight into the subtleties of self-assertion. Even the curious punctuation, the refusal to use quotation marks or capital letters, indicates a desire to be 'different'. There is something almost frightening about these conversations; one feels that when the desire for recognition and self-esteem becomes as acute as this, the author is treading fairly close to insanity.

The book ends as Stephen prepares to go abroad—to Paris— for the first time. 'Welcome, O life! I go to encounter for the millionth time the reality of experience and to forge in the smithy of my soul the uncreated conscience of my race.' The words are perhaps less meaningful than they sound. (Even if 'conscience' is used in its European sense—of consciousness— it is still not clear what he means.) Nevertheless, there can be no doubt that he is projecting an idealised self-image with a forcefulness that makes even Hamsun look modest.

When *Ulysses* appeared in 1922, it was immediately recog- nised as one of the most significant novels since *Pamela*. Although it was difficult to judge a work that was a quarter of a million words long and far from easy to read, it was still obvious that Joyce was trying to do something that no other novelist had attempted. Ever since Zola, writers had been trying to capture something of the texture and complexity of modern life. Readers had always felt ambivalent about these attempts at 'realism'; after all, the purpose of a novel is to take you on a mental voyage; so why should anyone want to be taken on a tour of his own back yard? The literary critics took a more tolerant view—reflecting their own uncertainty about the aims of the novel. Surely a serious literary form should be more than a vehicle of escapism? Surely the novel had a social role to fulfil? In which case, it ought to combine social documentation with the narrative? But in what pro- portion? So when Joyce produced a 750-page book that minutely documented the actions and thoughts of its charac- ters in a single day, everyone seemed to agree that something

of the sort 'had to come' sooner or later. Moreover, this novel
went further than ever before in detailing 'the truth' about the
sexual aspects of human nature. This also had to come. But if
there was no action, what did the author put in its place?
The answer was: language. You might say the novel is a kind
of film, and language is the camera. What Joyce wanted to do
was to slip a magnifying glass in place of the ordinary lens, and
show reality in a minute detail that had never been attempted
before.

The aim sounds admirable—but our definitions so far enable
us to see immediately what is wrong with it. The novel aims
at inducing 'wide-angle consciousness'. And Joyce was introducing a lens with an even narrower-angle than usual.

Now there is no harm in a novel attempting a greater realism
than usual: this is precisely what made *Pamela* such a sensation.
But it must also *get somewhere*. What bothered the early readers
of *Ulysses* was that it got nowhere. Of course, plenty of things
happen in it: there is a birth, a funeral, an adultery and two
fights. But there was apparently nothing to draw the reader
on from page to page, as there was in *Pamela* or *Clarissa*.

That, said the critics, is unimportant. T. S. Eliot explained
that, in borrowing the structure of Homer's *Odyssey* to impose
some sort of order on 'the canvas of anarchy that is modern
life', Joyce had set an example that many other writers would
be forced to follow. (It became known as 'the mythic method'.)
The argument he was implying goes something like this.
Modern life is impossibly complex and confused. The old
values—virtue, honour, decency, religion—are all under
attack. Novels like *Clarissa* and *Sir Charles Grandison* would
strike a modern audience as hopelessly old fashioned. But in
making the adventures of his heroes—Stephen and Bloom—
parallel those of Telemachus and Ulysses, Joyce was com-
menting ironically on the absence of these ancient virtues, and
therefore reflecting his own age with the same fidelity that
Richardson reflected the age of Johnson. . . .

That sounded convincing. In fact, it convinced far too many
novelists that plot was now obsolete. The trouble is that the
whole argument is based on a fallacy. Although the action

occupies only one day, *Ulysses* is by no means plotless. It has
at least as much plot as *Clarissa*. But this plot is concerned
entirely with Stephen Dedalus and his determination to become an artist. Even the sections about Leopold Bloom are
only there for the sake of the contrast of an ordinary, decent
but fundamentally second-rate man with the artist hero.

For just as the *Portrait of the Artist* was a re-working of
Stephen Hero, so *Ulysses* is a re-working of the *Portrait*. Wyndham
Lewis went to the heart of the matter in a deadly piece of
mockery in *Time and Western Man*. He pointed out that the aim
of the early chapters is to glorify Stephen, to build him up as
an artistic superman. And this is true. When we meet Stephen
again in the first chapter of *Ulysses*, he is just back from the
Paris trip on which he was embarking at the end of the *Portrait*.
He has been summoned back by a telegram announcing that
his mother is seriously ill. She has since died. Stephen is now
living in a Martello tower near Sandycove—a tower that was
built as defence against Napoleon—with a medical student,
Buck Mulligan, and an Englishman, Haines. Stephen has
apparently refused to kneel down and pray at the bedside of
his dying mother—determined to keep up his quarrel with the
Catholic church—and the story has got about. People feel he
is a heartless prig—a judgment with which the reader may
concur. Once again, as in the *Portrait*, Stephen feels himself
under pressure to conform. The climax of the book occurs in
the Night-town scene—in Dublin's brothel quarter—where
the drunken Stephen thinks he sees the ghost of his mother
rising through the floor and begging him to repent and save
his soul. His response is to smash the gas jet with his cane,
shouting '*Non serviam*'—I will not serve. Subsequently, a
drunken English soldier knocks him unconscious, imagining
that Stephen has insulted his king. At the end of the book,
after accompanying Bloom back home, Stephen decides he
cannot return to the Martello tower. Once again, he must go
into exile and forge in the smithy of his soul . . . etc., etc. The
book is intended to be the drama of the artist-outsider, having
to choose between compromise and integrity. In the course of
the book Stephen is several times identified with Hamlet, and

the scene with the ghost of his mother clinches the parallel. And in a long argument in the library scene, Stephen argues that Hamlet is actually Shakespeare himself, thereby adding another dimension to the parallel. Like *Stephen Hero, Dubliners,* the *Portrait, Ulysses* is a study of the artist in a hostile environment. Joyce is explaining and justifying himself to the world.

It is interesting to look more closely at the manner in which this is done. The opening chapter is basically about Stephen's conflict with Buck Mulligan, who reproaches him for refusing to pray at the bedside of his dying mother. Mulligan is represented as rich, complacent and shallow—as well as being 'in' with the Dublin literary crowd—Yeats, Lady Gregory and the rest. At one point, he asks Stephen to tell him frankly what he has against him. Stephen replies that he resents the way Mulligan once referred to him: 'It's only Dedalus, whose mother's beastly dead.' Mulligan replies that he meant no disrespect to Stephen's mother.

> Stephen, shielding the gaping wounds which the words had left in his heart, said very coldly:
> —I am not thinking of the offense to my mother.
> —Of what, then? Buck Mulligan asked.
> —Of the offense to me, Stephen answered.

It can be seen that he is still obsessed by the craving to be liked and admired. Mulligan has been invited to a literary party—with Yeats and others—later in the day, but Stephen has been pointedly excluded. The reader does not have to be a psychologist to sense that this really happened, and that Joyce has stored up his resentment for ten years before allowing it to overflow in *Ulysses.*

We accompany Stephen to the junior school where he teaches a history class; this is followed by a discussion with the headmaster, who is mildly reproachful of Stephen's bohemian life and habit of borrowing money. When he leaves the school he walks on the beach and meditates on his destiny.

The next time we meet Stephen, four chapters later, he is in the office of *Freeman's Journal.* (The intervening chapters have followed the activities of Leopold Bloom, a Jewish advertising agent, whose wife is unfaithful to him.) This chapter may be regarded as one of the most important in the book. A group of Dublin characters, including a professor of Latin and the newspaper editor, tell one another stories and anecdotes before moving off to the local pub. The chapter is structured around these anecdotes. First, someone reads aloud a speech by an Irish politician, full of Celtic sentimentality: 'the transcendant translucent glow of our mild Irish twilight . . .' and so on. (Dedalus senior, who is present, comments: 'Shite and onions.') Professor MacHugh then delivers a speech in praise of Greek idealism and against Roman materialism. After this, the editor tells a story of how a journalist brought off a celebrated scoop at the time of the Phoenix Park murders, telegraphing the movement of the assassins in a code based on an advertisement. Professor MacHugh caps this with an account of a speech by John F. Taylor, full of splendid rhetoric, in which Taylor compared the Fenian movement to the Israelites under the leadership of Moses.

Then, as they adjourn towards the pub, Stephen remarks quietly: 'I have a vision too.' He then tells a detailed but apparently pointless anecdote about two old ladies who go on an outing up Nelson's Pillar. The story could be regarded as an exercise in Flaubertian realism; it ends with the old ladies spitting the plumstones between the railings.

In order to fully appreciate the meaning of this chapter we need to know something about Joyce's theory of 'epiphanies': these are simply typical moments of everyday life, caught as if by a camera—verbal snapshots. The young Joyce intended to write a volume of epiphanies, and, in fact, *Dubliners* could be regarded as a volume of extended epiphanies. Like any good photographer, Joyce felt that such snapshots could contain the whole truth of any given situation. What he is saying, in this newspaper chapter, is that our linguistic habits, and our desire for a dramatic 'point', prevents us from grasping this fundamental truth about everyday events. This chapter is, in fact, an apologia for the whole of *Ulysses*, as well as for Stephen himself. The same point is made, in a different way, in the chapter describing the waiting-room of the maternity hospital. The chapter consists of a series of parodies, beginning with the *Anglo-Saxon Chronicle* and Sir John Mandeville, and continuing with Browne, Bunyan, Pepys, Sterne, Lamb, Dickens, Carlyle and many others. The point Joyce seems to be making is that all these writers interposed a veil of language between the object and the reader; he is trying to make the veil transparent.

However, we can observe an interesting contradiction here. I have pointed out that *Ulysses* has as much plot as *Clarissa*; yet here is Joyce deliberately confusing the situation by seeming to argue that he is not interested in plot: in fact, that plot falsifies the truth. Still, this is understandable. For, to put it bluntly and crudely, *Ulysses* is basically a piece of self-glorification: he is defending himself and getting his own back on his enemies. This insistence that a book should aim at total plotless realism is a clever red herring. Wyndham Lewis saw through it; but Joyce eventually got the best of the argument, for most critics have taken the view that Wyndham Lewis was motivated by jealousy and resentment. This is true; but he hit the nail on the head nevertheless.

One more episode in *Ulysses* should be mentioned. This is the episode in which Buck Mulligan and the Englishman Haines go to a tea shop and discuss Stephen. Mulligan explains that Stephen will never be a true artist—in the Greek tradition—because he has been permanently warped by his conflict with Catholicism. Haines asks whether Stephen writes anything for the Irish literary movement, and Mulligan explains, 'He is going to write something in ten years.' 'Seems a long way off,' says Haines. 'Still, I shouldn't wonder if he did after all.' The point Joyce wishes to underline is that in ten years' time, he was starting to write *Ulysses*. And its success, and the fame that followed, must have delighted him. He had made his point. He had become more famous than Yeats, Synge and AE put together. And he was hailed as a more serious artist. The triumph must have been sweet. Of course, it was not true that he didn't write for the movement because he was saving himself up for *Ulysses*. He had already made a determined attempt to become the Irish Knut Hamsun with *Stephen Hero*.

But the truth was that no one asked him to write for the movement; Yeats and the rest regarded him as a conceited fool. (Understandably: when he was introduced to Yeats, Joyce remarked portentously, 'We have met too late; you are too old to be influenced by me.')

Is *Ulysses* a great novel? The answer is probably yes, for Joyce had talent, and he poured more effort into it than Flaubert had poured into *Bovary*. Yet it has also been one of the most pernicious influences in twentieth-century literature. It was *Ulysses* that led critics to declare that the novel was now coming to an end: that it was impossible to go further than this. Joyce deliberately encouraged this view by implying that *Ulysses*—that vast epiphany—was the logical next step in the history of the novel. We have seen why it was in Joyce's interest to do this: to disguise the fact that the fundamental drive of *Ulysses* is ego-assertion; self-esteem. Unfortunately, this also involved a biased and highly personal view of the purpose of art. Joyce had always been inclined to violent reactions. Yeats, Russell and the rest were all admirers of Plato; so Joyce insisted that he preferred the hard-headed realism of Aristotle. The Irish literary movement admired Shakespeare; Joyce remarked sourly that he preferred Ben Jonson. The celebrated writers of the period (1900–10) were Shaw, Wells, Chesterton and (to a lesser extent) Oscar Wilde. All dealt in ideas. Joyce, in mulish reaction, insisted that ideas had nothing to do with art. (He mortally offended Yeats by telling him that he talked like a man of letters, not like a poet—implying that his head was stuffed with ideas about literature rather than the real thing.) The truth may well be that Joyce was basically a religious man who had lost his faith, and turned art into a substitute religion. Like all religious fanatics, he was inclined to distrust the intellect and despise mere ideas. But it was this dislike of ideas, which fitted in so well with the 'existentialist' temper of the period, that did most damage to the cause of the novel, and literature in general. Ideas are the result of man's mental activity as he confronts problems. The atmosphere of ideas tends to be optimistic because a man would not bother to think unless he hoped to solve the problem. The writer who declares that ideas are unimportant has committed himself to an attitude of pessimism. Joyce only deepened the pessimism that had settled on the novel since Flaubert.

This in itself was paradoxical: for not only was Joyce himself a man of ideas, but *Ulysses* is undoubtedly an optimistic book. Joyce was enough of an artist to recognise that the 'narrow-angle lens' is opposed to the basic purpose of the novel, which is to induce wide-angle consciousness. Therefore, as the book draws to a close, he deliberately 'draws back the camera', revealing wider and wider vistas. Bloom and Stephen look at the sky and see 'the heaventree of stars hung with humid nightblue fruit'. As Stephen walks away, Bloom feels 'the cold of interstellar space, thousands of degrees below freezing point . . . the incipient intimations of proximate dawn'. And in the last chapter, Mrs Bloom seems to turn into the earth itself, and the book ends with total affirmation: 'yes I said yes I will Yes.'

The *Portrait* and *Ulysses* are again full of ideas and discussions; but in the *Portrait*, Stephen insists that he is not interested in *new* ideas: only in the old-fashioned scholasticism of Aquinas. (In one of his poems he speaks of 'Those souls that hate the strength that mine has/ Steeled in the school of old Aquinas'.) In *Ulysses*, Stephen's intellectual brilliance is demonstrated in an erudite but barren discussion about Hamlet. In short, Joyce seems to be insisting that ideas are a mere gymnasium in which he exercises his intellect; they have no value in themselves.

All of which presented a menacing problem for anyone who wanted to carry the novel one step beyond Joyce. It meant that if they were to follow in the steps of the master, they weren't allowed to *think* about the problem: only approach it intuitively—via the solar plexus, as Lawrence might have said. But if a writer gropes intuitively to present reality as he feels it from the solar plexus, what he ends by writing about are his own emotions and the 'reality' at the end of his nose. This is why it is important to recognise that *Ulysses* is not an attempt to write *the* great objective novel of the twentieth century, but a highly subjective novel springing from Joyce's own emotions. If the compass of *Ulysses* is narrow, this is because the emotions

Joyce is writing about are narrow. This is not to assert that its
central argument about artistic integrity is invalid. The trouble
is that Stephen's idea of art is so narrow. He will write a number
of bitter little vignettes of Dublin, then a book glorifying his
own struggle in the nets of provincialism and Catholicism,
then a still larger book about his rejection of Dublin. At least
Knut Hamsun progressed beyond those intensely personal
early books to write a series of masterpieces on Norwegian life
in *Children of the Time* and *Growth of the Soil*. Joyce's work is so
personal that, having achieved his objectives so fully with the
publication of *Ulysses*, there was little else to do. In effect, he
was hoist with his own petard. He had set out to make *Ulysses*
such a technical *tour de force* that no one could ignore it. He
gave it everything he had. And, having compelled the world
to acknowledge his mastery, he was confronted by the same
problem that he had thrust upon his contemporaries. Where
could the novel go from there? What could he write next?
The great novel of Irish life? He knew nothing of it, having left
Ireland at the age of twenty-two; in any case, his art was too
essentially self-orientated to write about other people. The
incredible but sad truth was that his mind was basically trivial.
Admirers who came from great distances, hoping to hear
profundities—or at least, discourses on the art of the novel—
were disconcerted when he told jokes that dated from his
childhood, or reminisced about Irish singers of his youth.

Joyce had forgotten one of the cardinal rules of art: always
to leave a door open for further development. He had piled
so much into *Ulysses* that he had left nowhere else to go. It was
as if Beethoven had started his career by writing the Ninth
Symphony.

Then where, precisely, had Joyce gone wrong? For surely his
life had been devoted, with fanatical single-mindedness, to the
development of the self-image?

This is only partly true. A writer's central purpose is not
simply to discover who he wants to be, but where he wants
to go. It is no coincidence that Shaw's discovery of a self-image
—in *An Unsocial Socialist*—occurred when he had also identified himself with socialism. And the concern with social reform

later expanded into a more general concern with human evolution. It is the clarity of Shaw's self-image—the attitude of cool commonsense in a world of emotional confusion—that gives his plays their unique flavour. But this is only a *vehicle* for conveying his convictions about civilisation and evolution. Few people nowadays would deny that Shaw was an artist of considerable skill; but art is fundamentally the shaping of material. It must have material to shape. The artist's material is provided by his interaction with the world around him, and his attempt to digest it. The most painful and difficult fits of 'indigestion' often produce the greatest art. Joyce created a clear self-image, but he neglected to develop a *direction*—or rather, he chose a road that doubled back on itself.

And so it need surprise no one that his last book, *Finnegan's Wake,* is little more than an interesting rag-bag of linguistic experiments. He had left himself nothing to develop *except* language and technique. *Ulysses* had ended with a kind of universal vision, and if Joyce was to go further, he could only try to be more universal still. But the novel is not really suited to such purposes; music is altogether closer to it. Anyway, the real trouble was that Joyce had only one basic theme: himself. Or, to put it more charitably, the conflict between the idealistic artist and a materialistic society. And in *Ulysses*, he had also developed the technique of parallels: Stephen is Telemachus and Hamlet and Shakespeare; Bloom is Ulysses and Hamlet's father; Mrs Bloom is Penelope and Mother Nature. . . . Out of this rather small armoury of themes and effects, Joyce tried to develop the successor to *Ulysses*. The Buck Mulligan–Stephen opposition reappears in the brothers Shem and Shaun, who are also Cain and Abel and a dozen or so others. (For a complete listing, see Campbell and Robinson's *Skeleton Key to Finnegan's Wake.*) Shem is the idealist artist; Shaun is his worldly brother. Bloom becomes a kind of universal father-figure, Humphrey Chimpden Earwicker, while Mrs Bloom is metamorphosed into a kind of *ewig weibliche* called Anna Livia Plurabelle. Since the book attempts to unite all the world's legends in a vast dream-structure, it also tries to unite all the world's languages by means of endless puns. The final effect is not, as Joyce hoped, of some profound, universal work of art, but merely of six hundred or so pages of whimsy in the manner of *Tristram Shandy*, an ageing scholar amusing himself by making obscure jokes. Perhaps the most moving pages in the book occur in the Shem the Penman section, once again describing the outsider-artist (this time with a certain wry humour), and ending with something that sounds very like a confession of guilt and an act of contrition.

Finnegan's Wake was finished in 1939; Joyce was only fifty-seven years old—the age at which his idol Ibsen was writing his greatest plays; but he was artistically played out. He was almost blind and his health was poor—but this had been so since the publication of *Ulysses*. Where could he possibly go after *Finnegan's Wake*? Only into something still more universal and amorphous. He talked vaguely about an epic on the sea—presumably this would have been entirely without full stops or sentence structure—but he had still made no attempt to write it when he died two years later. He was like a contortionist who ties himself into a knot from which he cannot escape.

I have devoted so much space to *Ulysses* because it is the most famous—and most successful—of all experimental novels. But this analysis has revealed that it is hardly accurate to speak of it as an experimental novel. To begin with, *all* novels are experiments—thought-experiments. And secondly, *Ulysses* is no more experimental in its basic intentions than *The New Héloise* or *Obermann*: it is another subjective novel, the record of an odyssey of a soul.

But if *Ulysses* is not a true experimental novel, what is? Let us begin with a definition. The experimental novel is supposed to be a novel in which the writer tries new techniques to convey his own peculiar vision of reality. The implication is that this vision cannot be conveyed in any other way. Now when you have finished *Ulysses*, you know a great deal about the Dublin of 1904; but not much more than you could learn from a conventional book like *Dubliners*. You know a great deal about Joyce's obsessional sense of being an artist-outsider, but not more than you learned from *Portrait of the Artist as a Young Man*.

Most of the stylistic innovations are therefore not essential to its theme; they are hardly more than rococo decorations.

Let us make a short list of novels that most critics would agree to be 'experimental':

Proust: *Remembrance of Things Past*
Musil: *The Man Without Qualities*
Broch: *The Sleepwalkers*
Döblin: *Alexanderplatz, Berlin*
Dos Passos: *Manhattan Transfer* and *U.S.A.*
Hemingway: *A Farewell to Arms*
Beckett: The *Molloy* trilogy
Burroughs: *The Naked Lunch*
Burgess: *A Clockwork Orange*
Sartre: *Roads to Freedom*

It is a fairly short list, but I do not think I have missed any major 'experimental' work. We could, perhaps, stretch it by adding Simone de Beauvoir's *Mandarins*, and novels by Uwe Johnson, Gunther Grass, Thomas Pynchon, B. S. Johnson (who tried issuing a novel in separate sections, so that the reader could mix them up and read it in any order he liked) and Alain Robbe-Grillet, but most of these latter are experimental in form only, and fairly conventional in content.

I have placed Proust and Sartre at opposite ends of the list because they stand for two extremes: what might be called the conservative novel and the radical novel. I am not referring to the political opinions of the authors. But you only have to glance at any page in Proust to see that he has only carried on where Richardson left off. Richardson slowed the novel down, made it a vehicle for detailed descriptions and endless ruminations—or 'sentiment', as Johnson called it. Proust has done the same. It would be easy to divide his novel up into 'letters', like *Clarissa*, and then we would immediately see that Proust's experimentalism merely amounted to taking his time. The same is true of Musil's remarkable—and still unappreciated—masterpiece *The Man Without Qualities*, a panorama of pre-1914 Vienna that is really a mixture of a novel and a collection of essays. And Broch's *Sleepwalkers*, another panoramic novel of central Europe in a time of crisis, is another leisurely monster of a book. On the other hand Sartre, borrowing his technique from Dos Passos, gives an impression of speeded-up experience, a mad jumble of events that seem to fly past. This is also true of Döblin's *Alexanderplatz, Berlin* (the title itself tells us what Döblin wants to do), Burroughs's *Naked Lunch* and Burgess's *Clockwork Orange*. The odd-men-out on this list are Beckett, a discussion of whose intentions must be left to a later chapter, and Hemingway, whose chief innovation is a flat, precise prose designed to purge the novel of all emotional romanticism.

All these novels mentioned above have one thing in common: they are all about 'alienation'—a word invented by Karl Marx to describe modern man's sense of not belonging to a highly mechanised society. But then, if we remember, *this* was precisely what Rousseau was writing about. So even this cannot be regarded as a theme common to experimental novels.

However, we have to recognise that it is the feeling of alienation that drives most of these novelists to use experimental techniques. You could compare them to cubist painters. The novelist is trying to say that he cannot take the warm, easy, comfortable view of life that we find in Jane Austen, Trollope, even Wells. They take a certain stability for granted; the experimental novelist feels he is living in a confused, hectic and basically soul-less world. Musil's great *Man Without Qualities* begins: 'There was a depression over the Atlantic. It was travelling eastwards, towards an area of high pressure over Russia. . . .' And a few sentences later we read: 'Motor-cars came shooting out of deep, narrow streets into the shallows of bright squares. Dark patches of pedestrian bustle formed into cloudy streams. Where stronger lines of speed transected their loose-woven hurrying, they clotted up. . . .' And a few pages later, we encounter the hero, Ulrich, and are introduced to his dilemma. Ulrich was born with a vague sense of destiny, the feeling that he would one day be 'a man of importance'. He enters the army, and for a while is quite happy in this simplified world of old-fashioned virtues; then he becomes disillusioned and leaves. Next, he becomes an engineer—the kind of

engineer one often meets as the hero of Soviet novels: an en-
thusiast, a man who believes that engineering will one day
solve all humanity's problems. But he soon realises that engineers are ordinary human beings, not scientific supermen,
and abandons this profession too. But he does not abandon his
faith in science; it seems to him that mathematics is the perfect
science, and that it is therefore his destiny to become a mathematician. Which he does. Only to realise that to be a master
of numbers and quantities is not the same as being a master of
life. So as the novel opens, Ulrich is not sure what he wants to
become. And all that happens, in this vast novel, is that he
allows himself to become involved in a scheme to celebrate
Franz Josef's seventieth jubilee with a great patriotic campaign, and seduces a number of women. From the beginning,
Ulrich feels the campaign to be futile (and in fact, Franz Josef
died in 1916, two years before it would have come to fruition
anyway). So even if Robert Musil had not died before he
finished it, the novel would have reached no definite conclusion.

But from this summary, we can immediately see that
Ulrich's problem is that he is engaged in a search for a self-
image. He tries on different identities, like the heroes of Shaw's
early novels; but unlike Shaw, he never finds one that fits.
The only thing that *does* give him a certain sense of purpose is
sleeping with strange women, and before the end of the novel
he has seduced half a dozen, including his sister.

Let us compare this typical 'conservative' experimental
writer with a typical 'radical' novelist, John Dos Passos. Here
is a passage from *Manhattan Transfer*:

> The sun's moved to Jersey, the sun's behind Hoboken.
> Covers are clicking on typewriters, rolltop desks are
> closing; elevators go up empty, come down jammed. It's
> ebbtide in the downtown district, flood in Flatbush, Wood-
> lawn, Dyckman Street, Sheepshead Bay, New Lots Avenue,
> Canarsie.
> Pink sheets, green sheets, grey sheets, FULL MARKET
> REPORTS, FINALS ON HAVRE DE GRACE. Print squirms among
> the shopworn officeworn sagging faces, sore fingertips,

aching insteps, strongarm men cram into subway expresses.
SENATORS 8, GIANTS 2, DIVA RECOVERS PEARLS, $800,000
ROBBERY.

It's ebbtide on Wall Street, floodtide in the Bronx.

The sun's gone down in Jersey.

It can be immediately seen that, in spite of differences of
style, Musil's Vienna and Dos Passos's New York are per-
ceived by their respective novelists in much the same way. In
a review of *Manhattan Transfer* written in 1925, D. H. Lawrence
summarised its aim:

> If you set a blank record revolving to receive all the sounds,
> and a film-camera going to photograph all the motions of a
> scattered group of individuals, at the points where they
> meet and touch in New York, you would more or less get
> Mr Dos Passos's method. It is a rush of disconnected scenes
> and scraps, a breathless confusion of isolated moments in a
> group of lives, pouring on through the years, from almost
> every part of New York. . . . The scenes whirl past like
> snowflakes.

This description—of the record and the camera—also applies
to the newspaper-office scene in *Ulysses*, the first time in literature that this technique was used. It also applies, to a large
extent, to all the novels in the above list. In short, we see that
the experimental novel is not some special adventurous,
pioneering type of novel, but is simply a novel about 'not
belonging', not being able to find a self-image and purpose.
Once a writer has found a self-image and purpose, he ceases
to write experimental novels. The basic 'form' of every novel
is of tension and release-from-tension; its appeal to us is an
appeal to our instinctive craving for freedom. Most experimental novels fail to complete the cycle of tension and release.
Because of this failure, it also follows that most of them are
grimly pessimistic. In short, the experimental novel is basically
an unsuccessful thought-experiment.

*

In his review of *Manhattan Transfer*, D. H. Lawrence goes on to discuss the first book of a writer of short stories, Ernest Hemingway. It was called *In Our Time*; and, as Lawrence points out, is a succession of fragments. 'So short, like striking a match. . . .' The phrase reveals the affinity between Hemingway and Joyce; each had arrived at a theory of 'epiphanies'. In fact, the 'epiphany'—the brief snapshot, the lighted match—is the natural form for the experimental novel, which concentrates on the fragmentary, meaningless nature of human existence. *Manhattan Transfer* is a series of snapshots.

Lawrence immediately recognised Hemingway's merit as a writer, even if he disliked the Hemingway philosophy. ('It isn't fun any more'; 'Everything's gone to hell inside me.') He recognised that Hemingway was honestly attempting to convey his own curious, individual vision.

This is what distinguishes Hemingway from experimental novelists like Dos Passos or Döblin, or even Sartre. He is, in fact, trying to convey a vision of reality which is fundamentally different from that of the nineteenth-century novelists, although it has something in common with Maupassant. He is inclined to take a grim and pessimistic view of human existence. Death is the reality that overshadows all things. That flat, dry style—which became so famous—seems to imply: human beings are all idiots, emotional fools. But I tell the truth. . . .

At its best, this style conveys an almost frightening impact of reality. Here is the passage from *For Whom the Bell Tolls* describing the bombing that destroys El Sordo and his men:

> Then there were hammering explosions past his ears and the gun barrel hot against his shoulder. It was hammering now again and his ears were deafened by the muzzle blast. Ignacio was pulling down hard on the tripod and the barrel was burning his back. It was hammering now in the roar and he could not remember the act of contrition.
>
> All he could remember was at the hour of our death. Amen. At the hour of our death. Amen. At the hour. At the hour. Amen. The others all were firing. Now and at the hour of our death. Amen.

Then, through the hammering of the gun, there was the whistle of the air splitting apart and then in the red black roar the earth rolled under his knees and then waved up and hit him in the face and then dirt and bits of rock were falling all over and Ignacio was lying on him and the gun was lying on him. But he was not dead because the whistle came again and the earth rolled under him with the roar. Then it came again and the earth lurched under his belly and one side of the hilltop rose into the air and then fell slowly over them where they lay.

The planes came back three times and bombed the hilltop but no one on the hilltop knew it. Then the planes machine-gunned the hilltop and went away. As they dived on the hill for the last time with their machine-guns hammering, the first plane pulled up and winged over and then each plane did the same and they moved from echelon to V-formation and went away into the sky in the direction of Segovia.

This is writing of incredible power, and the flat, almost casual description of the planes flying away in the last paragraph gives it a feeling of photographic precision. No novelist before Hemingway had ever conveyed violence and death with such a sense of truth. This is 'vicarious experience' of a kind few readers had ever known.

Hemingway's greatest success, *A Farewell to Arms*, is certainly one of the finest novels of the twentieth century. This is because it uses this same 'photographic' technique to convey the reality of the 1914 war. ('Now in the fall the trees were all bare and the roads were muddy.') But that savage and violent reality is contrasted with a love affair between the hero and an army nurse—also told with the minimum of sentimentality. It is this sharp contrast between bleakness and warmth that gives the novel its emotional impact. Hemingway conveys the feeling that no one has ever told the truth so completely before. What is more, the photographic realism of the violence gives the beauty of Nature an almost unbearable poignancy. The almost visionary intensity of Hemingway's descriptions of the seasons seems to derive from his feeling that life is short—and also cheap.

The consequence of this heightened perception is that Hemingway seems to be singularly free of the smell of decadence that hangs over so many realistic novelists. He seems to go back to primal simplicities. His heroes are free of the usual neuroses. They have no crises of identity, no problems about the self-image. Without exception, they have a firm, solid sense of their own identity. They can look other men in the eye and, if necessary, knock them down. But they all have the same problem as Ulrich in *The Man Without Qualities*. They know who they are, but they have no idea of what they *want to become*. The Hemingway hero is stronger and healthier than anyone else in the novel, but he still has no sense of ultimate purpose. So he whiles away his time in fishing, big-game hunting, bull-fighting, and is basically thoroughly cynical and frustrated. At the end of *The Sun Also Rises*, Lady Brett says sadly: 'Oh, Jake, we could have had such a damned good time together', and Jake growls, 'Yes, isn't it pretty to think so.'

This fundamental pessimism blocked Hemingway's development as it blocked that of Proust, Joyce and Musil. His sense of values depends on the feeling that death lies just around the corner, so that everything to do with life becomes almost unbearably poignant. All his work could be regarded as an elaboration of Dr Johnson's comment: 'When a man knows he is to be hanged in a fortnight, it concentrates his mind wonderfully.' But in order to maintain this acute awareness of death, Hemingway had to deliberately seek out extreme situations: preferably wars. His cinematic technique requires the sharp contrast of life and sudden death, beauty and brutality. His two best novels—*A Farewell to Arms* and *For Whom the Bell Tolls*—are about war, and his next best—*The Sun Also Rises*—is about a man who has lost his sexual organs in the war, so that he is doomed to perpetual frustration. In *Death in the Afternoon* and *Green Hills of Africa* he tries to use bull-fighting and big-game hunting as 'moral substitutes for war' (William James's phrase), but neither could be called successful. His problem was not simply that his technique confined him to tragic subjects; it was that it prevented him from writing convincingly of anything *but* war and violence. Not only does it exclude comedy; it excluded almost every other subject that interested Richardson, Jane Austen, Balzac, Dickens, Tolstoy. . . . In short, Hemingway's peculiar achievement was to limit the range of the novel to about five per cent of its normal possibilities.

EIGHT

Ideas

SOME TIME IN the early 1950s, the science-fiction writer
A. E. Van Vogt became preoccupied with the question of
husbands who openly practise a double-standard: that is, who
demand total and strict fidelity from their wives, and who
make no secret of their love affairs with other women. What
interested him was how such men justify their behaviour *to
themselves*. And as he gathered stories about such behaviour,
he was amazed how far these men could go in sheer self-
deception. For example, a nurse who was about to marry
confessed to her prospective husband that she had had two
previous love affairs with doctors. He went almost insane
with jealousy. The next day, he arrived at her home with a
legal document in triplicate for her to sign, but he refused to
allow her to read it. She signed, and in due course they were
married. He then proceeded to misbehave himself fairly
openly. His business took him all over the country; he seldom
bothered to inform his wife where he was, or when he would
be home. He was always visiting his female employees in their
apartments, or driving female secretaries home and taking
hours to do it. If his wife dared to ask any question about
these activities, he flew into a rage and often knocked her
across the room. She finally became sexually frigid; they
divorced, and he set her up in a suburban home. But he made
a condition that she must not re-marry; she must devote her
life to being a good mother to their child. . . .

From his knowledge of other such types, Van Vogt was
reasonably certain that the document she signed contained a
'confession' that she was little better than a prostitute, and
that she had no legal rights as his wife.

Van Vogt labelled this type of man 'the violent man' or 'the Right man', because under *no* circumstances will he ever admit that he is in the wrong.

The most straightforward comment on the violent man is that he is immature. Freud once said that a child would destroy the world if it had the power; frustration of its wishes produces a blind and violent rage. As we grow up, we all continue to want our own way, but we realise that we have to take account of other people to get it. Purely for self-protection we have to learn to give as well as take. Many people are singularly slow to learn; or perhaps they simply don't want to learn. We all continue to want all kinds of things, and the world is full of people we dislike or disagree with. So there is a secret hankering in all of us for absolute power—to be able to re-arrange the world with a wave of the magic wand. Few human beings actually *want* to be reasonable, as an aim in itself. The right man simply goes further in this direction than most. He feeds his ego with secret fantasies of power; and, as far as he can, he puts them into practice with subordinates. His wife and family are ideal subordinates, since they depend upon him absolutely. So they are incorporated into the self-esteem fantasy; it is their business to be submissive and docile, while he—like an Eastern despot—does just as he likes.

But he is playing a dangerous game. For if the breath of reality blows into his fantasy, his foundations are destroyed. Van Vogt observed again and again that if the wife deserted 'the Right man', he might plunge into severe mental illness, or even die.

I spent most of a Creative Writing period discussing Van Vogt and his 'Right man' theories with my students, and the response was remarkable. All of the students had known at least one 'Right man'—or woman. (The condition is rarer among women than men, but it *can* exist. The mother of the novelist Turgeniev was a 'Right woman', who used to have her servants flogged for the slightest offence.) Two of them said their fathers were 'Right men'. And one girl had just separated from a 'Right man' with whom she had been living for years. (I wondered why she often appeared in class with bruises and scratches.)

And why *should* the 'Right man' theory be of any use to a novelist? For exactly the same reason that general equations are of use to a mathematician, or laws of nature to a scientist. A writer's material consists of other human beings—as well as himself. He tries to understand what motivates them—particularly under conditions of stress. It is not enough to observe human peculiarities; the writer must classify them, and then try to understand their general laws.

Maupassant possessed this kind of insight to an extraordinary degree. The odd thing is that he allowed it to operate only in flashes. He captured human peculiarities with the precision of a great photographer; but he never attempted to classify his photographs.

Let me offer three examples of the quality of Maupassant's observation.

At a masked ball in Montmartre, a tall, dandified-looking man is dancing with such enthusiasm that he suddenly collapses. When a doctor tries to remove the mask, he discovers it covers another mask, made of skin-like rubber. The face underneath is that of a withered old man. When he recovers consciousness, the doctor escorts him home, to a poverty-stricken lodging house. There the man's wife tells the doctor his story. As a young man, he was irresistible to women; and, as the assistant of a famous theatrical hairdresser, he had opportunity for endless *affaires*. When the white hairs and wrinkles began to appear, he was unable to accept that he was growing old. And now, when the craving for bare shoulders and half-naked bosoms becomes insupportable, he puts on his mask and blond wig, and dances frantically all night. . . .

Clearly, this is a form of 'Right man' behaviour. His wife has always been expected to accept his love affairs. He has lived in his fantasy world until time began to destroy it. And now, as it slowly crumbles, he clings to his self-esteem with a frenzy that will soon destroy him.

You feel that Maupassant relates all this with a touch of sadistic pleasure. If a man insists on living on illusions, he must be prepared to die when they are taken away. Yet the story is not merely a clinical report on self-delusion. Maupassant himself was a dandy; he also had endless love affairs. The story could be interpreted as a warning from one aspect of his nature to the other. It was a warning that served no purpose. Maupassant died insane.

In *The Revenge*, a man recognises his ex-wife—from whom he has just been divorced—in a hotel in Cannes; she is there on honeymoon with her new husband. The ex-husband accosts her, and they begin to argue. She finally admits that she was unfaithful to him, and that her lover was the man who has now become her husband. At this, the ex-husband delivers an ultimatum; either she agrees to take him as a lover, or he will go to her new husband and tell him that his wife was frequently unfaithful with other men. . . . At this moment, the husband's voice calls to his wife; she hurries off, agreeing to meet her ex-husband after dinner. . . .

In this case, the ex-husband is not necessarily a 'Right man' (although she divorced him for beating her). But his attitude towards women is typical of the 'Right man'—what would now be called male chauvinism. She has robbed him by giving herself to other men; now she can make restitution by robbing her new husband.

But the really interesting question is the one that Maupassant does not even bother to ask. Why *should* a man want to sleep with a woman he has slept with on a hundred other occasions? Particularly when they dislike one another? Because she is somebody else's wife; therefore she is 'forbidden'—and desirable. Maupassant is aware of this paradoxical element in the situation; but he takes it for granted.

In *The Unknown*, a young man-about-town recounts how he passed an attractive girl in the street, and found her so desirable that he turned and followed her. But he lost her in the crowd. During the next two years he sees her on a number of occasions, but never succeeds in getting acquainted. Then, one day, he collides with her in the street, and loses no time in asking when he might see her again. To his astonishment, she asks for his card, and promises to come to his house. A few days later, she keeps her promise. Within a few minutes, he is helping her to undress. And then, as her undergarments slip to the floor, he sees that she has a patch of dark hair on her back. Instantly, his desire vanishes; he becomes impotent. And the girl says irritably: 'There wasn't much point in putting me to all that trouble, was there?' and leaves. And from then on, whenever he sees her in the street, she passes coldly, refusing to acknowledge his bow. . . .

What has happened here is what happened to the hero of *The Chinese Room* when he glimpses Sidonie's deformed foot. But what precisely *has* happened? Maupassant's character is a hunter of women. He is the beast of prey; they are the victims. He does not enter into a *relation* with them as human beings. Their role is to act a part in a play he has written for them; they are creatures of his fantasy, reinforcing his vision of himself as a Casanova. When the girl offers to come to his home, this already worries him; it is too easy; she is not playing the game according to the rules. When she allows him to undress her within a few minutes of arriving, it again arouses a feeling of uneasiness. The patch of hair between the shoulders is enough to deflate his desire; it could have been a mole on her breast, a scar across her stomach. . . .

It can be seen that these three stories are delicate explorations of the paradoxes of the male psyche; it would be possible to write a whole book about their meaning and implications. For is it not true that *all* our human relationships have this element of play-acting? That all human beings prefer the forbidden to what is legitimately theirs? That even the nicest and most well-adjusted human beings live in a fantasy world, with bullet-proof armour-plating around their self-esteem? Maupassant observed these paradoxes brilliantly and accurately; but he never *thought* about them. This is why he never became a great writer.

For this is one of the most fundamental laws of creativity: to worry a problem until you see all its *implications*. Anyone can become a good writer by pondering Christopher Isherwood's remark, 'I am a camera', and training himself in accurate observation. But the difference between a merely good writer and a serious writer is that the serious writer is concerned with implications. Like a mathematician, he is concerned with general equations. And Van Vogt's 'violent man' theory, with which I opened this chapter, is a good example of a general equation. In the days when Joyce was writing *Ulysses*, Freud's theories about human sexuality had just become a part of the cultural background of educated people, and it would be no exaggeration to say that *Ulysses* could never have been written without them. (Leopold Bloom is intended as a kind of Everyman, yet he is a pantie-fetichist and a masochist; this would have been unthinkable twenty years earlier.) Freud had 'extended our knowledge of human nature' (as Johnson said of Richardson), and Joyce took advantage of the new knowledge. Yet it must be admitted that Freudian psychology is not an ideal example of the 'general equations' I am discussing. It contains too much guesswork and too much unsupported assertion. On the other hand, the basis of Van Vogt's 'Right man' theory can be observed around us—and inside us—all the time. As soon as we begin to think about it, to discuss its implications, we become aware of aspects of human behaviour that we had never noticed before. And *this* kind of knowledge is a part of a writer's essential equipment, as a saw and chisel are a part of a carpenter's.

Now these general equations are *ideas*, and they are the basis of all serious writing. For a long time now, writers have entertained the mistaken notion that ideas have no place in literature, because literature is about 'life', not abstractions. But this statement is in itself an idea. And it was upon this idea that Joyce and Hemingway based their literary practice. Unfortunately, it was a false idea—which is another way of saying that Joyce and Hemingway were muddled thinkers. We can study the nature of the fallacy more closely in a controversy between Hemingway and Aldous Huxley. In an amusing essay called 'Foreheads Villainous Low', Huxley accuses Hemingway of trying to create a cult of stupidity and inarticulateness. The Hemingway hero, he says, seems ashamed of his mind, and flinches at the least suspicion of culture. In *Death in the Afternoon*, Hemingway replied. A good writer, he said, tries to tell the truth about reality, and he has no business with fine feelings and abstractions. . . .

Both were wrong. Huxley was a novelist of ideas, and his serious novels are irritating because they are so unreal; you can almost see the characters walking out of Huxley's brain on to the paper. (This hardly matters at all in comedy, which is why his two comic novels, *Crome Yellow* and *Antic Hay*, are the best he wrote.) Hemingway was right to reject that kind of thing. But Hemingway's ideas were circular. Man lives by courage, but his courage is negated by death. Which means that he needs even more courage, which is also negated by death. Which means. . . . And so on. Hemingway's trouble was not that he failed to ask questions, but that he asked the wrong questions, and failed to follow up his answers. For example, in an early short story called *Soldier's Home*, he writes of a soldier who comes back from the 1914 war, and experiences the same kind of profound boredom and life-failure experienced by Saki's Bassington. Talking about his war experiences destroys their reality. 'All of the times that had been able to make him feel cool and clear inside himself when he thought of them; the times so long back when he had done the one thing, the only thing for a man to do, easily and naturally, when he might have done something else, now lost their cool, valuable quality, and were lost themselves.' This is penetrating psychological observation that reveals that Hemingway was a man of acute intelligence. And he now has a kind of equation: that when we do something in a time of crisis, our vitality responds to the summons, and we do it well. When we are in non-crisis situations, we tend to become bored and do things badly. It is civilisation that tends to produce boredom and indifference. . . . And now Hemingway has formulated an equation that we can also find in the work of Rousseau and D. H. Lawrence. What is the solution? Rousseau suggested that we get rid of civilisation—or at least, alter its basic nature. Lawrence thought that sex gave a clue to the answer, but never thought the problem through to the end. But Hemingway had come

closer to a solution than either by recognising that it is a strong
and deep sense of purpose that produces the feeling of being
'cool and clear inside'. Yeats had made exactly the same observation in a poem called *Under Ben Bulben*, where he observes
that 'when a man is fighting mad':

> Something drops from eyes long blind,
> He completes his partial mind.

That is to say, Yeats had recognised that our normal state of
consciousness is *somehow incomplete*—'partial'—and that sudden
crisis can lead us to complete it. It is as if everyday consciousness was like the moon in its last quarter; we *know* the rest of
the moon is there, but we can't see it. Under crisis, the whole
moon suddenly appears.

This in turn leads to the interesting question: are there
'methods' of completing the partial mind, apart from continually seeking out crisis? This completion of the partial mind
is what Abraham Maslow called the peak experience—the
moment of sudden absurd happiness—and Maslow noted that
the peak experience is always associated with fulfilled purpose
—*any* purpose. Hermann Hesse comments in *Journey to the East*
how 'a long time devoted to small details exalts us and in-
creases our strength'. Hemingway himself knew this; he knew,
for example, that he gained the same feeling of being 'cool and
clear inside' from watching his float bobbing in the water, or
sitting quietly in a brake, waiting for a wild animal to pass
by. . . . Unfortunately, Hemingway was not the reflective
type. So he never thought out the *implications* of his insights:
only kept on repeating them in book after book: *A Farewell to
Arms, For Whom the Bell Tolls, The Old Man and the Sea*. Sudden
crisis completes the partial mind. Good. So where do we go
from there?

Let us be clear about this. When I speak of ideas, I do not mean
the kind of ideas you find in the novels of Thomas Love Peacock
or Aldous Huxley, where intellectual men sit around a table
and argue about philosophy. An idea is something that the

whole work is saying, and *all* works contain an idea. If the author happens to be stupid or untalented, the idea may be a cliché—which may nevertheless be true. The only kind of work that could be totally devoid of an idea is automatic writing.

Let me give another example of the fruitful use of an idea in fiction. L. H. Myers was a remarkable English novelist who committed suicide in 1944. His greatest work, a trilogy, is called *The Near and the Far*, and the title is derived from its opening scene. The young Prince Jali has been travelling all day across the desert with his father; now they have arrived at their destination, the castle of the Great Mogul Abdul, and Jali stands on the battlements looking at the sunset. It occurs to him that there are *two* deserts, one of which is a glory to the eye, the other of which is a 'weariness to the foot'. Looking out at this gold and crimson desert in the sunset arouses a deep craving, a hunger for the magic of the distance. But if he tries to run towards the sunset, he will only get his shoes full of sand. The 'near' is always real and uncomfortable; the magic we crave always seems to be far away. Myers develops this image throughout a long novel which, in its first two-thirds at least, is as great as anything that has been written in the twentieth century.

The hero of Villiers de l'Isle Adam's play *Axel*, which we mentioned in Chapter Four, took the same view. ('As for living, our servants can do that for us.') Reality is always disappointing; the greatest pleasure lies in hopes and illusions and expectations. . . . It becomes possible to understand why Myers committed suicide.

And so when we talk about the 'idea' behind a novel, we mean the author's attempt to summarise his vision of existence. Or at least, his *attitude* to his own everyday life. Is he a natural winner or a natural loser? Does he believe that human reason and will-power can improve things, or does he feel that nothing we do has much effect—that we are creatures of circumstance (a view held by many noted writers including Thomas Hardy and Somerset Maugham). Is he compassionate about human suffering, or does it touch a secret spring of sadism—a feeling of 'it serves them right' (which is what we feel in Maupassant).

Above all, does he merely record the surface of human existence as we all see it, or does he try to get below it? Is he a describer or explainer?

I must emphasise this matter of attitude. If a literate Martian came to earth, and was handed novels by Balzac, Dickens, Trollope, Dostoevsky, G. K. Chesterton, Aldous Huxley, Ernest Hemingway, Graham Greene, William Faulkner, Evelyn Waugh—he would ask incredulously: 'Do you mean to say they are all writing about the *same* world?' To which the strictly correct answer would be: No. They are each writing about a world inside their heads—what you might call their individual Life-Worlds. (The term was invented by Husserl.)

All the authors whose names I mentioned in the above paragraph have highly individual Life-Worlds. On the other hand, if I compared a dozen stories by writers in my Creative Writing class, I would not find nearly so much difference of attitude. And this is because most of them would be writing about a Life-World they all share to a large extent. They watch the same television programmes, read the same newspapers and books, listen to the same professors. So what they are recording might be termed the Communal Life-World.

Which leads to the interesting recognition that all works of literature can be judged according to how far they share the Communal Life-World. You could draw a scale, like a ruler, and at the bottom end, mark it 'Communal Life-World', and somewhere towards the middle, 'Highly Individual Life-World', and then classify almost any novelist we have mentioned so far somewhere on the scale. You can take it for granted, for example, that almost every novel that has ever appeared on the best-seller lists belongs at the bottom end of the scale, for if it didn't share the Communal Life-World, it wouldn't be a best-seller. (There are very rare exceptions, but for the moment, I am dealing with the general rule.) This is not to say that such books are bad. *The Good Companions, Gone With the Wind, The Caine Mutiny, From Here to Eternity, Advise and Consent* and *In Cold Blood* are all books with a degree of literary merit; but although the authors of these books may be writing about an aspect of existence with which we are unfamiliar, they are still writing about the world we all know. They are describers. Jane Austen, Anthony Trollope and Arnold Bennett are also describers; but they also have their own individual, quirky way of seeing things and events. If our 'scale' was a twelve-inch ruler, then they would be around the two- or three-inch mark. Dickens would be around the four-inch mark, for although he is no man of ideas, his world is highly individualised. Hemingway, Greene and Faulkner would be at the six-inch mark—Highly Individualised Life-Worlds.

And what about the rest of the ruler?

That raises an interesting question. As we begin to move into the field of great writers—for example, Goethe, Dostoevsky, Tolstoy, Shaw—we are again moving out of the field of Individual Life-Worlds into something more general. As odd as it sounds, they are beginning to write about *the same* world. The breadth and intensity of their vision means that they are beginning to break out of the prison of Individual Life-Worlds into something more objective. They are still highly individual writers; yet at their greatest, they seem to be seeing—and saying—the same thing. They have a sense of life as something infinitely interesting, far more complex and fascinating than any human being has ever realised. For example, Dostoevsky has a parable—in *The Brothers Karamazov*—about a sinner who was also an atheist, and when he died and found there *was* a life-after-death, he was furious. For his unbelief, God sentenced him to walk a billion miles before he could be admitted to heaven. He flatly refused, and lay down on the road. He stayed there for thousands of years, until he finally got bored, and started walking. Finally, he completed the billion miles, and was allowed to enter heaven. He immediately declared that this was so beautiful that it would have been worth walking a million times as far for one single glimpse of it. . . . Dostoevsky's novels are full of suffering and misery—even masochism; yet beyond it all lies this vision of life as something infinitely meaningful. You find the same thing in Goethe, Tolstoy, Shaw, John Cowper Powys, David Lindsay—as well as many of the great philosophers, poets, mystics and saints. So it would prob-

ably be true to say that the top of the scale should be labelled:
Purely Objective Vision.

And where on the scale should we place Goethe, Tolstoy,
Dostoevsky and the rest? Probably at the seven- or eight-inch
mark—no higher. Which leads to the observation that critics
who think the novel has come to an end are clearly mistaken.
There are still four or five inches to go.

And what does the scale actually measure? What is it that distinguishes Jane Austen from Balzac, Charles Dickens from
Tolstoy?

Ideas—again, using that word in its broadest sense. A writer
who merely records what he sees in front of him is little more
than a camera; he is as devoid of ideas as it is possible to be.
Here is an example:

> My bedroom overlooks the main street of our district.
> Though it was a fine afternoon the paving blocks were
> black and glistening. What few people were about seemed
> in an absurd hurry. First of all there came a family going
> for their Sunday afternoon walk: two small boys in sailor
> suits, with short trousers hardly down to their knees, and
> looking rather uneasy in their Sunday best; then a little girl
> with a big pink bow and black patent-leather shoes. Behind
> them was their mother, an enormously fat woman in a
> brown silk dress, and their father, a dapper little man whom
> I knew by sight. He had a straw hat, a walking stick, and
> a butterfly tie. . . .

A paragraph like this could be continued: 'Etc, etc. . . .'
It gives the impression of going on merely for the sake of going
on. In fact, it is from Albert Camus's novel *L'Etranger* (called
in England *The Outsider*), and the effect is carefully calculated.
His hero, Meursault, lives like that, taking life as it comes. He
takes two pages to describe everything he does on a Sunday—
reading a newspaper, staring out of the window, smoking
cigarettes. This is an essential part of the plot of the novel, for
later, when he is on trial—for the shooting of an Arab—the

jury cannot believe that a man who is so bored and indifferent is not just cold-blooded, and Meursault is sentenced to death. But it is worth bearing in mind that most of us live like that for most of the time. The point of Camus's novel suddenly becomes clear in its last paragraph, when, after losing his temper with a priest, he feels an immense calm and happiness. He speaks of the 'benign indifference of the universe', and says that he suddenly realised that 'I had been happy and I was happy still'. This is a curious recognition for a man who has spent so much of his life in a state of boredom—yet if we remember Dostoevsky's sinner and his first glimpse of heaven, we begin to understand what he is talking about. Camus has deliberately contrasted the dull, close-up view of the Communal Life-World with the bird's-eye vision of a man facing death. The implication is that the everyday vision is untrue—untrue because it is incomplete. On the point of death, Meursault has 'completed his partial mind'.

Many other writers of the twentieth century have been preoccupied with this problem. For example, it lies just below the surface in *The Unbearable Bassington*. It is the subject of Eliot's *The Waste Land*, 'I see crowds of people walking around in a ring'.

It remained a lifelong concern of Hemingway. He treats it, for example, in a story called *A Clean Well-Lighted Place*, which simply describes two waiters in a café late at night. An old man is sitting drinking, and one of the waiters tells the other that the old man has recently tried to commit suicide. The younger waiter is anxious to get home to his wife. The older one has no desire to leave. He suffers from insomnia, and a sense of total meaninglessness. He can understand only too well why the old man tried to commit suicide, even though he has plenty of money. As he turns off the lights, he reflects on his own sense of emptiness. 'It was not fear or dread. It was a nothing that he knew too well. It was all a nothing and a man was nothing too. . . .' And he goes on to recite the Lord's Prayer and Hail Mary, substituting 'nothing' for 'Our father' and 'Mary'. . . . What Hemingway is saying is that the young waiter will hurry home to his wife, convinced that life is worthwhile and meaningful. The older waiter has seen the meaning leak away as he gets older, and he knows that one day he will also sit at a café table, like the old man, bored and secretly afraid, but unable to think of anything to do. . . .

Dostoevsky treated the same problem in his novel *The Devils.* The central character, Nicholas Stavrogin, is always doing strange and eccentric things, yet it seems clear that he is not insane. The reason, we discover, is that he feels life to be totally meaningless. So if he is shaking hands with someone, it seems just as logical to hit him in the face. Stavrogin eventually commits suicide because he admits that he finds it impossible to think of anything to *do* with his life. Unlike Camus's Meursault, he is not contented to be a kind of vegetable. (Camus was fascinated by the novel, and dramatised it.)

Sartre's earliest novel, *Nausea*, deals with a man who is always experiencing moments in which life seems absurd, devoid of meaning. He is a historian, and he is writing the biography of a historical character; but in these moments of 'nausea', he feels that he is *inventing* the meaning of the book. Our bodies and instincts endow life with a false meaning. We have to believe in meaning in order to live. But sometimes we catch a glimpse of the truth, and know that it is all illusion. . . .

This, then, is what we might call the primary level of experience—immediate, confused, undigested. The philosopher Whitehead liked to call it 'presentational immediacy', and the word immediacy describes it as well as any. Obviously, most young would-be writers are going to write about this world of immediacy. But it is worth bearing in mind that immediacy only *appears* to be meaningless, because it is so close-up. Closeupness inevitably robs us of meaning. If you looked at the greatest painting in the world with your nose half an inch from the canvas, it would strike you as meaningless. Most everyday experience has this quality, as if a camera was held too close to the object it is photographing, or as if a microphone is held too close to the mouth when speaking. The result is a blurry effect. The writer's problem is to *pull back*, to try to get the camera far enough away to see things whole.

Now two hundred years ago, this problem simply would not

have arisen. If a man decided to write a novel, he looked around for a good story, and told it. Novels in those days were 'Shakespearian fish'. Then came the romantic fish, pouring out their emotions and problems. And then the fish landed on the beach, and found themselves unable to get back into the sea. The first problem of the modern novelist is just to get himself into the sea.

I have tried to show that the first step is to attempt to create a self-image. He must recognise that what he is trying to do is to create a mirror in which he can see his own face. The next step is to recognise that the purpose of literature is not to record the world of immediacy, but to get beyond it, to achieve detachment from it.

And how precisely is this to be done? Each individual is bound to have his own answer to the problem, because each individual has a different set of experiences that make him feel 'cool and clear inside'. But *this* is basically the method. Once a writer has discovered what makes him feel 'cool and clear inside', he has also discovered his subject. For Hemingway it was war and human courage. For Lawrence, it was sex. For Hamsun, it was nature. For Conrad, it was the sea. For Saint-Exupéry, it was the air. For Joyce, it was the idea of the outsider-artist. For De Sade it was cruelty and defiance of the law. For Farnol, it was the open road. For Graham Greene, Catholicism. For H. P. Lovecraft, it was horror. (This sounds absurd, but it is true; concentration on horror 'saved' Lovecraft from the boredom of everyday life, from the triviality of everydayness.) Every major writer has his own symbols of *meaning*, and he contrasts these with the dreariness or chaos of the world of immediacy. A writer's 'symbol' is basically his own idea of *freedom*, and his work is about the journey towards freedom. This is the basic mechanism of creativity.

We shall look more closely at the actual workings of this mechanism in the next chapter. Here we are still concerned with the writer's fundamental problem: close-upness, immediacy, a 'reality' that suffocates like a cushion held over your face:

The day has gone by just as days go by. I had killed it in accordance with my primitive and withdrawn way of life. I had worked for an hour or two and perused the pages of old books. I had had pains for two hours, as elderly people do. . . . Taken all in all, it had not been exactly a day of rapture. No, it had not even been a day brightened by happiness and joy. Rather it had been just one of those days which for a long time now had fallen to my lot; the moderately pleasant, the wholly bearable and tolerable, lukewarm days of a discontented middle aged man. . . .

This is the beginning of Hermann Hesse's novel *Steppenwolf*. His hero lives alone. He has enough money to do what he likes, so in theory he ought to be free. Instead, he is bored; life drifts past meaninglessly, so he is often tempted to put an end to it. The problem that concerns him is the curious *limitation* of human consciousness. There are certain tape-recorders that have a special electronic control, so if the volume of sound gets too loud, they automatically reduce it by a half. Human consciousness seems to have a similar mechanism. No matter how pleasant our lives, no matter how much we have to be grateful for, we quickly fall into the old mental groove, that lukewarm condition of semi-contentment, semi-boredom. . . .

And yet two hours later, as Steppenwolf drinks a glass of Moselle wine in a restaurant, the limitation vanishes: 'a refreshing laughter rose in me. . . . It soared aloft like a soap bubble, reflecting the whole world in miniature on its rainbow surface, and then softly burst. . . . The golden trail was blazed and I was reminded of the eternal, of Mozart, of the stars. . . .'

But what soon becomes very clear is that Hesse has no idea of the solution of this problem. His hero walks into a 'magic theatre', gets involved with two women (of a type who, in real life, would not pay the least attention to a middle-aged scholar), and lives out a kind of Walter Mitty fantasy of sex and dissipation. This same criticism applies to most of Hesse's novels. He is inclined to make his heroes run away from their problems and take to the broad highway, in search of Life with a capital L. *Steppenwolf* is impressive largely because of its clear statement of the basic problem: the way that the sense of freedom arrives unexpectedly, giving us a sensation of looking down on life from a great height, and suddenly grasping all the hidden meanings.

In order to see why Hesse is such an unsatisfactory novelist, it is only necessary to compare him with his friend and contemporary Thomas Mann. Mann was obsessed by the same basic problem: the dreary meaninglessness of 'ordinary consciousness', and the sudden moments of intensity when meaning unveils itself. His earliest story, written when he was twenty, states the problem with superb clarity. It is called *Disillusionment*. The narrator is sitting in St Mark's Square in Venice when he falls into conversation with a fellow-countryman. The man asks: 'Do you know what disillusionment is? Not a miscarriage in small, unimportant matters, but the great and general disappointment which everything, all of life, has in store?' He tells how, as a small boy, the house caught fire; yet as they watched it burn down he was thinking: 'So this is a house on fire? Is that all?' And ever since then, life has been a series of disappointments; all the great experiences have left him with the feeling: 'Is that all?' Only when he saw the sea for the first time, he says, did he feel a sudden tremendous craving for freedom, for a sea without a horizon. . . . And one day, death will come, and he expects it to be the last great disappointment. 'Is this all?'

He is, of course, re-stating the problem of the 'near and the far'. The sea gives him a momentary glimpse of the magic of the horizon; mostly he is trapped in the meaninglessness of the 'near'.

Mann treated the problem at length in his first novel, *Buddenbrooks*, a vast 'family chronicle'. It concerns the rise and fall of a family of north German merchants; their decline begins when the sensitive and artistic Hanno is born into the family. In the mid-nineteenth century, many doctors held the belief that sickness makes people more sensitive, and the whole 'decadent movement' was based on this idea that art and sickness are closely related. In all his works, Mann explores this idea that art *is* sickness, and that stupidity is another name for

health. But, unlike Hesse, he thought about the idea and explored its implications. In his masterpiece, *The Magic Mountain*,
a young engineer goes to visit his cousin in a Swiss sanatorium,
and finds himself increasingly fascinated by the emotions and
ideas to which he is subjected. And—typically—when he under-
goes a routine check-up, it is discovered that he is also infected
with tuberculosis. Yet he feels no dismay about his sickness;
he is glad to remain in this poisonous, enchanted realm of
ecstasy and death. His sensibilities expand; the engineer is
transformed into a kind of artist. His cousin dies, but still he
feels no desire to escape; only the shock of the First World War
finally forces him to recognise that he cannot stay here for ever;
he has to return to the harsh, real world of action. But this
brief summary fails to do justice to the immense intellectual
complexity of the novel. With endless curiosity, Mann explores
every aspect of the problem. *The Magic Mountain* is one of the
great novels of the twentieth century because Mann is not
afraid of ideas. By comparison, Hesse seems limited. Yet the
basic themes in Mann and Hesse are almost identical. Mann is
the greater novelist because he thinks them through, explores
their implications. Even in the less successful works—the
Joseph novels and *Doktor Faustus*—there is an enormous sense
of range and power, which springs from the vitality of the ideas.

And now it should be possible to see why Joyce and Hemingway failed to develop beyond a certain point. It was not simply
that they were inclined to pessimism; a pessimist may have an
interesting development if he explores the implications of his
pessimism. It was because they both rejected ideas, insisting
that the novel should be 'about reality'. This is a fallacy, for
the way a novelist perceives 'reality' *is* an idea. And if his work
is to develop, the ideas must develop too.

Before we go any further, let us be quite clear what is meant
by the word 'idea'.

Imagine that you have just undergone a minor operation
under anaesthetic, and you are opening your eyes in a strange
room. For the first few seconds, you recognise nothing; you
are like a new-born baby. Then you recognise that you are in

a room, but have no idea where you are. You look around, still dazed from the anaesthetic. You recognise the window, the door, the bedside table. You are still not sure what time of day it is. Then it all comes back, and suddenly you know where you are and what has been happening.

When you first opened your eyes, you had no *ideas*. Just perceptions. But they were not attached together, like a string of beads; they were drifting around in your consciousness, *unconnected*. As soon as you recognised the window and door, a whole group of these disconnected impressions coalesced *into an idea*. And finally, when you recognised the place and re-membered where you were, your capacity for ideas was again functioning freely.

An idea is the thread that holds the beads together, and if that thread did not exist, you would be an imbecile.

Now consider again the paragraph describing Camus's Meursault looking out of the window. He is only a few degrees more conscious than a man waking from an operation. His is a 'worm's-eye-view' of the world. The hero of Sartre's *Nausea* comments about a café proprietor: 'When his café empties, his head empties too.' Again, he is remarking on the cow-like, almost imbecilic quality of ordinary consciousness. And in moods of 'nausea', his own consciousness also collapses into this state, so that things become as meaningless as they are for the patient waking from the operation.

The novelist *starts* with this 'worm's-eye' consciousness. His problem is to transcend it and move into bird's-eye consciousness.

On a hill by the Mississippi where Chippewas camped two generations ago, a girl stood in relief against the cornflower blue of Northern sky. She saw no Indians now; she saw flour-mills and the blinking windows of skyscrapers in Minneapolis and St Paul. Nor was she thinking of squaws and portages, and the Yankee fur-traders whose shadows were all about her. She was meditating upon walnut fudge, the plays of Brieux, the reasons why heels run over, and the fact that the chemistry instructor had stared at the new coiffure which concealed her ears.

A breeze which had crossed a thousand miles of wheatlands bellied her taffeta skirt in a line so graceful, so full of animation and moving beauty, that the heart of a chance watcher on the lower road tightened to wistfulness over her quality of suspended freedom. . . .

This is not great prose, but it has a quality of poetry. Not surprisingly, the book of which it forms the opening paragraph —Sinclair Lewis's *Main Street*—became an immediate bestseller and launched its author to fame.

The same thing happened to J. B. Priestley after publication of a novel that began:

There, far below, is the knobbly backbone of England, the Pennine range. At first, the whole dark length of it, from the Peak to Cross Fell, is visible. Then the Derbyshire hills and the Cumberland fells disappear, for you are descending, somewhere about the middle of the range, where the high moorland thrusts itself between the woollen mills of Yorkshire and the cotton mills of Lancashire. Great winds blow over miles and miles of ling and bog and black rock, and the curlews still go crying on that empty air as they did before the Romans came. There is a glitter of water here and there, from the moorland tarns, that are now called reservoirs. In summer you could wander here all day and never meet a soul. In winter you could lose your way in an hour and die of exposure, perhaps, not a dozen miles from where the Bradford trams end or the Burnley trams begin. . . .

And so Priestley swoops down, like a giant camera, closer and closer:

At first the towns only seem a blacker edge to the high moorland, so many fantastic outcroppings of its rock, but now that you are closer, you see the host of tall chimneys, the rows and rows of little houses, built of blackening stone. . . . Down there are thousands and thousands of men and women who are stocky and hold themselves very stiffly, who have short upper lips and long chins, who use emphatic consonants and very broad vowels and always sound aggressive. . . .

And so, finally, we come down to Bruddersford, and the crowds streaming out of a football match on a Saturday afternoon, and finally, to the hero of *The Good Companions*, Jess Oakroyd.

A literary critic might remark cynically that this is the best-selling manner; it soothes the reader like a mother saying: 'Now, children, tuck up in bed and I'll tell you a story. . . .' But what is more important is that it performs the basic function of a novel: of inducing 'wide-angle consciousness'. Neither Carol Milford nor Jess Oakroyd could have seen themselves as Sinclair Lewis and J. B. Priestley saw them. The novelist is exercising his privilege of the god's-eye view, and providing the consciousness of the reader with a kind of holiday from his own life.

Having said which, we must immediately admit that both *Main Street* and *The Good Companions* are books about the Communal Life-World. The reader is soon involved in quite ordinary events, of the kind he might watch on any soap opera on television. Both are fine novels, but if you tried to read through either of them in one sitting, they would leave you depressed, with a feeling of moral dyspepsia. Mann's *Magic Mountain*, Musil's *Man Without Qualities*, Broch's *Sleepwalkers* may be far harder going (and it would be impossible to read more than a few chapters at a sitting), but they leave you exhilarated, as if you had been rock climbing. They set out to induce a bird's-eye view, not merely of everyday life, but of human existence itself.

It might be objected that *no* novel can be written entirely from the bird's-eye view. Priestley may begin above the Pennines, but he has to bring the camera down to the individual in a football crowd. He could not tell Jess Oakroyd's story—of leaving home and joining a theatrical company—if the camera stayed up above the mountains.

But there *are* novels that succeed in combining the two visions, the near and the far. E. M. Forster calls them 'prophetic novels', and cited George Eliot's *Adam Bede*, Dostoevsky's *Brothers Karamazov* and Melville's *Moby Dick*. By prophetic, Forster means a novel that tries to convey this broader view of human existence. (Apparently it never struck him that, in this sense, *all* novels are prophetic.) His list is understandably short. But six years after the publication of *Aspects of the Novel* (1927), there appeared a prophetic novel that, for sheer breadth of vision, surpassed anything mentioned by Forster: John Cowper Powys's *A Glastonbury Romance*.

Powys is a mystic, and the first thing to note about the book is that it appeared when he was sixty. This kind of vision could not have been achieved by a young man; the young tend to be trapped in immediacy. In the course of his six decades, much of which had been spent lecturing in America, Powys had developed an increasing sense of the oneness of man and nature. He would not have been in the least surprised by the discovery made by the experimenter Cleve Backster that plants can apparently read our minds; in Powys, trees, grass, even rocks, possess their own strange, dim consciousness. Human beings alone are cut off from this universal consciousness by their narrow, intense perceptions, although Powys prophesies that this will cease to be so, that there will soon be a 'catastrophic change in human psychology itself' which will cause certain human beings to experience a sense of oneness with the 'subhuman organisms in nature'.

Powys fills his enormous canvas—the book is nearly twelve hundred pages long—with an almost Shakespearian panorama of humanity. But no matter how absorbed we become in these human beings, we remain aware of the vast, overarching nature above them.

A blue haze was over everything, so thick and intense, that it was as if the blueness in the sky had fallen upon the earth, leaving only a vague grey hollowness in the upper air. This blue haze invaded everything. It crept through gaps in hedges; it floated over old crumbling walls; it slipped into open stickhouses and haysheds. And though it was blue in colour, it smelled strongly of brown mud and yellow apples. This blue mist, reeking of cider juice and ditches, seems to possess a peculiar somnolent power. . . . Sleep seems to emanate from this district like a thin, penetrating anaesthetic, possessed of a definite healing power. . . .

As John and Mary Crow lie against the roots of an ash tree as they make love, the tree is intensely conscious of them; but when they direct a prayer for happiness to the First Cause, it somehow becomes lost in the evil aspect of the 'Janus-faced Force', condemning them to suffering.

It may sound an impossible notion—to write a novel about human passions against this background of the whole of nature; but it works triumphantly. Apart from *War and Peace*, *A Glastonbury Romance* is one of the least claustrophobic novels ever written; the smells of the countryside seem to blow through it. But it must be admitted that, structurally speaking, it is far from perfect. The reason should be obvious. Its 'subject' is the connection—and contrast—of human beings with the universal forces that surrounds them. So it has no logical beginning or end. Powys gives it a typically novelistic opening —with the reading of a will—but as it moves from character to character, it is clear that there can be no natural climax. To say 'They lived happily ever after' would be to narrow the focus down to particular human beings, which is the reverse of Powys's intention. He contrives a kind of ending to the story with a natural catastrophe—a flood—but it fails to serve its purpose. We know that far more important things have happened in the course of the book—Sam's vision of the Holy Grail, Geard's miraculous cure of a woman with cancer—than this mechanical climax. (Powys encounters the same problem in all his major novels: *Wolf Solent*, *Weymouth Sands*, *Maiden Castle*—and never finds a satisfactory solution.) But then, the ordinary mechanics of a novel have never seemed less important than in *A Glastonbury Romance*. To become absorbed in its serene forward-flow is like drifting down a broad, peaceful river; time ceases to matter, and the reader is likely to spend half an hour lingering over some detailed description of dead leaves or the moss on an old tree-trunk. I have occasionally even turned back to the beginning of a chapter, merely for the pleasure of dawdling over the same ground, like a favourite walk. More than any other novelist, Powys has mastered the secret of inducing wide-angle consciousness.

Which enables me to offer a summary, not merely of the present chapter, but of the main thesis of this book.

Human consciousness has a curious in-built limitation. It is too easily hypnotised.

If you take a chicken, and press its head gently against the floor, then take a piece of chalk and draw a straight line from the beak across the floor, you will discover that the chicken will remain in that position, its eyes fixed on the chalk. It is hypnotised.

But why? What has happened? No one knows for certain. All that is certain is that our consciousness usually has a certain freedom of choice, like the ability of a car driver to turn the steering wheel. The more relaxed and wide-awake we are, the more freedom we have. If you get overworked, and concentrate on some objective with a tension rooted in exhaustion, you are very close to the hypnotic state. A few quick passes by a trained hypnotist would have you in a trance. As it is, you may break off work, stare at the opposite wall, and go into a kind of frozen daydream.

Consciousness *locks*. It is as if the steering wheel of the car suddenly locked, so it could not be turned. All hypnotists achieve their effect by making use of this peculiarity of consciousness. They persuade the subject to stare fixedly at some object, or to place his hands on his knees and concentrate wholly on the feeling of the cloth against his fingertips. And when it is narrowed down in this way, consciousness easily 'locks'.

But the locked state is not peculiar to moments of actual hypnosis. It happens all the time, for ninety-nine per cent of every day. It is so common that we do not even notice it. Or if we do, it is in a mere brief flash, soon forgotten. Perhaps you leave home for the office on a bright spring morning; the air smells so fresh that it reminds you of other times and other places—summer holidays, childhood expeditions. And for a few seconds or even minutes, your consciousness swings free.

There is a sense of lightness and exhilaration, and you are aware that you could pursue any one of a thousand lines of thought. You could recall days of childhood, places you have visited, girls you could have married. . . . And *any one* of these 'thought-experiments' would be as interesting and relaxing as a good book.

Then you climb on the bus or train, open your newspaper—and the freedom-feeling evaporates. The steering wheel is locked. But you don't notice. You merely remember the walk as a pleasant interlude. For the odd thing is that we do not take our freedom for granted. We do not feel that our minds are cars—or even helicopters—that ought to be able to travel freely in any direction. We take it for granted that they are trains, which run on rails, and can only go forward.

Each thought of *necessity* can destroy our feeling of freedom. Let us say that, as you are about to leave for work, you remark: 'Well thank God I've got this evening free. I want to finish that book and hear some music. . . .' And your wife replies: 'No, don't you remember, we've promised to go to the Greens' for dinner.' 'I thought that was tomorrow?' 'No, tomorrow you've got to attend the parents' meeting at the school. . . .' And suddenly all sense of freedom vanishes; boring necessities seem to block your horizon. You feel trapped. If such feelings happen to come in the middle of the night, when your vital powers are low, you can begin to see *all* life as an endless series of dreary necessities which keep us all trapped from birth till death. . . .

When I am in this 'fixed' or 'locked' state of mind, it is as if a part of my mind is anaesthetised. Like the chicken, my eyes are fixed on each thing I do, and I go through various activities quite mechanically. But now, supposing that, as I am prepared to plod mechanically through the next few hours, some sudden crisis arises—let us say, I suspect I have left some vitally important document in a phone booth. It may only take a few minutes for me to realise that it is not lost after all; but when it happens, I experience a sweeping sense of relief—and my consciousness suddenly 'unlocks'. Everything becomes more real. As I go through my routine tasks, I am thinking how lucky I am to be able to do them rather than searching the town. . . .

Crises always have this effect of making us aware of the immense horizons of freedom. Tolstoy has an episode in *War and Peace* where Pierre stands in front of a firing squad, and suddenly recognises how free we normally are. Dostoevsky actually went through this experience—sentenced to death for revolutionary activities—and he puts a description of it into the mouth of Prince Myshkin in *The Idiot*. Graham Greene's drunken priest, in *The Power and the Glory*, suddenly realises, as he stands in front of a firing squad, 'that it would have been so easy to be a saint'. For the flat, simple truth is that human consciousness *is* free, a thousand times more free than we normally realise. Yet because the moments of freedom are so brief, we accept the 'locked', narrow state as the norm, and the glimpses of freedom as some freakish illusion.

This curious tendency to 'lock' is inherent in all consciousness, as we can see from the chicken. But at a fairly recent stage in his evolution, man discovered various tricks for 'unlocking' it. As long ago as 900 B.C. we know that a blind minstrel called Homer travelled around Greece, reciting epic poems—probably to a kind of harp—and his enormous success is evidenced by the fact that these savage, scarcely literate people carefully preserved his immense narratives of the fall of Troy and the adventures of Odysseus (both are obviously part of a far longer work) in the exact words in which he sang them. No doubt it was the Neolithic hunters, sitting around a camp fire, who had first made this discovery that a tale of adventure can induce the 'freedom feeling'.

It took more than two and a half thousand years after the *Iliad* for the narrative of adventure to be finally perfected in the form of the novel. The human imagination soared. It was one of the most extraordinary evolutionary leaps in the history of the race. And then, absurdly, the novel fell a victim to the very defect of consciousness it was intended to cure. The novelist pressed his nose firmly against reality. And, like the chicken, his eyes glazed. His sense of freedom evaporated. He became trapped in the mechanical forward movement of the narrative. Lucien de Rubempré, Emma Bovary, Anna Karenina, the Baines sister, all plod grimly towards death like a convict marching to the scaffold. Only Tolstoy had the stature to recognise the absurdity of what he was doing; as Anna Karenina is in the act of flinging herself under a train, she realises that this is stupid; she doesn't want to die. But it is too late. And it was also too late for Tolstoy, who had come to the end of his novel about the tragedy that arises from adultery. Less intelligent novelists were not even aware of the absurdity; Zola made a virtue of his limitations by explaining that his novels were based on the scientific discovery that human behaviour is totally determined by heredity, and that therefore free will is an illusion. . . .

Because this problem has never been dragged into the daylight of consciousness, it has remained as a conflict at the heart of the novel. The novel was intended to be an exploration of the laws of freedom, release from our normal limitations. We know that such an investigation is best conducted according to a rigorous logic. The trouble is that if you stumble into a state of hypnosis—two-dimensional consciousness—your logic will lead you inevitably to the conclusion that death is the end of everything and that freedom is an illusion. That is why the novel should try to recognise that its aim and precondition is three-dimensional consciousness. If this is recognised, it can at least save the novelist from becoming the victim of a false logic, and ending in any one of a hundred different *cul de sacs*—the Flaubert *cul de sac*, the Hemingway *cul de sac*, the Joyce *cul de sac*, the Sartre *cul de sac*. . . .

This insight can be conveyed most simply by saying: the novel tends to find itself stuck in immediacy, like a fly on a fly paper, unable to extricate itself from mere description of passing events. Most of the world's novels—the 'great' novels as well as the fairly commonplace—are little more than a series of snapshots taken with a narrow-angle lens.

The novelist's task is a spiritual one: to free himself from this narrowness, to achieve 'wide-angle' vision, and to convey this to his readers.

NINE

Structure and Technique

FROM THE MOMENT a child emerges from its mother's womb,
it begins to experience the coldness and harshness of physical
reality. All living creatures feel that warmth and comfort are
their birthright; instead, they find themselves in a world that
frequently torments them beyond endurance. Most animals
accept this state of affairs with resignation. Only man asks
indignantly what he did to deserve it. And the most rebellious
members of the species are the philosophers and artists. Shaw,
talking about the miseries of the poor, says: 'It is only the poet,
with his vision of what life might be, to whom these things are
unendurable. If we were a race of poets, we would make an
end of them before the end of this miserable century.' Similarly, Omar Khayyam speaks of shattering the world to pieces
and re-building it 'nearer to the heart's desire'—which may be
regarded as a clear and convenient expression of the basic aim
of the novel.

Not that many novelists are concerned with practical
re-building—unless we except certain works of social purpose,
like William Godwin's *Caleb Williams*, Edward Bellamy's
Looking Backward and B. F. Skinner's *Walden Two*. But every
serious novelist has his sense of what is meaningful and important, and he contrasts this with the things he considers to
be stupid and unimportant. There is a fine example of the
technique in Christopher Isherwood's novel *Prater Violet*.
Isherwood describes how he was hired to work on the script of
a musical comedy by a British film company. He is working
with Friedrich Bergmann, a great German director who has
been forced to leave Germany by the Nazis. The plot of the
musical is unutterably silly and trivial; they wrestle with its

monumental banality. Meanwhile, Bergmann's mind is back home in Germany, brooding on the rise of the Nazis and the European holocaust he knows to be inevitable. He is particularly obsessed by the Reichstag fire trial:

> Bergmann enacted the entire drama and represented all the characters. He was Dr Buenger, the testy embarrassed President of the Court. He was Van der Lubbe [the accused], doped and apathetic, with sunken head. He was the earnest, harassed Torgler. He was Goering, the straddling military bully, and Goebbels, lizard-like, crooked and adroit. He was fiery Popov and stolid Tanev. And, in the biggest way, he was Dimitrov himself [the Communist leader who was accused of inspiring the crime]. . . .

Bergmann enacts the courtroom scene between Goering and Dimitrov. Clearly, *this* is the kind of thing he ought to be making a film about. Then he re-creates the cross-examination of the semi-imbecile, Van der Lubbe:

> He stands before his accusers, with his huge stooped shoulders and hanging hands, the chin sunken on the chest. He is scarcely human: a wretched, clumsy, tormented animal. The President tries to make him look up. He does not move. The interpreter tries. Dr Seuffert tries. There is no response. Then, suddenly, with the harsh authority of an animal trainer, Helldorf barks out: 'Head up, man! Quick!'
>
> The head jerks up at once, automatically, as if in obedience to some deeply hidden memory. The clouded eyes wander around the courtroom. Are they searching for somebody? A faint gleam of recognition seems to flicker in them for a moment. And then Van der Lubbe begins to laugh. This was really horrible, indecent, terrifying. The heavy body quivers and heaves with noiseless laughter, as if shaken by its death-agony. Van der Lubbe laughs and laughs, silently, blindly, his mouth open and dribbling, like an idiot's. Then, with equal suddenness, the paroxysm ceases. Again, the head falls forward. The grotesque figure

stands motionless, guarding its secret, unapproachable as the dead.

And then with no transition, Isherwood goes back to the musical *Prater Violet*:

> We were at work on the sequence in which Rudolph loses his future kingdom of Borodania through a palace revolution. A wicked uncle deposes his father and seizes the throne. Rudolph returns to Vienna, a penniless exile. He is now, in reality, the poor student he had pretended to be at the beginning of the story. But Toni, naturally, refuses to believe this. She has been deceived once already; she has trusted him, she has loved him, and he has left her. (Unwillingly, of course, and only because his faithful chamberlain, Count Rosanoff, reminds him with tears of his duty to the Borodanians.) So Rudolph pleads in vain, and Toni angrily dismisses him as an imposter. . . .

The contrast could not be more brutally effective. Without invective, satire or open ridicule, Isherwood has reduced *Prater Violet* to its true dimensions, something utterly vapid and frivolous, an example of Thorstein Veblen's conspicuous waste.

But perhaps 'true' is the wrong adjective to use in this context. To begin with, like most leftists of the 'thirties, Isherwood assumed that the Nazis themselves had set fire to the Reichstag in order to 'frame' the communists. Dimitrov himself said of Van der Lubbe: 'There stands the miserable Faust. But where is Mephistopheles?' Evidence since then has shown that Van der Lubbe *did* fire the Reichstag of his own accord. And we are aware of the unconscious irony when Dimitrov asks Goering: 'Is the Herr Reichminister aware that those who possess this alleged criminal mentality are today controlling the destinies of a sixth part of the world, namely the Soviet Union—the greatest and best land on earth?' Besides, why should we assume that *Prater Violet* is going to be bad and trivial? Directed with vitality and imagination, it might be as effective as an operetta by Strauss or Lehar—that is, completely valid in its own terms.

These comments only serve to remind us that the effectiveness of a work of art does not depend on its 'truth', any more than a good painting has to be an accurate representation of reality. What produces the galvanising effect—what Edmund Wilson called 'the shock of recognition'—is the effectiveness of the *contrast*. In the passage from *For Whom the Bell Tolls*, quoted on p. 138, the effectiveness springs from the contrast between religious emotion—the Hail Mary and Our Father—and the violence of the action. T. S. Eliot obtains the same effect in a far briefer compass in 'The Hollow Men':

> Is it like this
> In death's other kingdom
> Waking alone
> At the hour when we are
> Trembling with tenderness
> Lips that would kiss
> Form prayers to broken stone.

Here the flat, objective effect is increased by the lack of punctuation; if Eliot had used a question mark after 'kingdom', and an exclamation mark after 'broken stone', this effect would have been totally destroyed. (Writers should remember—as a general hint—to use exclamation marks as little as possible; they always produce an effect of naïvety.)

I have already pointed out that *Ulysses* achieves some of its best effects by the use of this contrast device. (The book could be studied as a compendium of practically every technical device known to novelists.) In the opening pages:

> Stephen, an elbow rested on the jagged granite, leaned his palm against his brow and gazed at the fraying edge of his shiny black coat-sleeve. Pain, that was not yet the pain of love, fretted his heart. Silently, in a dream, she had come to him after her death, her wasted body within its loose brown graveclothes giving off an odour of wax and rose-

wood, her breath, that had bent upon him, mute, reproachful, a faint odour of wetted ashes. Across the threadbare
cuffedge he saw the sea hailed as a great sweet mother by
the wellfed voice beside him. . . .

Here the contrast is between the brightness of the morning, the
cheerful inconsequence of Buck Mulligan (the 'wellfed voice')
and the tragedy of Stephen's mother. It is worth observing
how many false notes Joyce strikes in this passage: he speaks
of Stephen's 'brow' instead of his forehead, using a word that
strikes us as affected; he 'gazes' at his fraying coat-sleeve (you
could almost imagine an orchestra playing 'Hearts and
Flowers'). 'Pain, that was not yet the pain of love, fretted his
heart' is downright sentimental. And breath cannot 'bend' on
anybody. The technique is untidy, the sneer at the 'wellfed
voice' unfair (after all, it's not Mulligan's fault that Stephen is
suffering pangs of conscience about his mother); but the
passage is still remarkably effective. Precision is less important
to a writer than a clear knowledge of what he wants to achieve.
The meaning comes across in spite of technical defects.

The same technique of contrast is used in the newspaper-
office chapter, where Stephen's precise, objective account of
the old ladies is contrasted with the sentimentality and bombast
of earlier stories. For sheer technical effectiveness, the Gertie
Macdowell chapter is a showpiece. Gertie is a sentimental daydreamer who has been brought up on cheap novelettes; so the
language of the first half of the chapter is of the cheap novelette.
'The summer evening had begun to fold the world in its mysterious embrace. Far away in the west the sun was setting. . . .'
Occasionally, reality breaks through the romantic haze: 'Her
figure was slight and graceful, inclining even to fragility, but
those iron jelloids she had been taking of late had done her a
world of good much better than the Widow Welch's female
pills and she was much better of those discharges she used to
get and that tired feeling. The waxen pallor of her face was
almost spiritual in its ivorylike purity . . .' etc. As she sits daydreaming of weddings, Gertie notices Bloom watching her.
'He was in deep mourning, she could see that, and the story of a

haunting sorrow was written on his face.' As she dreams of the dark-eyed stranger carrying her off, she leans backwards so he can see her underwear. Then, as she walks off the beach, the focus shifts back to Bloom, who is in a normal masculine state of sexual excitement, and who masturbates as he recollects what he has just been watching. 'Mr Bloom with careful hand recomposed his wet shirt. O Lord that little limping devil. . . .'

For sheer dramatic effect, the most stunning scene in *Ulysses* is the brothel chapter, a nightmare phantasmagoria written in play form. This enables Joyce to manipulate the reality-unreality effect with every shade of virtuosity, reaching a climax as the prostitutes sing and dance drunkenly to a pianola, and the ghost of Stephen's mother rises through the floor, 'in leper grey with a wreath of faded orange blossoms and a torn bridal veil, her face worn and noseless, green with grave mould'. As she calls on him to repent, he shouts, 'Break my spirit all of you if you can! I'll bring you all to heel!', and smashes the chandelier with his walking stick. 'Time's livid final flame leaps and, in the following darkness, ruin of all space, shattered glass and toppling masonry.' Stephen's act of destruction becomes a kind of Last Judgment, the end of the world. The whole chapter is presented continually on two levels, and derives its power from the counterpoint.

We should note, in parentheses, that a work of literature need not contain the elements of contrast *within* itself. The very fact that the outside world exists, and that we all live in it, can provide the bass line of the counterpoint, so to speak. A writer of fantasy may choose quite simply to create his own world on his own chosen level: for example, William Morris in his fantasy novels (*Well at the World's End*, etc.), Tolkien in *Lord of the Rings*, Mervyn Peake in his *Gormenghast* trilogy, H. P. Lovecraft in his horror stories. All these works are *implied criticisms* of the 'triviality of everydayness'. Arnold Bennett's *Old Wives' Tale* is apparently a straightforward, realistic narrative, devoid of the cymbal effects of Joyce or Hemingway. But it is time *speeded up*, and this is contrasted with the slow-moving time in which we actually live, producing the bird's-eye effect. Or a writer may deliberately 'darken' his reality, making it gloomier, more

tragic or sordid than the world most of us know: Zola, Dostoevsky, Céline, Faulkner, Beckett, many Russian novelists.
(P. G. Wodehouse writes about a Russian in whose novels
'nothing happens until page 500, when the *mouzhik* commits
suicide'.) E. M. Forster recognised Joyce's affinity with this
type of novelist, calling *Ulysses* 'a determined attempt to cover
the universe with mud', which is by no means an unfair comment. You could say that these writers are 'criticising reality'
by a technique that has something in common with slander.
Graham Greene could be added to this list; but Greene is also
a master of the internal-contrast: for example, he is fond of
fairgrounds as a setting for crimes.

It is clear, then, that all serious literature derives its power
from the contrast between the writer's symbols of value and the
world he rejects. A man who feels perfectly at home in the
world, who accepts life as it comes and sees no reason for complaint, will be almost certainly incapable of producing interesting literature.

On the other hand, it is not enough just to *feel* dissatisfied
with 'this sorry scheme of things'. A writer needs to have some
idea—no matter how vague—of what he would actually prefer.
The 'symbol of intensity' may be precise or general. In the
novels of E. M. Forster, for example, it is simply a feeling about
human decency, freedom from artificial constraints and conventions. In the American novelist James Gould Cozzens, it
is a feeling about 'socially responsible' individuals, the managers
and administrators whose job is to see that society runs
smoothly. The same is true of the novels of C. P. Snow. This
is as far as possible from the novels of Maxim Gorky or B.
Traven, in which the workers and revolutionaries are the
heroes and the 'ruling classes' the villains. In Faulkner, the
'symbol of intensity' is the Old South and its ideals of honour.
And there are many novelists who look back nostalgically to
some epoch of the past—for example, G. K. Chesterton,
J. R. R. Tolkien and T. H. White (the author of *The Sword
in the Stone*) all share the same nostalgia about the age of
chivalry and feudalism.

On the other hand, readers of such modern American classics as Upton Sinclair's *The Jungle* (about foreign immigrants in the stockyards of Chicago), Dos Passos's *U.S.A.* or James T. Farrell's *Studs Lonigan* will note that there is a lack of 'symbols of intensity'. All three writers are committed to some form of socialism; all three are concerned with social injustice. But apart from some vague social justice, they have no clear idea of what they want. There is no equivalent of Hemingway's preoccupation with courage, or Lawrence's with sex, or Eliot's with religion, to counterbalance the 'Communal Life-World' they are writing about. The interesting result is that although the novels I have mentioned are impressive, these writers simply failed to develop. It seems that mere social purpose is not, in itself, enough to provide a writer with the intensity he needs to develop. The same thing applies, to a large extent, to Albert Camus, whose 'symbol of intensity' is his concept of justice. His output is small, and one gets the feeling that this is because, although he has remarkable integrity, he doesn't actually *believe* in anything very strongly. It is worth comparing these writers with Bernard Shaw and H. G. Wells, who were also committed socialists, but who also believed strongly in something *more* than socialism: in Shaw's case, evolution, in Wells's, science.

Ezra Pound wrote in the *Cantos*:

> What thou lovest well remains,
> the rest is dross
> What thou lov'st well shall not be reft from thee
> What thou lov'st well is thy true heritage.

In saying this, he had stated the artist's basic credo. His starting point is 'what he loves well'; like the spring that is the source of a river, all his work flows from it.

In *Classics and Commercials*, the critic Edmund Wilson has an article called 'The Boys in the Back Room' in which he discusses a number of writers—like John O'Hara, John Steinbeck and James M. Cain—whose style and subject-matter all derive from Hemingway. The article was written in the 1940s;

nowadays, we would find it difficult to see the resemblance between Hemingway and Steinbeck or O'Hara. And this is mainly
because these writers have no 'symbol of intensity' to compare
with Hemingway's obsession with courage and death. Steinbeck's
Grapes of Wrath, O'Hara's *Appointment in Samara*, strike us as
brilliantly observed and reported, but they lack something
which is *not* lacking in Joyce or Hemingway or Thomas Mann.
The French novelist André Gide once said that American
writers 'lack soul', and he was obviously trying to put his finger
on this same deficiency. It is the lack of the 'symbol of intensity'—'What thou lov'st well'—which should be the core of
the writer's creative urge.

Once a writer has arrived at his 'symbol of intensity', his
next task is to present it as clearly as possible in contrast to the
world of immediacy, the Communal Life-World. This sounds
straightforward enough, but there are complications. It is not
a simple matter of clashing them together, like two cymbals.
For example, if we compare Hemingway's *A Farewell to Arms*
with the later *Across the River and Into the Trees*, we can see that
both use the same basic symbols: both contrast the warmth of
love with the cold of death. Yet the first is a masterpiece, the
second an almost embarrassing failure. The answer is absurdly
simple: one novel has a story, and the other hasn't. *A Farewell
to Arms* tells how an American soldier falls in love with a nurse,
gets wounded, has an affair with her, deserts the army, and
finally loses her in childbirth. *Across the River and Into the Trees*
is merely 'about' an American colonel who is having a love
affair with a beautiful young Italian countess, and nothing
much happens except that he dies. There is nothing wrong
with Hemingway's *symbols* in *Across the River and Into the Trees*,
but he simply fails to deploy them effectively. If you think of
the writer as a movie-projector, then his 'symbol of intensity'
is the light behind the projector lens; but his problem is to
throw this intensity on to a screen where everyone can see it,
which involves a story, characters, dialogue. In short, a pattern
of events.

In a famous essay on *Hamlet*, T. S. Eliot suggested a name for
this pattern of events. He called it the 'objective correlative', a

clumsy and abstract expression for a simple concept. Eliot argues that *Hamlet* is such a mysterious and ambiguous play because Shakespeare was trying to 'project' an emotion for which he could find no satisfactory equivalent in characters and events. 'The only way of expressing emotion in the form of art is by finding an "objective correlative"; in other words, a set of objects, a situation, a chain of events, which shall be the formula of that *particular* emotion. . . .' Hamlet, says Eliot, is dominated by an emotion of disgust towards his mother—probably (although he does not say so) an incestuous feeling—but his mother is no tragic heroine, no Cleopatra or Lady Macbeth, so these violent emotions aroused in the son by the death of his adored father and his mother's marriage to a lesser man (Freudians can have a field day here) cannot be purged by some spectacular death scene. There is also another problem which Eliot leaves untouched: the fact that Hamlet's intelligence and insight—which ought to make him superior to stupider men—only lead to indecision and self-disgust: the Outsider problem. If Shakespeare had tried to solve the problem by making Hamlet's mother wickeder—perhaps actively involved in her husband's murder—it would have ruined the play. The whole point is that she is a typical mother: gentle, self-effacing: in fact, rather a nonentity; *this* is why Hamlet feels such a powerful, possessive feeling towards her. If Shakespeare had made her wicked, she would have ceased to be a typical mother. Now Lady Macbeth and Cleopatra are highly successful pivots of their individual plays because they are so positive; Shakespeare can paint them in primary colours, and they make 'good theatre'. This is not so in the case of Hamlet's mother. In a sense, the most important scene in the play is the one in which Hamlet pours out his disgust to his mother and draws tears of repentance; it ought to be the climax of the play, but it is not spectacular enough. And so the most important scene of the play remains, by necessity, tucked away into a corner, so to speak.

Hemingway has a similar problem in *Across the River and Into the Trees*. He wants to write about a battered old soldier who has suffered a great deal, who has learned to come to

terms with necessity, who has long ago ceased to expect life
to be a golden daydream. And here, when he is almost too old
to appreciate it, life has handed him a beautiful girl who
adores him and simply wants to become his property, to feel
she belongs to him. It is deliciously sweet; it almost reconciles
him to life, to the hurts he has received. In an attempt to
exorcise some of the old bitterness, he visits the scene of a
battle, lowers his trousers, and excretes on the spot where he
had been wounded in the First World War. Then he buries a
ten-thousand-lire note in the earth, as an ironical payment for
the medals he received. The scene *ought* to be tough and manly
—the brave soldier rejecting the usual lies about the glory of
war. . . . Instead, it has the effect of making the reader wrinkle
his nose. Admittedly, a writer *needs* the kind of boldness to dare
to write a scene like this; but in this case, it fails to come off. A
similar scene in *A Farewell to Arms* is wholly successful: where
the hero, just before an operation, is given an enema by the
nurse he is in love with; this produces the feeling that Hemingway has the courage to tell the exact truth about love, without
sentimentalising it.

Hemingway is the master of understatement; the fact that
all the emotions of *A Farewell to Arms* are understated seems to
make them more authentic. In *Across the River and Into the Trees*,
he tries the same technique: of describing the *surface*, and
leaving the reader to infer the torment that lies below it. There
are many conversations, all fairly trivial, jokes with bartenders
and so on. And finally, when he dies, it is all carefully understated. He has a heart attack while driving back from a duck
shoot:

> The Colonel started to speak but he stopped while it hit him
> the third time and gripped him so he knew he could not live.
> 'Jackson,' the Colonel said. 'Pull up at the side of the road
> and cut to your parking lights. Do you know the way to
> Trieste from here?'
> 'Yes, sir. I have my map.'
> 'Good. I'm now going to get into the large back seat of
> this god-damned, oversized luxurious automobile.'

That was the last thing the Colonel ever said. But he made the back seat all right and he shut the door. He shut it carefully and well. . . .'

What is wrong with that? It is hard to explain, but there is something phoney about it. It reminds you of this:

He put his shoulders back and his heels together. 'To hell with the handkerchief,' said Walter Mitty scornfully. He took one last drag on his cigarette and snapped it away. Then, with that faint, fleeting smile playing about his lips, he faced the firing squad, erect and motionless, proud and disdainful, Walter Mitty the Undefeated, inscrutable to the last.

Hemingway has exposed himself to this reaction by trying to cut the novel down to its bare bones. His attempt at simplicity misfires—as in the atrocious phrase 'He kissed her true'.

The moral seems to be that if the device of understatement is to be effective, you must have something important to understate. Roy Campbell stated this with epigrammatic precision in 'Lines on Certain South African Novelists':

You praise the firm restraint with which they write.
I'm with you there, of course.
They use the snaffle and the curb all right,
But where's the bloody horse?

This problem of creating a precise objective correlative brings us to another matter of central importance: structure. For example, if the most important scene of *Hamlet* is not the climax of the play, it indicates that something is wrong with the structure of *Hamlet*.

Eliot invented the term 'objective correlative', but certainly not the idea. That credit should probably go to Henry James, whose book *The Art of the Novel* (in fact, his collected prefaces) goes to enormous length to explain precisely how he decided to embody the 'idea' of each novel in characters and events.

James was fascinated by these problems; he was as dedicated to the art of writing as Flaubert had been; and he explains himself with enormous gusto. The style is sometimes difficult, and it is probably necessary to have some acquaintance with the novels he is discussing; but *The Art of the Novel* is probably the most important and rewarding single volume ever written on its subject.

But even in James, we can see the difficulties of trying to tailor the 'objective correlative' to fit the basic idea. It is not difficult to pinpoint James's symbol of intensity—what he 'loves well'. It is Europe and its culture, with all its 'sense of the past' (the actual title of his last novel). His feelings about America—his home land—were ambivalent; he admired the American directness and honesty, and deplored its lack of subtlety and its materialism. One of his earliest attempts to dramatise the conflict is to be found in his novel *The Europeans*, written when he was thirty-five. A baroness—wife of a mid-European prince—arrives in Boston with her brother, on a visit to American cousins. The novel has immense charm and vitality—one of the most readable things James ever wrote— and you can tell that this is because James is deriving such enormous pleasure from engineering this confrontation between the old world and the new. He likes and admires his Puritanical New Englanders, but he obviously feels that it's about time they learned how the rest of the world lives. And he, Henry James, has appointed himself spokesman for the European point of view. He never loses his sense of balance; even the later works—when his anti-American feeling had grown—are full of innocent Americans being betrayed by sophisticated Europeans. But his deeper sense of values is undoubtedly represented by European culture. For James, Europe symbolised freedom.

Nevertheless, *The Europeans* is light-weight. There is a happy-ever-after ending, with most of the characters getting suitably married—with the exception of the baroness, who finds Boston a little too much for her. Clearly, a minimum of planning went into this novel. It gives the impression that when James started to write, his sole idea was to introduce his rather bohemian Europeans to his sober New Englanders, and see what happened.

When, a quarter of a century later, James planned *The Ambassadors*, he obviously regarded it as his major statement about the relation between Europe and America. And in structure, it comes as close to perfection as anything James ever conceived. His hero, Lambert Strether, is a middle-aged American editor who is engaged to marry a rich widow, Mrs Newsome. (She also happens to own the magazine he edits.) This lady is concerned about the moral welfare of her son Chad, who is living in Paris, and who seems determined to remain there. They are convinced that he is leading a life of dissipation—probably in the hands of some loose woman. Strether is despatched to bring him back to Woollett, Mass. —by force if necessary.

From the moment he lands in England, Strether's moral certainties begin to waver. He finds himself falling under the insidious spell of the 'old world'. In Paris, he has to acknowledge that he is beginning to experience a delightful sense of escape. When he finally meets Chad, he finds him greatly improved—clearly he has been subjected to some 'civilising influence'. The only women in Chad's life seem to be a countess, Madame de Vionnet, and her pretty daughter, and Strether finds them both charming. A point comes where he has to face his own feelings: that Paris already means a great deal more to him than Woollett, Mass., and that Madame de Vionnet and the values she represents are in every way preferable to Mrs Newsome and her fortune. Besides, Strether is half in love with Madame de Vionnet. Now his position and Chad's are reversed. Chad is willing to return, and Strether advises him to stay. Strether summarises what he has learned—too late in life: 'Live, live all you can. It's a mistake not to.'

Mrs Newsome sends more ambassadors—her daughter and son-in-law—to bring home the errant New Englanders. Strether has now burnt his boats. But the attraction of Madame de Vionnet holds him in Paris, until it dawns on him that she is Chad's mistress. Only then does he reluctantly make up his mind to return—still advising Chad to stay. He also decides against marrying another woman he has met in Europe, on the grounds that it would hardly be fair to acquire another bride on an expedition financed by Mrs Newsome. And so, on this note of subdued resignation, the book ends.

Structurally speaking, then, *The Ambassadors* is close to perfection. It is in twelve perfectly proportioned books, and each one carries the action a stage further. By the end of Book Six, Strether has decided against persuading Chad to return home. In Book Nine, he hears that Madame de Vionnet's daughter is about to marry, and realises that it is her mother with whom Chad is involved. It is all so perfectly planned that you could believe James used a pair of compasses and a ruler to work it out. The shape is, as E. M. Forster pointed out, that of a cross or an hour glass. James carefully avoids loose ends—for example, Chad's American fiancée—who comes to fetch him back—ends by marrying Chad's best friend. It has the neatness of an equation.

All of which should not blind us to the book's imperfections. To begin with, it is written in James's most tiresome later style which sounds absurdly affected ('She sighed it at last all comically, all tragically, away. "I can't indeed resist you."')

This kind of language only comes between the reader and the object. James's defenders argue that he is striving for accuracy, but the impatient reader comes to suspect that he is trying to cover up his defects. For example, Madame de Vionnet is the pivot of the novel: she is supposed to symbolise culture, grace, feminine wisdom: in short, James's own values. And she is unconvincing. Few of the characters emerge as real human beings, and those who do—like the Pococks—the daughter and son-in-law—only emphasise James's failure to 'realise' the others.

But a more serious defect lies at the heart of the novel. It is intended to be James's 'credo', with Paris as his symbol of 'meaning', and Mrs Newsome and Woollett, Mass., as his symbols of immediacy and material values. The contrast between them is highly effective. Which leads us to look more closely at James's own values. What is he actually offering? 'Live all you can. It's a mistake not to.' That formula is hardly more satisfying than Axel's 'Live? Our servants can do that for us', or Hemingway's comment that only a bull-fighter lives his life 'all the way up'. What would be Strether's ideal solution? To marry Madame de Vionnet and spend his days sipping French wine and admiring French architecture? This hardly seems to be the spiritual revolution James hints at. And then, Strether *doesn't* decide to 'live all he can'; he returns to Woollett and a doubtful future. Which reminds us that most of James's novels have this unfortunate tendency to fizzle out, with the hero or heroine glumly accepting second best. So many of his novels begin with the implication that life holds out marvellous rewards for those who face it with courage and determination. Then, as we press him for further details, his imagination seems to fail, and he tries to convince us that the whole thing was intended to be a cautionary tale about the effect of moral indecisiveness. Clearly, James himself would have been embarrassed if someone had pressed him to explain 'Live all you can'. As a gentle, hypochondriacal American who spent his days commuting between Paris and London, he had no clear ideas on how to live life up to the hilt. The consequence is that his novels have a slightly unreal quality that tempts one to describe him as a male Jane Austen.

The moral is not that structure is unimportant; only that it is, perhaps, less important than other qualities, such as imagination and vitality. Structurally, *The Ambassadors* is a far more impressive performance than *The Europeans*; but it is less alive, and most readers will settle for vitality. The novels of George Meredith are among the worst constructed in the English language; he wastes too much time on preliminaries, underplays climactic scenes, holds up the action for philosophical discussions, and tends to make a mess of the endings. But this is partly because he is trying to do something new in fiction: to create a blend of comedy, romance, drama, philosophy and poetry; so no matter how exasperating, his novels are seldom dull. Scott, Balzac and Dickens all treat structure with the indifference of a man in a hurry; they are still great novelists. James was a victim of what we might call the Flaubertian fallacy: the notion that so long as the structure is neat and symmetrical, nothing else matters. This is untrue; a great deal else matters. What makes so many of Balzac's novels unsatisfying is not so much makeshift structure as makeshift thinking. We are impressed when he sends his characters off in search of the absolute, and irritated when he kills them off before they get there. We feel that he ought, perhaps, to have given more thought to the whole enterprise. And *this* is the meaning of structure: *the thought the novelist gives to the whole enterprise and all its implications.* James was basically right, of course; a novel should grow from its basic idea as inevitably as an oak tree from an acorn. But the idea itself should also be probed and extended. What is the good of writing a novel about a 'young person confronting life' unless you are willing to ask Wells's question: 'What ought we to do with our lives?' Anyone who answers: 'But James was not a philosopher' is missing the point. *Roderick Hudson* and *Portrait of a Lady* are damp squibs precisely because James failed to probe the question deeply enough. He developed his 'idea' within thoroughly conventional limits. Both books begin beautifully; then, like underpowered rockets, crash back to earth. I am not suggesting that James should have made Roderick or Isobel join a revolutionary movement, or undergo religious conversion: only that he should have made an effort to increase their *awareness*. (This, for example, is what distinguishes Powys's *Glastonbury Romance* and later works from early novels like *Wood and Stone*; they create an illusion of *freedom*; whereas, after the first few chapters, Roderick and Isobel seem as predetermined as trains running on a single track rail.)

Finally, a word about the development of technique in the novel.

In the days before Defoe, when writers were all 'Shakespearian fish', the novelist was inclined to write as if he were God: that is to say, he told the story as if he had access to all the thoughts and feelings of all the characters. He told the story just as he felt inclined: digressing, philosophising, exhorting the reader.

Whether by chance, or design, or pure literary instinct, Defoe changed all that. He wrote in a tone of flat, realistic reportage which nowadays sounds like an amazing anticipation of Hemingway and Dos Passos. This may have been because he *was* a reporter; but to our ears, it sounds marvellously convincing. The only other pre-modern writer who commanded this same tone of unexaggerated realism was Prosper Merimée, best known for *Carmen*, which might easily pass for a 'true narration'.

Richardson, as we know, chose the epistolary form by chance, but found that it suited his purpose admirably. It wasn't *quite* as realistic as Defoe; after all, you cannot really believe that Clarissa would snatch up her pen as soon as she had been raped, and describe the experience in detail. Still, it worked. After all, the novelist wants to be 'believed'—at least if he is being serious rather than comic—because the power of his climaxes depends on how far the reader believes him. We have pointed out that Richardson outdistanced various rivals—Fielding, Smollett, Sterne—precisely because his *impact*: it struck readers as *realler* than anything they had read before.

Those early romantics—Rousseau, Goethe, Senancour—took care to use the techniques developed by Richardson. But romanticism was pulling in the opposite direction: towards the daydream. You can see the tug-of-war in Scott and Balzac. Both take care to set the scene in a tone of flat, informative reportage, sometimes taking a whole chapter to set the scene with minute realism. But long before the end of *The Bride of Lammermoor* or *Lost Illusions*, the action is straining our credulity. (Kleist's short novel *Michael Kolhaus* is an interesting study in this respect; it begins as flat reportage—the story of how injustice turns a reasonable man into a rebel—and ends as a kind of fairy story.)

By the time Dickens began *Pickwick Papers* in 1836, most novelists seemed to agree that one of the basic aims of the novelist was to show how clever he was. It was arguably a disaster for literature that Dickens began his career with *Pickwick*. For the aim of comedy is bathos, deflation. *Pickwick* begins:

The first ray of light which illumines the gloom, and converts into a dazzling brilliancy that obscurity in which the earlier history of the public career of the immortal Pickwick would appear to be involved, is derived from the perusal of the following entry in the Transactions of the Pickwick Club, which the editor of these papers feels the highest pleasure in laying before his readers, as a proof of the careful attention, indefatigable assiduity, and nice discrimination, with which his search among the multifarious documents confided to him has been conducted.

This kind of pompous language is admirable for comedy, if a little tiresome. But Dickens continued to use it on every occasion. This is from the second paragraph of *David Copperfield*, a serious autobiographical novel:

In consideration of the day and hour of my birth, it was declared by the nurse, and by some sage women in the neighbourhood who had taken a lively interest in me several months before there was any possibility of our becoming personally acquainted, first, that I was destined to be unlucky in life . . . etc.

Dickens influenced every major nineteenth-century writer who came after him, from Thackeray to Carlyle, Dostoevsky to Shaw. A writer would have been ashamed not to sound literate. Meredith, Gissing, Wells, Bennett, Galsworthy. . . . The involved 'comedic' style spread like a cancer of language.

Joyce was one of the first to throw it off, to insist that language should re-focus on its object. The newspaper-office chapter of *Ulysses* is one of the most revolutionary pieces of writing of this century; for Joyce writes as if there was a camera in one corner of the office, and a tape-recorder in the other, and as if his task was simply to utilise their materials. Although Isherwood invented the phrase, it was Joyce who invented the concept of being a camera.

It was not a moment too soon. The novel was becoming an undisciplined mass of free-association. Shaw satirised it in an article written in 1916—at about the time Joyce was writing the newspaper chapter. It was called 'Mr Arnold Bennett Thinks Playwriting Easier than Novel Writing', and Shaw quotes the whole of Macbeth's death scene, then re-writes it in the style of a novel 'by Arnold Bennett, John Galsworthy or Anybody'.

> He was to fail, after all, then. The day was going against him. His men were not really fighting. They had conveyed to Old Siward that they were open to an offer of quarter; and the hint had not been lost on that ancient campaigner, whose son he had just slain. . . .'

And so on. 'What an exquisite morning it was! Was there anything so blue as a blue sky, anything so white as a white cloud. . . .' It is true. This is not narrative, but a kind of diarrhoea.

Unfortunately, Joyce's 'camera', which looked as if it would re-vitalise the novel, led it straight into a blind alley. But this must be the subject of a separate chapter.

TEN

Limits

A PHOTOGRAPH IS obviously more 'authentic' than a painting or drawing of the same subject, for the artist always selects and distorts, while the camera can only record. On the other hand, the content of a painting can be so much greater than that of a photograph. A country scene by Constable may *look* 'photographic', but you could spend an hour staring at it and finding new matters of interest, details of technique. Few photographs remain of interest for more than a few minutes. Of course, a photographer chooses his 'meanings', just as a painter does, by choosing his subject. But he has to look further, and take his photograph at exactly the right moment.

The naturalists discovered the power of photographic writing. It is more convincing, and therefore potentially more moving, than Once-upon-a-time storytelling. But it has the same disadvantage as photography. Nowhere can this be studied more closely than in *Ulysses*. The whole book aims at a new level of realism, a new kind of detailed precision:

—Mrkrgnao! the cat said loudly.
She blinked up out of her avid shameclosing eyes, mewing plaintively and long, showing him her milkwhite teeth. He watched the dark eyeslits narrowing with greed till her eyes were green stones.

We observe here the care Joyce has taken to get the exact sound of a cat's mew; the whole description of Bloom feeding the cat—too long to quote here—is a superb example of photographic realism.

But by the time we reach the newspaper office, it has become altogether more difficult to maintain this precision, because so much more is happening. Doors burst open, newsboys rush through, telephones ring, several people speak at once, and we have Stephen's interior monologues as well as Bloom's. Not only is this difficult to follow; but Joyce is obviously being forced to simplify and select in a way that contradicts the principles of photographic realism—which tries to *look* non-selective. The thought of a whole book written in this style is unbearable. So Joyce obviously realised; for after plodding on grimly for another four chapters, he begins the series of parodies and language-experiments that occupy more than half the book.

What is the *excuse* for these parodies? Well, Joyce is apparently presenting us with a treatise on language. 'In my first dozen chapters I showed life as it appears to pure, detached observation. Now I shall show you the hundreds of ways in which language can falsify this reality. . . .' And in the final chapter, we return to detached observation, as Joyce inserts a microphone inside Mrs Bloom's head and records her thoughts. . . .

But with *Ulysses* behind him, Joyce had not only exhausted his potentiality for self-image-building; he had also exhausted his subject-matter. *Ulysses* is a prose-movie about Everyman living his Everyday Life. What else was there to write? Faced with a similar problem after *Madame Bovary*, Flaubert turned to the past and produced a historical novel; but since he knew less about ancient Carthage than about modern France, the result was inevitably something of an anti-climax. Joyce was determined not to make a similar mistake. Besides, the photographic technique would have been useless trying to describe the battle of Marathon. Yet beyond all doubt, history *is* as real as the present moment. And the unconscious mind is as important as the conscious. Logically speaking, Joyce should have given up writing and turned to film-making—preferably in three-dimensional Technicolor; then, with a combination of images and music, he might have succeeded in creating the logical counterpart to *Ulysses*, a work about history and the unconscious. Instead, he tried to do it with language—in

spite of the fact that the second part of *Ulysses* had been a pro-
tracted demonstration of how language *falsifies* reality. Joyce
wanted to turn language into a kind of music; but music is
'universal', and Joyce's weird mixture of a dozen or so languages is ultra-private. Music appeals to the emotions; Joyce's
endless puns appeal to the sense of the ridiculous. Worse still,
they produce an effect of mere facetiousness. *Finnegan's Wake* is
an immense miscalculation.

But the real fallacy behind it lies in Joyce's notion that language is a kind of magical sea, full of strange creatures. This
was merely confused thinking. Language is an instrument, like
a pair of compasses or a ruler. It can be used for describing
reality, even exploring reality; but it is not, in itself, a form of
reality. In the same way, the language of mathematics enables
us to explore the mathematical truths of our universe; but you
could spend years juggling with Egyptian, Roman and Arabic
numerals without making a single mathematical discovery.
What matters is not the language, but the reality it corresponds
to. Sometimes it may be necessary to create new words; but
only if we find something for which no old word exists. For
example, if a biological mutation made our eyes sensitive to
infra-red and ultra-violet rays, we would see new colours, for
which no word at present exists; *then* we should need a new
word. The deeper we look into reality, the more fine shades of
meaning we observe, and each shade requires a new word—or
new combination of old words. This is the way language
'grows'. It is a kind of fungus *on* reality, not a reality in itself.
And this is the final objection to *Finnegan's Wake*; it is not an
attempt to express new shades of meaning; only a language
game, like a kitten playing with a ball of wool.

So far as the novel is concerned, Joycian linguistics are a
dead end. Novelists seem to realise this instinctively, and few
of them have even tried. Anthony Burgess is the most notable
exception; his *Clockwork Orange* is a bravura performance that
uses a highly inventive slang (drawn mainly from Russian) to
capture the state of mind of a young thug in some future
Welfare State. But although Mr Burgess makes no secret of his
admiration for Joyce and his preoccupation with language,

he is not at heart an experimenter. His other novels make it clear that he belongs to the classic tradition of novelists with a moral concern. He lacks the obsessive single-mindedness of Joyce, the devotion to an artistic logic—which probably explains how he has managed to avoid the Joycian *cul de sac*.

There are many other kinds of *cul de sac*. Twentieth-century novelists have been fertile in discovering new ways of arresting their own development. Yeats's 'strand' is covered with every kind of fish, from whales to tadpoles. But the lure that tempted them on to the beach is always the same: realism, the desire to grab the reader by the shoulders and shake him until his teeth rattle.

As a particularly remarkable example of the technique, we may consider the story *Christ in Concrete* by Pietro di Donato, expanded into a novel in 1939. Originally published in *Esquire*, its impact was immense. It describes the collapse of a half-finished building, with a number of Italian workmen. In the first few pages, the author describes the men as they work at top pressure, slave-driven by the American manager, who is indifferent to safety regulations. The foreman, Geremio, is unusually cheerful; after twenty years in America, he has just paid the deposit on a house. He is just wondering whether all workmen are doomed to perpetual fear of unemployment, and praying to God for guidance, when the building starts to collapse. '. . . her supports burst with the cracking slap of wooden gunfire. The floor vomited upward. Geremio clutched at the air and shrieked agonisingly. "Brothers, what have we done? Ahhh-h children of ours!" With the speed of light, balance went sickeningly awry and frozen men went flying explosively. . . . Walls, floors, beams became whirling, solid, splintering waves crashing with detonations that ground men and material in bonds of death.' But this is only the beginning. For four more pages, Donato relentlessly describes Geremio's death agonies, sparing nothing. He is impaled on a steel rod; he splinters his teeth gnawing at a beam. Then concrete pours in on him and slowly hardens, squeezing his skull out of shape.

Possibly this is the most powerful short story ever written. Few people could read it without feeling as if they have been hit with a bludgeon. Critics might have been forgiven for feeling that a writer who could produce that kind of thing was a literary genius of the first order. It was Donato's first published story.

The full-length version that followed convinced anyone who needed convincing that there is an abyss of difference between a good story and a successful novel. To begin with, a climax so violent tends to make everything that goes before seem trivial. In the story version, the opening pages were brief. In the novel, the life of Geremio had to be expanded out of all proportion. But it was not possible to expand the death scene to the same length. The author's solution was to interpose scenes of domestic Italian life—with the emphasis on human warmth and affection—with scenes of violence and sudden death. But this is crying wolf too often. The story remains a classic; the novel is now forgotten.

The same basic formula was applied with far greater success by William Faulkner. Heavily influenced by Hemingway, Faulkner was, in fact, two years his senior. The central emotion of all his work is his romantic nostalgia for the old South. The parallel with Hemingway is underlined by the first novel *Soldier's Pay*, about the war hero who returns to his home town, horribly disfigured. (In *The Sun Also Rises*, the hero has been sexually maimed.) In *Sartoris* (1929), the theme is again the despair of an ex-soldier who has been 'burnt out' by his war experiences. Unlike Hemingway, Faulkner had not been in the war; but clearly, he wanted to say something to his readers about tension and sickness and despair that could be symbolised by war-wounds and shell-shock.

Sartoris was followed in the same year by *The Sound and the Fury*, the first typically Faulknerian novel. The language and structure of the earlier novels had been conventional; now Faulkner begins to strain the language and fragment the structure to express his sense of tragic tension. The central character is another young man under severe mental strain, Quentin Compson, and the main event of the novel is Quentin's suicide.

Like Shakespeare in *Hamlet*, Faulkner needed a symboli 'reason' for Quentin's despair; he chose Quentin's half-incestuous relationship with his sister Caddy (although, to prevent any simplistic interpretation, he insisted that Quentin was not interested in Caddy's body, only in some idea of family honour symbolised by her maidenhead). Caddy has been seduced by one young man, then married to another to cover up her pregnancy. Quentin's jealousy, the morbid obsession with his sister's lost virginity, is devouring his sanity. But this is only the immediate cause of his mental tension. He regrets the disappearance of the old South, and the steady decline in his family's fortunes—a pasture belonging to his idiot younger brother had to be sold to send him to Harvard. The father is a dipsomaniac who spends his days in an empty office reading Latin poetry. The mother is a neurotic snob, and her brother is an alcoholic sponger. The whole novel is positively Elizabethan in its atmosphere of impending doom.

The main section of the novel consists of Quentin's long interior monologue on the day he commits suicide. And the core of this monologue is a scene in which Quentin and Caddy discuss a suicide pact. She lies on her back in the damp grass as he holds the point of a knife against her throat, and she urges him to push it in. The sexual overtones are obvious. But the incest that might seem the natural climax never occurs. Faulkner is anxious *not* to reach a climax; the reader has to be kept in a kind of tragic suspense.

When *The Sound and the Fury* appeared, the few critics who paid any attention were understandably baffled and irritated. A writer who begins his novel with a long interior monologue told by an idiot is asking to bore the reader. They wanted to know why Faulkner has to jump back and forth in time so erratically, why he seems to want to turn the novel into a do-it-yourself jigsaw puzzle that needs half a dozen readings. Joyce once said: 'I ask nothing more of the reader than that he should devote his life to reading my works.' Faulkner seemed to have the same idea.

In retrospect it is easy enough to see why Faulkner wrote it as he did. Like Shakespeare, he was unable to find the right 'objective correlative' to convey the emotion. His aim is to create a sense of tragedy and waste that will leave the reader shattered. The climactic tragedy of the novel is to be Quentin's suicide, and this is to be set against the background of the decline of an old southern family. In fact, the emotion that lies behind the novel is the same as the emotion behind the poetry of so many nineteenth-century romantics—the feeling that all greatness and nobleness lie behind us in the past, that the world is drifting into a mechanical, soul-less era. W. B. Yeats had quoted Ruskin as saying that as he walked to the British Museum, the faces of the people became daily more corrupt. Faulkner's work embodies the same feeling. But for an American of the bootleg era, the contrast must have been more jarring than for a European. What had Henry Ford and Al Capone in common with the 'beautiful, noble things' of a bygone age? So the novel is basically a gesture of loathing towards the modern world. This explains why it leaps back and forth between two dates, 1910 and 1928. In 1910, the year of Quentin's suicide, there was still something of the old South left, even though the family *is* in decline; by 1928 (the year the novel was written) it has all gone. Caddy's loss of her virginity was the beginning of the end. Quentin tried to renew his self-respect by ordering her seducer to leave town, but fainted as he tried to hit him. The sensitive 'gentleman' is ineffectual in the modern world. Quentin commits suicide. Caddy marries, but her husband divorces her when he realises their daughter is not his own child. The daughter is sent to live with the Compson family, and finds life there as intolerable as Caddy and Quentin had. The remaining brother, Jason, is a mean, dishonest materialist. When the idiot brother Benjy frightens some schoolgirls, it is Jason who insists that he be castrated. In the last section of the novel, the illegitimate daughter runs away, taking Jason's savings (as well as money he has stolen). It seems fairly clear that she is destined to end on the streets. . . .

The truth is that the plot is as crude and melodramatic as an early Elizabethan tragedy. This is underlined by the notes on the characters that Faulkner wrote for a later edition. Of Caddy: 'Doomed and knew it, accepted the doom without either seeking or fleeing it.' But it is not quite clear why she is 'doomed', since she marries a film magnate, lives in Paris, and apparently ends as the mistress of a German general during the Second World War. And Faulkner describes her face 'ageless and beautiful, cold, serene and damned'. All this brings to mind Tolstoy's comment on the writer Andreyev: 'He keeps shouting boo, but he doesn't frighten me.' Faulkner is too sophisticated to shout boo; he tries to work up a sort of *Gotterdämmerung* atmosphere by repeating words like 'doomed' and 'damned' in a sepulchral voice, and trying to keep the action so ambiguous that the crudities will pass unnoticed.

What is wrong with *The Sound and the Fury* is quite clear. Faulkner had failed to find the train of events to objectify the emotion. A work of art *holds* an emotion as a bottle holds wine. Faulkner was unable to create a bottle to hold this particular emotion. Quentin's talk about family honour deceives no one; his real desire is to become his sister's lover, and what drives him to suicide is jealousy. In which case, Faulkner should have had the courage to bring it into the open, instead of pretending the novel was about something else. The ambiguity at the heart of the novel—it would hardly be unfair to call it evasiveness—makes it ultimately unconvincing.

The relative failure of *The Sound and the Fury* decided Faulkner to try and write a novel that would make money, a 'shocker'. *Sanctuary*, according to Faulkner, was written in three weeks, and was an attempt to write 'the most horrific tale I could imagine'. When he saw it in proof he tore up the galleys and re-wrote it; but the result is still fairly horrific. Temple Drake, a judge's daughter, is taken to a gangster's hideaway to collect bootleg liquor. Her boyfriend deserts her, but she ignores advice to leave before dark. A gangster named Popeye shoots the man who is trying to guard her, then—being impotent—takes her virginity with a corncob. After this, he takes her to a brothel in Memphis, finds her a lover, and gains a kind of perverted satisfaction from watching them make love, while he lies on the end of the bed wearing his hat. When the lover tries to see her alone, Popeye kills him. Later, at a murder trial, she falsely accuses a bootlegger of raping her and killing the man who was protecting her; the mob break into the jail and burn the man alive. Popeye is finally executed for a murder he did not commit.

Again, the story is told in such an obscure and elliptical way that it is difficult, on first reading, to tell exactly what is happening. This was partly due to fear of censorship, but mostly to Faulkner's desire to sustain the *grand guignol* atmosphere with mysterious hints and conspiratorial whispers—as if what he was saying was too horrifying to be said straight out. This time, he has found an 'objective correlative' for the horror he wants to convey—but, unfortunately, not for his romanticism, his sense of meaning and value. Of course, there is also the objection that the whole thing is downright unbelievable: that Temple would not passively allow herself to be violated with a corncob then ravished repeatedly in a Memphis brothel, that she would not testify against an innocent man, and so on. But all this would hardly have mattered if he had succeeded in bringing his positive values into the book. These are only there by implication—in his obvious loathing of the world he was portraying. (And even then, it is fairly clear that he is secretly enjoying the rape of Temple much as Richardson enjoyed the violation of Clarissa.) The violence in *Sanctuary*, like the violence in *Christ in Concrete*, is a negation of values, and therefore a kind of dead end.

The problem is clear. The novelist cannot have it both ways. If he wants to write about an old, stable world of human values—of the kind we find in Jane Austen or Trollope—then he must give up the attempt to batter the audience into submission with shock tactics. The two refuse to mix. The writer's sense of meaning—the things he loves and values—must be *exactly* counterbalanced by the things he hates or rejects. So, for example, in the novels of Dostoevsky, we have a world of misery and violence counterbalanced by a world of humanity, goodness and self-sacrifice. Murder and suicide are counterbalanced by flashes of mystical insight into the absolute value of life. In a famous chapter of *The Brothers Karamazov* entitled 'Pro and Contra', Dostoevsky actually tries to weigh all the world's evil against all its good, as if placing them in opposite balance pans of a pair of scales. Faulkner's 'values', like Hemingway's, are not positive enough to counterbalance the violence and misery. He believes in the decency and power of endurance of ordinary people, and in the aristocratic values of the old South; but they are too light, and the balance pan kicks the beam. Any perceptive critic who understood this principle could have predicted, after *Sanctuary*, that Faulkner would never write a wholly successful book—not necessarily a masterpiece, but even a book that satisfactorily objectifies all his values.

This is true. *As I lay Dying* and *Light in August* are more artistically successful than *The Sound and the Fury* and *Sanctuary*, but this is because Faulkner has reduced his scale; he is no longer trying to convey the romantic sense of 'beautiful, noble things' that have been destroyed or supplanted by modern materialism. His most extensive portrait of the old Deep South, in *Absalom, Absalom!* is almost as full of cruelty and violence as *Sanctuary*. Like *The Sound and the Fury*, it ends with the raving of an idiot. And then, for the next two decades (1937–59), Faulkner devoted himself to a trilogy of novels about the 'supplanters', the small-minded, calculating Snopes clan, the new masters of the South. The first of these, *The Hamlet*, has some excellent comic episodes—suggesting that Faulkner was losing the gloomy obsession that had almost turned him into a great novelist. In fact, he never regained the power that flickered and rumbled below the surface of the early novels. Much of the later work is laboured and mannered, as if he is trying to compensate for lack of inner tension with portentousness of style.

In retrospect, it seems fairly clear that the turning point in Faulkner's development was *Sanctuary*. Precisely what went wrong? It was basically the problem that had first made its appearance nearly a century earlier, with the appearance of naturalism: the paradox of the microscope and the telescope, the near and the far. Naturalism uses the 'narrow-angle lens' to create an illusion of reality. Faulkner is not basically a naturalist; he is a romantic. But he recognised that, if he wanted to make an impact, he had to use the devices of naturalism—particularly its favourite device, the shock effect. In *The Sound and the Fury*, he tried to reconcile the two with the time-shift mechanism, so that although each individual fragment is 'close-up', the fragments come from different times and places, giving a kind of wide-angle vision. *Sanctuary* tries a new formula: an apparent surrender to naturalism, but with shock effects so violent (the sexual perversion, burning alive, etc.) that the whole thing is lifted beyond realism, into a realm of almost Gothic fantasy. It was a dangerous formula; to begin with, it meant that he had type-cast himself as a novelist of grimness and violence, which in turn meant that he had to keep looking further for images of violence. So in *Light in August* we have another Elizabethan plot involving a frigid spinster who takes a half-negro lover and becomes a nymphomaniac; the lover murders her, and is in turn murdered and castrated by a lynch mob. This was merely a variation of the *Sanctuary* theme of violation (Temple's name underlines the theme), nymphomania and murder. Obviously, there was a limit to the way these themes could be used. If you have kicked somebody in the stomach and then hit him on the head, it becomes difficult to produce any further impression by mere violence.

A few novelists *have* tried. After Faulkner's death, in 1962, literary censorship virtually disappeared. Nabokov's *Lolita* had dealt with the theme of sex with a ten-year-old girl without appearing to condemn it. It became possible to publish openly sadistic novels like *The Story of O* and *The Image*. Terry Southern's *Candy* ends with the heroine having intercourse with her own father. William Burroughs's 'beat' novel *The Naked Lunch* (the title suggested by Jack Kerouac) became an underground classic long before it appeared in America in 1962. The book professes to be memories of his delirium during drug-addiction. It uses the same basic technique as the Night Town chapter of *Ulysses*—fantasies swirling and dissolving as if in a dream. The fantasies involve detailed descriptions of acts of sexual perversion and sadism. Ten years earlier, it would have struck everyone as incomprehensible that such a book should ever be published, except by a 'private press', or possibly—for scientific reasons—by some psychiatric association. After all, the novel is basically a form of entertainment; and although *The Naked Lunch* is not devoid of literary brilliance, only the Marquis de Sade would have found it entertaining. But Joyce, Hemingway and Faulkner had implied that the novel has a deeper purpose than entertainment: to 'tell the truth'—even if it is only the author's own 'private' truth. The interesting result was that *The Naked Lunch* was able to be published and sold openly, without a murmur of protest. The critics, presumably, felt that it represented an interesting new milestone in the history of the novel, that it went 'further' than any previous novel. Yet with Burroughs' subsequent novels—*The Soft Machine*, *The Ticket that Exploded*, *Nova Express*—it has become clear that Burroughs, like Faulkner, had defined his own limit, and was unable to move beyond it.

One more example will suffice. In 1972, a Toronto publisher brought out a novel called *The Garbageman* by Juan Butler. Butler's first novel, *Cabbagetown Diary*, had been sub-titled 'a documentary', and had been an apparently autobiographical account of a writer living in a slum section of Toronto; there had been a great deal of sex and violence, but a strong feeling of authenticity. It had received a good critical reception. The second novel again deals with a bored and frustrated intellectual, this time living with his family in Toronto. Boredom and frustration have driven him close to insanity. On page 5 the shock effects begin: he caves in the cat's skull with a poker. But this is apparently fantasy, for half a page later, he kills it again with a knife. From then on, the violence erupts at intervals. There is a long description of a fight in an alleyway, which ends when the narrator blows the top of the man's skull off, then plunges his hand into his brains and throws them over the wall. But the climax of the book is the scene describing how the narrator picks up a girl, takes her out for a country walk, and then murders her. The details of the torture of the girl are described lovingly for some dozen pages. The narrator has several sexual climaxes before he kills her.

Whether—like the earlier attack on the cat—this murder is intended to be another sick fantasy is beside the point. The

novel itself is a fantasy, so it would be a sophistry to say that
the scene only takes place inside the narrator's brain. The
'justification' for such a scene as this is that it 'tells the truth',
and that it is the novelist's duty to tell the truth as he sees it.
Now certainly this scene describes something that happens
with horrible regularity in our society, something we prefer
to know about only at second or third hand, through newspaper reports; and there can be no doubt that the author has
also revealed a certain ghastly originality. But again, it is
based on the artistic fallacy that the writer's business is to try
to make the reader's eyes water and his teeth rattle. *If* that is
so, then a novelist would be justified in making an even greater
impact by abandoning the novel for the film business, and
presenting the scene of torture visually, preferably in Technicolor. And the ultimate impact would be made by actually
committing such a murder in front of an audience. . . . But
then, the purpose of the novel is not mere 'impact'. It is to
combine wide-angle vision and narrow-angle vision, the near
and the far. Instead of evoking 'meaning', the close-up vision
of extreme realism destroys it, leaving the feeling that man is
stranded in a brutal and empty universe.

The conclusion could be expressed in this way: that the basic
law of the novel is Newton's third law of motion: that every
action should have an equal and opposite reaction. In Samuel
Richardson, the shock effect of the seduction and rape is
counterbalanced by an equally strong sense of morality and
goodness—positive rather than passive goodness. In Dostoevsky, cruelty and violence are counterbalanced by a mystical religious affirmation. In Hemingway, the sense of brutality
and alienation is counterbalanced by human love and the sheer
joy of being alive. In all successful works of art, two forces pulling in opposite directions unite to create a third force at right
angles. The unity of a great novel is created out of a tension of
opposing forces.
    All major novelists recognise this instinctively. Lesser novelists
are inclined to the fallacy that provided the novel has one
single, powerful thrust, this will create the required effect of

unity. And indeed, for a short time it *does*. This is why so many 'single-force' novels, from De Sade's *Justine* to Faulkner's *Sanctuary*, are successful within certain limits. But the single-force soon dissipates itself; it reaches a limit, and there is no 'beyond'. De Sade's *120 Days of Sodom* is one of the cruellest novels ever written, Artsybashev's *The Breaking Point* one of the gloomiest, *Finnegan's Wake* one of the most linguistically complex, *The Naked Lunch* one of the most nightmarish, *The Garbageman* one of the most violent. And each one represents a dead end, like a chemical reaction that has burnt itself out, and contains no further possibility of change or development.

A chapter dealing with limits and dead ends could hardly end better than with a brief account of Samuel Beckett. Beckett, a Dubliner (born 1906), moved to Paris, where he became for a short time Joyce's amanuensis. The historian of drama, Martin Esslin, has recorded that Beckett frequently stayed in bed all day because he could see no reason to get up; he also mentions that Joyce's daughter Lucia was infatuated with Beckett, who remarked that it was no good because he was 'dead inside' and had no feelings. Psychologically speaking, Beckett was a 'man without motive', immersed in boredom. And so it is hardly surprising that his first novel, *Murphy* (1938), begins:

> The sun shone, having no alternative, on the nothing new. Murphy sat out of it, as though he were free, in a mew in West Brompton. Here for what might have been six months he had eaten, drunk, slept, and put his clothes on and off, in a medium size cage of north-western aspect commanding an unbroken view of medium-sized cages of south-eastern aspect. . . .

This contains all the seeds from which Beckett's later work was to spring: the emphasis on the boredom and futility of life, lack of belief in human freedom, the sense that we are all trapped in cages—all expressed with a certain dry Irish wit and charm, suggesting a man who knows his own mind. Murphy does nothing and can see no reason for doing anything. A Chelsea prostitute to whom he proposes insists that he get a job, and Murphy becomes a male nurse in a mental home on the outskirts of London; there he feels completely happy among human beings who decline to acknowledge the reality of the outside world. Murphy would like to do the same, but has never achieved it. Eventually, he is killed when his gas-fire explodes, and a friend scatters his ashes on the floor of a public house. The language is ironic and precise; the plot is deliberately absurd—with various Irishmen setting out in search of Murphy. But although the book is comic, Beckett is very clearly saying: 'Live? Our servants can do that for us.'

Beckett has now established his own comic manner: which consisted of earnest and precise descriptions of trivial or absurd events. (Damon Runyon was doing the same kind of thing, making his gamblers and hoodlums express themselves with elaborate courtesy.) The underlying assumption is that life is preposterous: not necessarily grisly or tragic, but nevertheless quite meaningless. Like Camus, Beckett feels that the universe is totally indifferent to us, and that therefore all our emotions are absurd—somehow disconnected, like a man carefully running a comb over a bald head, or an opera singer opening and closing his mouth without sound. There is also more than a touch of the ponderous precision of a policeman giving evidence in court: 'The victim was then seen to remonstrate with the accused, who addressed him as a cur and struck him on the head with a golf club. . . .' The technique is developed in *Watt* (1944), in which a series of fairly pointless events are described and discussed with this manic earnestness. Watt, another one of Beckett's homeless transients, set out on a journey to the house of Mr Knott, to whom he is to become a servant. On the way, he lies down in a ditch, and a lady throws a stone at him. . . . It reads like a collaboration between Kafka, James Joyce and Dickens. When, at the end of the book, Watt has departed on a train, a group of railwaymen sit and discuss 'life'. 'And they say there is no God, said Mr Case. All three laughed heartily at this extravagance.'

There is an appendix of meaningless fragments, and the author explains in a footnote that 'only fatigue and disgust prevented its incorporation' in the book itself.

What is now clear is that Beckett shares Kafka's sense that life is a kind of nightmare. But Kafka's language is flat and inexpressive. Beckett has discovered a new literary trick—or, rather, revived the old Dickensian trick of underlining the absurdity of the action by describing it with a kind of heroic pomposity. But even in *Watt*, the trick is becoming a little tiresome. It is easier to see its point where the action is more obviously comic, as in *Murphy*. The reader who opened *Watt* casually in the middle would find it very difficult to understand what Beckett was trying to do, for the elaborate descriptions of unimportant points are not self-evidently funny. The tension between the manner and the matter is disappearing.

In *Molloy* (published 1951) it has disappeared completely. The first half of the book is a rambling interior monologue of a dying man in his mother's room; he does not seem to be sure how he got there or what he is doing there. There is no structure, no attempt to tell a story; everything is intentionally ambiguous and nightmarish. The second part of the book seems to be told by a kind of private detective called Moran, who is ordered (by whom is not clear) to go and look for Molloy. He sets out with his son. The journey has the confused quality of a dream that we have now come to expect from Beckett. He is re-stating, at considerable length, his conviction that life is meaningless. He continues to re-state it in the two sequels to *Molloy*, *Malone Dies* and *The Unnameable*, the last of which differs from the other two largely because it has no paragraphs and few full stops. 'I'm mute, what do they want what have I done to them, what have I done to God, what has God done to us, nothing, and we've done nothing to him, you can't do anything to him, he can't do anything to us, we're innocent, he's innocent, it's nobody's fault . . .' and so on. The book ends: 'you must go on, I can't go on, I'll go on.'

What had happened, between the publication of *Molloy* and *Malone Dies* is that Beckett had suddenly achieved fame with the performance (in Paris) of his play *En Attendant Godot*. *Waiting for Godot* is Beckett's most amusing and effective presentation of his central idea. For two long acts, his two tramps stand under a tree, holding preposterous conversations and amusing themselves in various ways. Once again, there is inner tension between matter and manner; the tramps belong to the tradition of knockabout comedians, and they deliver their lines with the tremendous artificial vigour of music hall comics: 'Which of you two stinks?' 'He's got stinking breath and I've got stinking feet.' Pozzo, the 'capitalist pig' who leads in his servant, Lucky, on the end of a rope, makes speeches that sound like the platitudes of a politician:

> The tears of the world are a constant quantity. For each one who begins to weep, somewhere else another stops. The same is true of the laugh. *(He laughs.)* Let us not then speak ill of our generation, it is not any unhappier than its predecessors. *(Silence.)* Let us not speak well of it either. *(Silence.)* Let us not speak of it at all. *(Silence.)* It is true that the population has increased.

But perhaps the most effective episode in the play is the scene where Lucky is ordered by his master to 'think', and pours out a torrential, incoherent monologue full of fragments of philosophy and theology—literally 'a tale told by an idiot'.

Even so, *Waiting for Godot* is far too long. The second act can only repeat the effects of the first. For Beckett, this was a point worth making—that life goes on—and on and on and on— repeating itself. But we can immediately see the artistic contradiction that lies at the heart of his work. If his point about the meaninglessness and dreariness of life is to be made effectively, it must be made interestingly and amusingly, to produce the basic 'counterbalance effect'. He may imagine that it would be more effective to make the point deliberately boring, but this is simply a failure to understand the rules of art: that there must be two opposing forces that produce a third force at right angles. A single force always fizzles out.

And Beckett now proceeded to repeat, in the realm of the drama, the mistake he had already made in the novel. In the next play, *Endgame*, two characters sit gloomily in dustbins and discuss the meaninglessness of life as they await death. Even the title reveals Beckett's curious tendency to miscalculate; the

original title was *Fin de Partie*, and the most effective translation
would have been *The Party's Over*; by comparison, *Endgame* is
dull, unevocative.

Anyone who had followed Beckett's development as far as
Endgame could have foretold that he would soon reach his own
dead end. Without inner tension, there was no possibility of
further development. He had said all he had to say, and exhausted his resources. Like a pendulum coming to a standstill,
his work could only swing in smaller and smaller arcs. Says one
admiring commentator: 'One should not underrate the persistence of this author in continuing to write when there seems
nothing further to write about.'

Texts for Nothing begins, predictably: 'Suddenly, no, at last,
long last, I couldn't any more, I couldn't go on', and then goes
on in the same manner for seventy pages. *How It Is* has no full
stops; a character called Pim makes some kind of a journey
through the mud, and ends by lying in it. A play called *Play*
has three characters in jars, only identified as 'Woman 1',
'Woman 2' and 'Man', and they all stare in front of them and
fail to communicate.

For future generations, the chief interest of Beckett will probably be that he is the ultimate example of faulty artistic logic
taken to its false conclusion. His work begins from the premise
that 'the near and the far' are irreconcilable: that men may
catch glimpses of meaning—probably an illusion—but are
doomed to remain stuck on this meaningless flypaper of the
present. The 'far' remains present, in the form of references to
some incomprehensible God, but the work becomes a long-
drawn-out complaint about the meaninglessness of the 'near'.
Beckett's two most successful works remain his first novel,
Murphy, and his first play, *Waiting for Godot*. Then the meaninglessness closes in, like darkness, and the work finally sub-
sides into silence. Hardly a moment too soon.

ELEVEN

Fantasy and New Directions

TOWARDS THE END of 1918, Oswald Spengler published the first volume of *The Decline of the West*, which argued that civilisations are born and die, exactly like living organisms. It may seem that this book has presented a similar thesis about the novel. It was born in Spain in 1499—the year of the publication of *La Celestina* (known in English as *The Spanish Bawd*) by Fernando de Rojas. For two and a half centuries, it grew as slowly as an acorn; and then, quite suddenly, it was a full grown tree. A mere century later, it was already showing signs of premature ageing. With the death of James Joyce in 1941— almost exactly two hundred years after the publication of *Pamela*—it seemed to many critics that it had reached the end of its life cycle. In fact, it has shown no significant advance since the age of the great experimenters—Proust, Musil, Joyce. A few writers have continued to experiment: Sartre, Beckett, Alain Robbe-Grillet, Gunther Grass, B. S. Johnson, Thomas Pynchon: but never as boldly—or as successfully—as Joyce. Most of the best-known post-Joycian novelists have been traditionalists who have observed the same basic rules as Balzac or Dickens: Graham Greene, Evelyn Waugh, Saul Bellow, Bernard Malamud, Isaac Bashevis Singer, Heinrich Böll, Alexander Solzenhenitsyn.

There has been another interesting, but scarcely encouraging, development. Defoe, Richardson, Scott, Dickens, were all 'best-sellers' as well as serious novelists. Without attempting to produce self-conscious masterpieces, they wrote as well as they could, and the result was acceptable to immense audiences. But even before the appearance of *Waverley* in 1814, an ominous development had taken place: hack writers had begun to produce cheap imitations of the horror novels of Monk Lewis and Anne Radcliffe. The poet Shelley wrote a couple; Balzac began his career with half a dozen. By the mid-nineteenth century, the 'penny dreadful' was the most widely read form of fiction in England (in America they were called 'dime novels'). Published in weekly parts, they were entirely without literary merit—a lowest-common-denominator, a deliberately debased form of what more serious novelists were doing. Most of these hacks never became known to the public by name. (The title-page would read something like: *The Virgin's Curse*, by the author of *The Goblet of Gore*.) But in the twentieth century, the hack began to rival the 'serious novelist' for popularity. Finally, the 'best-seller' became a distinct literary *genre*. The curious consequence is that we now have two classes of writer, who seem to have little in common except that they both use words. A list of the most important novels of the eighteenth and nineteenth centuries would also be a list of their best-sellers. In the twentieth century, few 'important' novels have appeared on the best-seller lists, and vice-versa. The names of most of the best-sellers of the early twentieth century are now as forgotten as the names of the writers of 'penny dreadfuls', and it seems likely that today's best-sellers will be forgotten in fifty years' time. I am not arguing that all best-selling novelists are commercial hacks; only that there is now a gulf fixed between the 'popular' and the 'serious' novelist, and that few writers have been able to bridge it. All of which deepens the gloom that surrounds the prospects for the serious novel.

Yet the 1960s and early '70s have seen one interesting change in the taste of readers: the revival of interest in fantasy. George Macdonald, H. P. Lovecraft, E. R. Edison, C. S. Lewis, David Lindsay: all are now easily available in paperback. Tolkien's *Lord of the Rings*, popular with only a few enthusiasts for a decade after its first appearance in the 1950s, has been in the best-seller class for ten years or more. Science-fiction, once strictly a pulp-magazine industry, has become so much a cult that whole shops are devoted to it in most major cities. Horror stories and 'gothic' tales also proliferate in paperback; practically every half-forgotten writer mentioned in Lovecraft's *Supernatural Horror in Literature* has been revived, many of them after a century of oblivion. All this runs parallel to a general revival of interest in magic, mysticism and the occult which began in the early 1960s, and which still shows no sign of slackening fifteen years later.

The obvious explanation is that this is a movement of escapism, of flight from the alarming and violent realities of our world. But we have already observed that escapism can be a thoroughly misleading concept. The readers of *Pamela*, *Julie* and *Werther* were not merely 'escaping'; they were embarking on one of the most exciting voyages ever taken by the human imagination. The 'first Romantics'—Goethe, Schiller, Wordsworth, Rousseau, Jean Paul—sensed that the human spirit was on the point of a new breakthrough. But by the end of the century, the hope had evaporated—often undermined by self-pity and a self-indulgent pessimism. Besides, science was achieving incredible successes, and most scientists held firm to the belief that one day the universe will be entirely explained in terms of physical laws. Imagination found itself on the defensive; most serious people regarded it as a faculty for avoiding reality and inventing lies.

I have pointed out earlier that Abraham Maslow's 'hierarchy of values' applies as much to societies as to individuals. The most primitive societies are concerned solely with survival; once this is achieved, they become concerned with security and territory. As soon as a society has evolved beyond a certain point, it enters the stage of sexual romanticism. This is where we find European civilisation when the novel first appeared. (*The Spanish Bawd* is a kind of Romeo-and-Juliet tragedy.) It was *still* in the sexual-romantic stage when *Pamela* appeared two and a half centuries later. Within fifty years, the novel had developed beyond recognition. The Byronic poet shook his fist at heaven and declared that man is basically god-like. But his roots still lay in sexual romanticism (which tends to be pessimistic in nature—most of the world's great love stories end in tragedy). It is typical that Goethe declared that 'the eternal womanly' draws us upward and on. He found it hard to conceive of fulfilment in anything but sexual terms. And so the 'first romanticism' collapsed into the despair of the 'tragic generation' of the 1890s.

In the nineteenth century, the world was not ready for romanticism, with its belief in a new breakthrough for the human spirit. Besides, most members of society were still near the bottom rung of the 'hierarchy of needs'; while Goethe was writing the second part of *Faust*, Burke and Hare, the Edinburgh body-snatchers, were murdering transients and prostitutes for the sake of the few guineas paid by the medical school for the corpses. Even the poets and artists lived under constant threat of starvation, and the death rate was high. The facts of everyday life seemed to flatly contradict the notion that man was evolving into something more god-like.

By the second decade of the twentieth century, the facts were no longer so contradictory—largely due to the advance of scientific technology. The majority of people in the civilised countries had more security than ever before, and their children were all within reach of university education. Which meant that most people were in the position—if they were so minded —to explore the realm of imagination. Anyone with a capacity to daydream had the means at hand: in a novel, on the stage, on a flickering screen, on the radio. Novels like Dreiser's *An American Tragedy*, Sinclair Lewis's *Main Street* and *Babbitt*, are significant because they reflect a whole society that has reached the self-esteem stage of Maslow's hierarchy. And nowadays, a novel about social issues or politics is as likely to sell as a novel about romance or sex or violence. After the Second World War, America led the world in a new trend, the political best-seller: novels like Robert Penn Warren's *All the King's Men*, Alan Drury's *Advise and Consent*; such non-fiction works as David Riesman's *The Lonely Crowd*, J. K. Galbraith's *The Affluent Society*, or various books on 'The Making of the President'. Man-in-society, man at the self-esteem level, is the subject in the novels of C. P. Snow and James Gould Cozzens; their heroes sit on committees and discuss public welfare. You have only to try and imagine Homer or Virgil—or even Shake-speare—writing about the administrative problems of a general, to grasp the enormous mental gulf that exists between their society and ours.

The significance of all this is not simply that 'political man' has become a hero, but that the readers who turned these books into best-sellers were themselves 'men-in-society', able to 'identify' with committee men and administrators. By the time the political best-seller emerged in the late 'forties, the trend had been apparent for a quarter of a century; two generations had been obsessed by politics. Even a dedicated romantic like Thomas Mann could declare that 'in our time the destiny of man presents itself in political terms'.

All of which seems to suggest that by the mid-twentieth century, society as a whole—or at least, large portions of it—had reached Maslow's self-esteem stage; which in turn suggests that the self-actualisation stage may not be far off. The swing back to romanticism and mysticism may be more than an 'escapist' reaction; this time it *could* be the next step forward.

It is conceivable, then, that future generations may see the publication of *The Lord of the Rings* (1954–6) as one of the cultural watersheds of the twentieth century. In England it was the period of the 'Angry Young Men'. In the universities of Europe and America, logical positivism still dominated the philosophy departments. All writers were expected to be 'committed'. This three-volume fantasy, in which men and hobbits and elves and dwarfs live side by side, seemed to be an irrelevant freak, a piece of 'don's whimsy'. The author was apparently so convinced of the narrowness of his appeal that he did not even bother to register the copyright in America—which proved inconvenient ten years later, when the book suddenly became a best-seller on the campuses.

J. R. R. Tolkien was an Oxford professor who disliked the twentieth century and looked back with nostalgia to the Middle Ages. In an essay on 'Fairy Tales', he had argued passionately against the notion that fairy stories are 'escapist'. 'The notion that motor cars are more "alive" than, say, centaurs or dragons is curious; that they are more "real" than, say, horses is pathetically absurd.'

And so *The Lord of the Rings* conforms to the basic necessity for a 'serious novel'; it is a clear expression of the writer's standards of value. And what of that other essential element: the values the writer *dislikes*? This is, in fact, also present. The villain Sauron, with his lust for absolute power, sounds sufficiently like a modern dictator to give the novel a menacing sense of urgency. And so Tolkien has avoided the chief pitfall of the fantasist: the failure to present an 'alternative world', a 'far' without a 'near'.

The result is that, purely as a novel, *The Lord of the Rings* must be regarded as one of the most successful works of art of the twentieth century. This is not simply because Frodo's long journey from the Shire to Mordor is enormously inventive, but because Tolkien has been able to state his own values with such conviction. If we compare it with Faulkner's *As I Lay Dying*— another story of a journey—we can immediately see the essential difference; Faulkner—another romantic—can only *imply* his values, while he shows us a harsh and materialistic modern world. Tolkien can devote his full attention to creating the world he prefers; the world he detests hangs menacingly in the background; but he obviously prefers writing about the cosy home-comforts of the Shire, or the magical world of Lothlorien, to the smouldering slag-heaps of Mordor. Faulkner was forced to spend his life describing the slag-heaps.

The Lord of the Rings has its faults. I have read it aloud to my children several times; on the second reading, the sentimentality became oppressive, and the mock-heroic speeches boring. But the sweep and vitality remained breath-taking. It is significant that a work of so much imaginative vitality should have been produced when critics had been talking for years about the 'end of the novel'. If Joyce had jammed the novel in a *cul de sac*, Tolkien had found his own method of backing it out. And in fact, Joyce himself had been groping towards something like *The Lord of the Rings* in *Finnegan's Wake*: a timeless realm of myths—or what Jung would have called 'archetypes'.

At the time Tolkien was writing *The Lord of the Rings*, another writer was also exploring the imaginative possibilities of pure fantasy. Mervyn Peake was an artist, who also found the modern world oppressive. (It finally drove him insane.) The first volume of his Titus Trilogy, *Titus Groan*, appeared in 1946, the second *Gormenghast*, in 1950, the third, *Titus Alone*, in 1959. Compared to Tolkien's mountains and broad rivers, the castle in which most of the trilogy takes place is oppressive; but although Gormenghast castle may seem airless, it is as real, in its nightmarish way, as those vast imaginary prisons of the artist Piranesi. The hero, Titus, finds his home stifling, but when he finally escapes from it, the outside world is equally menacing, with the same echoes of totalitarianism that we have observed in *The Lord of the Rings*.* The Titus Trilogy reflects Peake's own feeling of being trapped; but again, it establishes its own reality, its own sense of values, with an authority that seemed lost to the twentieth-century novelist.

Yet although fantasy may be the ideal vehicle for releasing the powers of the imagination, it also has its own inherent limitations. These can best be seen by considering the life-work of the Scottish novelist David Lindsay.

Lindsay was, in fact, born in London in 1878, although he spent much of his youth in Scotland, and the Highlands are obviously the inspiration for much of the scenery in his masterpiece, *A Voyage to Arcturus*. Lindsay won a scholarship to a university, but his grandmother insisted that he go into business —as an insurance broker in the City. He was conscientious enough to make a successful businessman, but he always hated the life. He read Nietzsche and Schopenhauer, listened to Beethoven, walked in the Highlands, and dreamed of freedom. At the age of thirty-eight, he married a girl eighteen years his junior, and decided to give up insurance to become a writer. With the 'golden handshake' from Lloyds, they were able to move to Cornwall, and Lindsay wrote *A Voyage to Arcturus*, which was published in 1920. It should have made him famous; in fact, it was either attacked or ignored. The second

---

* Tolkien once told me—in a letter—that he had no symbolic intentions in *The Lord of the Rings*; the Nazgul were not supposed to be proto-Nazis. But for someone who began the book in 1937, the parallel must have been present, if only unconsciously.

novel, *The Haunted Woman*, appeared in 1922, and was simply
ignored. So was *Sphinx*, which appeared a year later. After this,
Lindsay began to have difficulty finding publishers. The book
he regarded as his masterpiece, *Devil's Tor*, finally appeared
in 1932—to meet an even stonier silence. He published nothing
more in his lifetime. His wife supported the family by running
a boarding house in Hove; Lindsay became increasingly depressed and embittered; he died, completely forgotten, in 1947.

Arcturus is the greatest imaginative work of the twentieth
century—possibly in all literature. Then why was it overlooked by Lindsay's contemporaries? Because, in spite of his
genius, Lindsay was a writer of amateurish clumsiness. (If only
for this reason, his novels should be studied in every Creative
Writing course; it will cheer struggling amateurs to know that a
totally incompetent writer can still produce great works.) The
level of his style seldom rises above that of a second-rate magazine writer. 'The host, eyeing him with indolent curiosity, got
up, and the usual conventional greetings were exchanged.
Having indicated an easy chair before the fire to his guest, the
South American merchant sank back again into his own.' We
can see at once what is wrong. A writer has to transport the
reader from A to B, like a train, and he has to describe what to
put in and what to leave out. Lindsay is like a train that stops
at every wayside station, whether anyone wants to get on or
not.

The opening chapters of *Arcturus* take place on earth; then
the hero is sent in a space-ship to the star Arcturus. From the
moment Maskull lands on Arcturus, the style ceases to matter.
(A glance at any part of the book will show that it does not
actually improve; but Lindsay has the reader so completely in
his power that it ceases to be noticeable.)

To create imaginary landscapes and imaginary events
sounds easy; to see how difficult it is, you have only to try and
do it for five minutes. The imagination quickly tires. Lindsay
keeps up an incredible and unflagging level of invention for
over two hundred pages. There are no dinosaurs or bug-eyed-
monsters; only strange landscapes, strange creatures, and a
haunting overall sense of strangeness. Lindsay's purpose is to

explain his feeling that the universe we live in is somehow false and illusory—in fact, a 'conjurer's cave' of illusions—but that a real universe lies behind it. The world we live in is fundamentally trivial, petty and rather frivolous; but we catch glimpses of another form of reality in sublime things: mountains, forests, vast landscapes. 'I *must*, before I die, find *some* way to say the essential thing that is in me . . . the very breath of life, fierce and coming from far away, bringing into human life the vastness and fearful passionless force of non-human things.' This is not Lindsay, but Bertrand Russell; but it expresses the essence of Lindsay's work. Human beings are afraid of this non-human force; they want comfort, cosiness, little pleasures that are not too demanding. The human soul contains an element that is allied to the sublime world of the non-human—hence the love of science, mathematics, philosophy, music—but it is continually being tempted to forget it and wallow in the trivial. All the different world of Arcturus, the strange landscapes Maskull passes through in his quest for the absolute, appear to be glimpses of a deeper reality, and all turn out to be illusions of the devil, 'Crystalman', the spirit of triviality and pleasure.

When Lindsay had finished *Arcturus*, he must have known that he had written one of the greatest books of the twentieth century. He had convinced himself that he was indifferent to acclaim; all the same, the total lack of interest must have been a shock.

And now he encountered the basic problem of the fantasist; the problem Tolkien would encounter on finishing *The Lord of the Rings*. How could he go on from there? His purpose was to contrast the 'triviality of everydayness' with the world of the sublime that is glimpsed by mystics. *Arcturus* does this so magnificently that it seems to leave nothing unsaid.

Lindsay chose the only possible direction: he moved 'back to earth', even though he felt thoroughly out of place there. And although *The Haunted Woman* is more noticeably clumsy than *Arcturus*, it is, in its way, very nearly as successful. Once again, Lindsay needed symbols for his 'two worlds', two standards of value. He chooses ingeniously. The heroine,

Isbel Loment, visits an old Elizabethan manor house and, as she explores it alone, finds a flight of stairs to an upper storey. The part of the house in which she finds herself is obviously hundreds of years older than the rest, and the landscape outside the window is not the landscape she could see from downstairs; she has walked into another dimension, and gone backwards in time. In this strange upper storey, she meets her host, Henry Judge. But they are two different people, aware of the 'other rooms' of consciousness, no longer trapped in rigid social conventions. They realise they are in love. Yet when they get back to the lower part of the house, all memory of the upper storey vanishes, and they hardly attract one another. In the same way, the mystic, returning to ordinary consciousness, can no longer remember why he wanted to shout: 'Of *course*.'

But in spite of this superb image, Lindsay had no idea of what to do with his plot and characters. The central problem lay in his pessimism. In *Arcturus* he had insisted that 'this' world is false, from top to bottom, and that the world of reality and sublimity is inexpressible. His rejection of 'this world' is so total that he left himself no room for manœuvre. The only way he can find room for manœuvre in *The Haunted Woman* is by retreating several steps. Now the world of false values is the social world, and the world of reality seems to be an idealised version of medieval England. The reader finds himself hoping that Lindsay is going to allow his leading characters to climb out of the windows and explore this fascinating world of the past; but when they do so at the end, they only encounter tragedy: the implication is that the world of reality is too fierce for human beings.

What is now clear—and what might have been deduced from the style of *Arcturus*—is that the author is rather a prim and proper man, who has never been able to escape a certain awkwardness and embarrassment in his social relations. When Isbel looks at herself in a mirror in the upper storey, she is startled by her image: 'It was not so much that she appeared more beautiful as that her face had acquired another character. Its expression was deep, stern, lowering, yet everything was softened and made alluring by the pervading presence of sexual sweetness. . . .' In other words, it is herself as she might be if she could achieve self-actualisation, complete self-expression of her potentialities. '. . . It was even a little awful to think that this was herself, and still she knew that it was *true*.' This is D. H. Lawrence's theme: that social life distorts us and prevents self-realisation; but he would solve the problem by sending the vicar's daughter to bed with a gypsy. Lindsay finds sex just as alluring (when he finally owns up to it), but he knows the answer is less simple.

In *Sphinx*, he is still searching for an image that will express this sense of two worlds of value that seem to be contradictory. This time, he chooses the world of dreams to symbolise the underlying reality. His hero, Nicholas Cabot, is a young inventor who takes a lodging in a suburban house full of pretty girls. He is engaged in perfecting a machine that will record dreams. The substance of the novel concerns his involvement with various women, in particular, with a composer, Lore, and an attractive widow, Celia. Lore has a capacity for writing great music—music that reflects the world of reality—but is forced to write sugary drawing-room pieces for money. Lindsay is intrigued by the problem of the artist who sells out. The 'sphinx' of the title is the goddess of dreams, and her riddle is 'Why are we alive?' The 'dream machine' seems to reveal that the world of dreams is common to all human beings—Jung's collective unconscious. Nicholas's dreams reveal his knowledge that Lore is trapped and needs help. Yet in real life, he is not deeply attracted to her. At the end of the book, Lore has committed suicide by drowning. A dream-recording of another character reveals Nicholas and Lore riding off on horseback. When they go to Nicholas's room, they find him dead.

Again, Lindsay's theme is that the life we live in the everyday world is a distorting mirror; this is why life is so messy and unsatisfactory. But there is another reality which is a true mirror; if we wish to know ourselves as we really are, we have to seek out this reality. . . .

Lindsay's next novel, *The Violet Apple*, never found a publisher during his lifetime (and is only now being published in America, together with the unfinished fragment, *The Witch*).

We now know enough of Lindsay to know that his novel will be about the 'unreality' imposed on us by 'the triviality of everydayness', and that he will need a fresh symbol for the world of reality. In *The Violet Apple*, the symbol is two tiny apples, grown (apparently) from two seeds of the original apple of good and evil eaten by Adam and Eve. The hero is a successful West-End playwright (again, the serious artist who has sold out), engaged to a girl named Grace. He is not much attracted by a perverse, rather mischievous girl named Haidée, engaged to his best friend. But when both Haidée and Anthony eat the apples from the tree of knowledge, they realise, like Isbel and Henry Judge, that they are soul-mates. When he looks at his fiancée Grace, he finds her unbearable because her eyes can 'only communicate with his frightful, earthy, mortal nature, which was like an invitation to share a common coffin. . . .' In spite of its clumsy style, this is a strange, disturbing work—although, like *The Haunted Woman* and *Sphinx*, it fails to reach a satisfying conclusion.

Devil's Tor is Lindsay's most ambitious, and most badly written novel. It takes place on the magnificent, bleak landscape of Dartmoor. Lindsay seems to have moved towards a curious, pagan sexual mysticism. He loathes the modern world and everything about it with a raging intensity. (The same loathing led H. P. Lovecraft to create his tales of monstrous horrors, and also led him dangerously close to a kind of fascism based on his distaste for Jews, Negroes and Latins.) He dreams of the coming of a new messiah or avatar who will lead the world away from its degrading materialism. The heroine of the novel, Ingrid, realises finally that she is destined to be the mother of the avatar; she is an embodiment of the Great Mother. The long, involved plot concerns a magical stone, broken into two pieces; the uniting of their two halves will release tremendous primitive forces and inaugurate the new age. When the two halves are finally joined, they explode into stars; Ingrid and the hero, Saltfleet, recognise that it is their destiny to produce the avatar; and the novel ends in a thunder of Wagnerian prose.

Understandably, Lindsay was exhausted after this effort,

and discouraged by its total failure. He spent the remaining fifteen years of his life writing another obscure dinosaur of a book called *The Witch*; he re-wrote it so many times that it is not clear whether the manuscript is complete or not. The witch of the title is Urda, the earth goddess. Lindsay seemed to have decided finally that he should face the greatest challenge: to describe that sublime world of reality that exists beyond our world. This is the realm beyond death, which is also (in some way) the realm of music. The hero, Ragnar, enters this realm after going to Urda's house—Lindsay's symbol of the junction between the two worlds, like the dream machine, the two halves of the magic stone, etc.—and the book moves into a strange realm of symbolism and mystical metaphysics. Lindsay does his best to make the prose approximate to music.

It is possible that *The Witch* will be one day regarded as Lindsay's supreme masterpiece; but one thing is certain, that only the most devoted Lindsay enthusiasts will succeed in reading it to the end.

In the novels of David Lindsay, we see the struggle of a man of genius to express a sense of values that is fundamentally mystical. And yet it would be true to say that *all* values are ultimately mystical, and that therefore Lindsay was only striving to realise the fundamental possibilities of the novel in general. He fails for the same reason that Faulkner failed: because his work had to reflect the everyday world, and his real interest lay elsewhere. Yet in no other novelist is it possible to study the processes of creation so closely. Like all major artists, Lindsay rejects the world he is living in. (If they didn't, they wouldn't try to 'rebuild it nearer to the heart's desire' in their work.) His problem was to find a series of symbols—the 'objective correlative'—to express the world that *did* interest him. The clumsiness of his technique actually enables us to appreciate the skill and imaginative boldness with which he attacked the problems.

One thing emerges clearly from the study of Lindsay's work; fantasy is not another name for free-floating imagination. It is a highly disciplined faculty that uses imagination to explore ideas; and its laws are as rigorous as the laws of mathematics. But then, this is true of the novel in general; it applies to *Clarissa* as much as to *The Castle of Otranto*, to *Pride and Prejudice* as much as to Mary Shelley's *Frankenstein*. It was because the novel began to lose sight of this fundamental truth that it began to lose its range and flexibility.

Lindsay understood that purpose: the extension of the human faculties by means of thought-experiments. That is why, in spite of his technical shortcomings, he may be one day recognised as one of the most significant writers of the twentieth century.

TWELVE

Conclusions

IN THESE FINAL pages I intend to state some personal views and conclusions on the novel. But first of all, let me summarise the central ideas of this book.

The novel is an attempt to create a mirror, in which the novelist will be able to see his own face. It is fundamentally an attempt at self-creation. 'Describing reality' and 'telling the truth' are only secondary aims, the novelist's credentials—his authority for demanding the reader's attention. His real aim is to understand himself, to grasp his own purpose, and in doing so, to enable the reader to understand himself and grasp his own purpose. This is not to say that the novelist's aim is not *ultimately* 'truth'; but this truth can only be achieved through the clearer and clearer definition of the self-image.

This is to say that the purpose of art is not to hold a mirror up to Nature, but to your own face. And not your everyday face, but the 'face behind your face', your ultimate face.

Shakespeare also failed to specify what kind of mirror he had in mind. There are plane mirrors, which merely reflect what is placed in front of them, and are therefore little better than the average pair of eyes. There are convex mirrors, which will only show you your own face vastly distorted, like a bull-frog. They are admirable if you want to examine your wrinkles and the bags under your eyes. But they can hardly be called truthful.

Then there are convex mirrors, like certain driving mirrors. These have one enormous advantage: within their narrow confine, they can reflect a wide area of reality. They have a 'wide angle' of reflection. And the novelist's aim is to be a wide-angle mirror—or, if you prefer the photographic metaphor, a wide-angle lens.

The aim of this wide-angle lens, or mirror, is not simply to show the world more truthfully, but *to make the reader aware of his freedom.* Einstein points out that city dwellers go to the mountains at weekends because the broad vistas give them a sense of freedom. This is exactly what the novelist is attempting to do. For each one of us, freedom lies at the other end of a maze—like those puzzles in children's newspapers where you have to draw a continuous line through a labyrinth of corridors. Freedom is the same for all human beings, but the maze inside each of us is different. The novelist's aim is to reach the freedom at the end of his own maze.

As to the 'rules'—the tricks of style and structure and characterisation—these are something the writer picks up as he goes along, or learns from reading other people's novels. Basically there is only one rule: to avoid blind alleys. Most of the writers who have landed in blind alleys—from Flaubert to Beckett—have done so because they placed too much faith in artistic intuition, and too little in thought. What is important above all is for the writer to understand the basic aims and purposes and methods of the novel: not merely to understand what Richardson was trying to do and how he did it, or what Lawrence was trying to do and how he did it, but what aims and methods Richardson and Lawrence had in common. This is less complicated than it sounds; it merely depends on recognising the *basic* aim of Richardson and Lawrence: that is to say, the way in which each of them conceived his *freedom.* That notion of freedom dictates everything else in the novel.

Finally, the novel is not intended to be a self-contained and insulated world. It is essentially a thought-experiment, a kind of dummy-run for actual experience. If you wish to solve a complex sum, you use a sheet of paper and a pencil. If you wish to solve a complex personal problem, you could hardly do better than write a novel about it. For all the great novelists, writing was an aid to the digestion of experience. Or—to use another metaphor—a scientific instrument, like a microscope or a telescope—designed to increase the powers of our rather limited faculties. Ultimately, it would probably be true to say that the novel is about education, that its aim is education— of the writer as well as the reader.

In the course of this book, I have tried to restrict myself to the field of the novel and avoid general ideas. But the general ideas have occasionally risen fairly close to the surface, and in these final pages, I think they may be allowed to emerge.

In the final pages of *The Stranger*, Camus expressed his profoundest insight: Meursault's recognition that 'I had been happy, and I was happy still'. Everyone has experienced this sensation: a kind of glowing inner pressure, Proust's moment of 'ceasing to feel mediocre, accidental, mortal', Steppenwolf's sudden recognition of the existence of Mozart and the stars.

There is an element of paradox in this. If Meursault was really happy when he was staring dully out of the window, why didn't he realise he was happy? Is it possible to be happy without realising it? Clearly, yes. We are always looking back on some past time and suddenly thinking: 'That was a happy time . . .', although we were not particularly aware of it when it happened.

What happens is that these moments of intensity suddenly bring our happiness *into focus*, as a slight twist on the adjustment wheel of a pair of binoculars can make a scene stand out sharp and clear. Steppenwolf knew that Mozart and the stars existed before he drank the glass of wine; the wine made him *realise* it.

This leads to the interesting recognition that most of our values—the things we love—are hidden most of the time, as if in a mist. We all have at least several hundreds of reasons for happiness, beginning with being alive. We value our homes, our security, our families, our possessions; yet except in rare moments of sudden delight—what Maslow called peak experiences—these values remain below the threshold of consciousness. Even a thoroughly contented man only allows a tiny percentage of his values to emerge into consciousness. If you were to ask him why he is contented, he might give a dozen *personal* reasons, but he would never think of giving an impersonal reason: 'Because Mozart existed,' 'Because leaves in the rain look shiny.' Only if, in a moment of intense happiness, he happened to hear a few bars of Mozart or see a wet leaf in the rain would he suddenly realise that these are also among his 'values'.

In fact, poets and mystics *do* recognise that many 'impersonal' things are among their reasons for happiness: for example, Rupert Brooke devotes a long poem called 'The Great Lover' to listing dozens of them. And, oddly enough, novelists possess this capacity for making 'hidden values' flash into consciousness like shooting stars. We have already touched on this in discussing *Pamela*: that Richardson had discovered that ordinary people enjoy reading about ordinary people like themselves, because it heightens their perception of themselves, and for a moment they also cease to feel 'mediocre, accidental, mortal'. Merely by inducing a self-reflective process, the novel can produce a mild and continuous state of peak experience. This means that, in a sense, no subject is unsuitable for a novel. Even the total nihilism of Beckett's later novels might bring a glow of satisfaction to someone who feels that life is utterly futile.

But the central problem of human consciousness is connected with the 'robot', the mechanical part of us. As highly complex beings, we need to be able to do a great many things mechanically, from breathing to driving the car and talking foreign languages. In fact, our 'robot' does most difficult things far better than we can do them 'deliberately'. I typed very badly when I was learning to type; now my fingers do it automatically, and I only have to think about what I am actually going to say. If I tried to think about my fingers as I typed, I would do it badly again.

When I have finished my day's work, I shall switch on the television news, and pour myself a glass of wine; and after that, I shall listen to some music. All this will be a signal for my robot to go off duty, and allow 'the real me' to take over again. The wine will aid the relaxation. But if I have been working too hard—and I am an incorrigible, obsessional worker—I shall sit there in my armchair feeling vaguely dissatisfied, not really enjoying the music, wondering if there's something interesting on TV or whether I should be reading a book. . . . What has happened is that my robot is still on duty. He tends to take over when I am tired, just as a thermostat switches on the central heating system when the temperature sinks below a certain level. So although 'I' seem to be looking out of my eyes and listening with my ears, it is actually the robot who is doing most of the seeing and hearing. Sometimes, I can forget things that I did only a few minutes ago—wonder whether I closed up the garage or put away the lawn mower— because it was the robot that did them, not 'me'.

This robot can be extremely dangerous sometimes, for a reason I must briefly explain. When I do something with interest or pleasure, it has the effect of charging my vital batteries, just as a car's batteries are charged when you drive it. When I do things 'automatically', there is little or no charge or 'feedback'. If I get overworked, or into a state of depression, the robot takes over by means of the 'thermostatic control', and I may live for weeks or months, or even years, in a de-vitalised, mechanical state, never putting enough energy into anything to realise that this state is abnormal. If such a state is complicated by anxieties and fears, the result may be nervous breakdown or severe mental illness. In such cases, the robot is to blame—or rather, we are to blame for failing to realise that it is *we* who are supposed to be doing the living, not the robot. Beckett's characters have stumbled into this vicious circle: boredom leading to a sense of futility, futility leading to 'mechanical' living, which in turn leads to more boredom and futility. . . . One of his characters (in *Endgame*) complains that the world is becoming darker, and he has never seen it 'lit up'. But the peak experience is practically impossible for anyone who lives in a state of passive misery; the vital batteries remain permanently flat.

On the other hand, once we recognise that the intensity which which we 'see' the world depends completely on the amount of 'interest' we put into the perceptive process, we begin to gain a kind of precarious control over our own moods and peak experiences. I say precarious because self-conscious-ness is a fairly new stage in human evolution, and to begin with, we are likely to find this kind of control as awkward as walking a tightrope.

The philosopher Edmund Husserl made the basic discovery that all perception is 'intentional': that is, that when you look at something, you *throw* your attention at it, like a stone. If you stare at it passively, without this effort, you fail to notice it—like reading a page of a book when your mind is elsewhere, and being unable to remember what you have read. We *grasp* meaning, as the hand grasps an object. The important corollary is that if we wish to see *more* meaning, we have to tighten the grip, heighten the 'intentionality'. It is easy enough to see, for example, that boredom is 'intentional'; when some repetitious task presents itself, you often groan and *say*: 'How boring.' You accompany this with a movement of inner disgust, a feeling of rejection, of refusal to make an effort. If such a task *has* to be done quickly before you can get on to something more rewarding, you may 'hurl' yourself into it—and discover, to your surprise, that you have enjoyed it. Yet although everyone has experienced this, we fail to learn from it. The habit of thinking that certain things *are* 'boring' and that others *are* interesting is too deep-seated; the mind can only grasp for a few seconds the notion that boringness and interestingness are values that *we* confer upon an object; then we slip back instantaneously into the old 'passive fallacy'.

And what has this to do with the novel? A great deal. Compare *Robinson Crusoe* with *Clarissa*, and you see that what Richardson has brought to the novel is increased 'intentionality'. Defoe is obviously absorbed in what he is writing, and he goes into considerable detail; but there is an over-all feeling of objectivity, as if he is telling you something that someone told *him*. Richardson brings a minute, obsessive interest to everything he describes, and although it sounds realistic enough, we are aware that this is a world of his own creating. It is already halfway to the fantasy world of Gormenghast or Arcturus. The writer has ceased to be a reporter or entertainer, and become a kind of god or demiurge. The romantics quickly realised that this obsessive quality was peculiar to the novel— the power to put life under a magnifying glass, as it were. But, as we have already seen, they were undone by romantic gloom and defeatism. In masterpiece after masterpiece, from Balzac to Knut Hamsun, we have the same formula: the novelist's own reality, brilliantly and carefully rendered; and then, in the final pages, the defeat and death of the hero, with whose fortunes the reader has been identifying so closely. There was actually something paradoxical and self-contradictory about the whole formula. Swept along by the power of the writing, the reader finds himself lost in admiration for the creative vitality of the human imagination, its capacity to transcend reality. And at the end, he discovers that the novelist is asking him to pity man for his helplessness. Bernard Shaw noted the same paradox about Wagner's music: that its surging power seemed a tremendous life-affirmation, yet that most of the operas end tragically.

It was this inherent self-contradiction that caused the decline of the novel. I am not suggesting that tragedy is somehow invalid, or that a happy ending is inherently preferable to a tragic one. An *Oedipus* or *Lear* with everyone living happily ever after would obviously be an anomaly. The fact remains that in many of the great nineteenth-century novels—perhaps the majority of them—the tragedy was simply a convenient way of rounding off the story, and side-stepping the fundamental questions raised by it. Balzac's *Lost Illusions*, Stendhal's *Red and the Black* and Flaubert's *Bovary* have one thing in common: they are all about young people 'fronting life', longing for more freedom than they possess. We know that Stendhal and Flaubert started with the intention of killing off Julien Sorel and Emma Bovary, because they based their novels on real incidents. Yet we may still be left with the feeling that they have failed to explore the possibilities of the subject. They have gained the reader's interest by asking: 'What *could* such a person do in this situation?', which implies: 'What is the ideal solution of the problem?' Then, instead of offering this solution, they merely tell us what actually happened: that Emma got depressed and committed suicide, that Julien tried to murder his mistress and was executed. It is as if a mathematician posed an interesting problem, then ended by offering the wrong answer—admitting that it *is* wrong, but explaining that he doesn't know the right one.

It is true that in the case of famous novels, the plot seems inevitable because we know it so well. A less well-known work may illustrate the point more clearly. George Simenon's *The Hatter's Ghosts* is about a man who has murdered his nagging wife—an invalid who never receives visitors—before he realises that, on her birthday, all her former classmates come to visit her. If he is to remain undetected, he has to murder all the classmates before the next reunion. And so the town has an epidemic of murders of old women. The murderer even carries on a correspondence with a local newspaper; a journalist has described the killer as a madman, and he writes to explain that, on the contrary, he kills out of necessity. These letters are composed of words carefully clipped from newspapers, and glued to a sheet of paper.

The novel opens superbly. The murderer (a hatter) and his neighbour, a little tailor, always go to the same café for a drink at the end of the day; they always nod but never speak, for the tailor is the hatter's social inferior. One day, the tailor sees something white on the hatter's trousers, and politely picks it off—then realises that it is a fragment of newspaper, clipped with scissors. With horrified incredulity, he realises that his respectable neighbour is the murderer. . . .

From this point on, the reader is absorbed; for, odd as it sounds, he 'identifies' with the hatter. It may seem strange that readers should feel sympathy for a killer of old women. Yet this is the essence of the novel: the 'thought-experiment'. And Simenon is here exploring the most basic of all problems: the problem of freedom. The hatter has killed his nagging wife; now he realises that seven old women still stand between himself and freedom. We wonder: will he succeed? And what will he *do* if he succeeds? This question is the real challenge to the novelist's imagination. And Simenon evades it. The maid-servant discovers that the hatter's wife is no longer in her bedroom; he is forced to kill her too. Then, for no apparent reason, he kills his mistress, and makes no resistance when the police come to arrest him.

During the time when he is killing the old women, the hatter has a strange feeling of invulnerability, the confidence of a sleepwalker. At one point, he reflects that he has never been so happy, except in the Air Force, when he also did 'what had to be done'. Simenon is touching on a problem we have discussed in the chapter on Ideas: the moments of intensity when a man does 'the one thing, the only thing for a man to do, easily and naturally. . . .' But he fails in the novelist's central task: to develop its *implications*. Instead, there is the mechanical ending, which 'completes' the story, but which leaves the essence of the novel undeveloped, almost untouched. It could be labelled 'the cop-out'.

Simenon was merely following the example of far greater forerunners. Even Richardson cannot be absolved of succumbing to the temptation of the 'cop-out'. Clarissa's death is not really the inevitable consequence of her seduction; in fact, it is downright improbable that a healthy girl would die of 'shame'. Because of its power, *Clarissa* is a borderline case; but this is not true of dozens of other 'tragic' novels, from *La Nouvelle Héloise* to *A Glastonbury Romance*. (In the latter, the final catastrophe—the flood—and the death of Geard seem to be almost arbitrary.) One critic accused Bernard Shaw of cowardice because he concluded *Pygmalion* without marrying off Eliza Doolittle to Higgins. In fact, Shaw showed artistic courage in refusing to distort his sense of reality for a tidy ending. He realised that, in real life, Higgins would never fall in love with Eliza, and preferred to leave the last act of the play 'open'— that is, unfinished. He recognised that life goes on, and that 'artistic truth' would best be served by admitting this. In the same way, Dostoevsky left 'open' the ends of his two greatest novels, *Crime and Punishment* and *The Brothers Karamazov*, because these novels are about men with an appetite for freedom, and he recognised the illogicality of killing them off.

The truth is that we all know about meaninglessness and 'contingency' and defeat and tragedy, because they are a part of everyday life. Art is an attempt to focus a pair of binoculars on a distant meaning, on a flash of absurd freedom. Sir Julian Huxley has pointed out the enormous role played by art in the

evolution of mankind. When man discovered art he also discovered that he was, in some paradoxical sense, a god. He was
not merely a creature of circumstance, a victim of everyday
events; he could create, and the part of his being that was involved in the act of creation was somehow higher than the part
that went hunting or tilled the earth. Creation allowed him to
withdraw from everyday life. It seems probable that animals
experience such moments of intensity only in sexual fulfilment.
Man learned to experience them in many other ways: through
religious ritual and dancing, by the imbibing of certain plants
(like *peyotl*) and fermented liquids. All animals strive for comfort and security; *man became the first who strove for these flashes of
intensity*. He achieved them in war and destruction, but also
in invention and creation. This urge for *more* than security,
for some ecstasy of achievement, has driven him up the evolutionary ladder faster than any other living creature on earth.
He has progressed further in ten thousand years than the horse
in ten million. And his most spectacular advances have been
in the past few hundred years—since the desire for the achievement of mental intensity became conscious. His painting, his
music, his literature, became directly concerned with producing
strong emotions, heightening his consciousness. The paintings
of Michelangelo and Leonardo display this new self-conscious-
ness, so do the plays of the Elizabethans and the music of
Monteverdi and Bach. For the Elizabethans, tragedy was one
of the most effective ways of creating an emotional impact, and
we still experience a tingling of the scalp as we hear:

> . . . Goodnight, sweet prince
> And flights of angels sing thee to thy rest.

Shakespeare was already enlarging the scope of the play beyond
the Greek unities of space and time, because he wanted to
include more of life. The novel was the logical next step. *Don
Quixote* and *Gil Blas* present a whole country, a whole epoch, as
if seen from a mountain-top with a telescope. Then came
Richardson, with his microscope, revealing that everyday life,
when examined in detail, is more fascinating than any mere

tale of adventure. The human spirit had taken one of its most decisive steps since the discovery of art. Suddenly, art began to aim consciously at new states of intensity of consciousness. Romantic poets, novelists, musicians and painters strove to capture the moments of ecstasy, the absurd moments when man sees life as if from a great distance above it.

But romanticism was a hothouse plant; it grew too quickly and exhausted itself. As it outstripped its means of expression, it began to cultivate neurosis as a new mode of intensity. Balzac led to Flaubert and Dostoevsky, and eventually to Joyce and Beckett. Berlioz and Wagner led to Mahler and Schoenberg, and eventually to Boulez, Stockhausen, and a dozen other composers whose idiom is incomprehensible to the concert-going public. Delacroix and Turner led to the Impressionists, then to Picasso, Mondrian, Kandinsky. . . . In each case, we can trace the same curve of development: the desire for intensity at any cost builds up towards neurosis, then recognising the dead end, tries to retreat towards abstraction, in an attempt to regain control and sanity.

We are now in a position to see that romanticism did not *have* to collapse. It brought about its own collapse by assuming that the only road to intensity led through hysteria. This swelled out of control, and led to disintegration. In the three-quarters of a century since Max Nordau's *Degeneration*, all the trends he examined have reached their limit. At the moment, there is pause for stocktaking—not only in art, but also in science and philosophy.

If I write a book too quickly, the worst consequences show themselves in the last pages, which look hasty and illogical. In that case I have to re-trace my steps to the point where it began to go wrong—sometimes the beginning—and re-work it from there. In effect, the novel has been an over-hastily written book. It took the wrong turn almost immediately, into a facile pessimism, which soon led to what we might call the First Romantic Collapse (Schiller, Novalis, Hoffmann, Byron, Coleridge, Shelley, etc.). After a decade or so it tried a new direction, into realism. For reasons we have already explained, this was even more of a wrong turn, for it abandoned romantic idealism without abandoning its pessimism. With a few rare exceptions, the post-Joycian novelists decided to return to the old ways, and wait and see what happened. And so most of the best-known names of the post-war era have been traditionalists who write as if Joyce, Kafka, Gertrude Stein and Hemingway had never existed. If there *is* to be a 'new direction', no one so far seems to have found it.

At this point, it may be relevant to say something of my own personal approach to the problems of novel writing.

I began my first novel when I was eighteen, in 1949; it was published—as *Ritual in the Dark*—just over ten years later.

Most writers learn more from their first novel than any other, and I was no exception. At that time, *Ulysses* was my bible. When I went into the RAF that year, I had with me Thomas Mann's newly published *Doktor Faustus*, Hemingway's *The Sun Also Rises*, and *Finnegan's Wake*; for some years, together with *Ulysses*, these remained the major influences on my approach to the novel. Hemingway fascinated me because of the economy of means; Mann because he had produced the only great novel of ideas since the war. As to Joyce, it was clear that he recognised that the way forward had to be through ideas—reversing the position of *Ulysses*—and that *Finnegan's Wake* was an attempt to create some ultimate unity of ideas and *existenz*. It still seemed to me possible that the novel might evolve a totally original language, and evolve into a new form allied to music. I persevered for a dozen or so pages with a 'novel' in a purely impressionistic language—based on in-tuition—before it struck me that it was not *saying* anything in particular.

I was fairly clear about what I wanted to say. It seemed to me that the main trouble with modern civilisation was that it was full of fools and sleepwalkers. I agreed with Eliot that what was needed was a return to religious values, and I spent a great deal of time wandering around churches and cathedrals, and reading Christian mystics. The problem was to try and shake people into wakefulness. The kind of novel that floated at the back of my mind was a cross between *Crime and Punish-*

ment and *The Waste Land*, and I suppose that if I had been asked to define my ambition, I would have said: 'To be an English Dostoevsky.' I wandered around London in a permanent state of rage at the 'false values' that stared out of every newspaper placard and advertisement. The kind of novel I had in mind would be a series of confrontations of false values with the brutal reality—as in Isherwood's Reichstag trial scene in *Prater Violet*. The story was to concern a Jack the Ripper-type murderer—that struck me as having the necessary shock value —taking place against the background of the 'unreal city', city of dreams and crimes.

By 1952, after three years of struggling with this novel, it was still a series of fragments. I tried to impose a certain unity by basing it upon the structure of the Egyptian *Book of the Dead*, as Joyce had used the *Odyssey* in *Ulysses*, but it struck me as arbitrary and unsatisfying. One day, I spent several hours in the Reading Room of the British Museum, brooding on what I wanted to say. What emerged were several themes, all closely linked. First, and most central, there was the problem of 'outsiders' in modern civilisation, the romantics and visionary idealists who feel completely out of place: Nietzsche, Van Gogh, T. E. Lawrence. It seemed clear that modern civilisation, with its mechanised rigidity, is producing more outsiders than ever before—people who are too intelligent to do some repetitive job, but not intelligent enough to make their own terms with society. The second major theme was sexual: the fact that our society offers more sexual stimulation than at any time in history, and that most healthy young men spend their days in a permanent state of sexual desire. But in fact, the goods are behind a sheet of plate glass. No one could live his sex-life 'all the way up' except an Eastern potentate with a harem. The hero of Barbusse's *Hell* says: 'It is not a woman I want; it is *all* women.' An American judge, sentencing a rape-murderer to death, remarked that Nature has endowed man with a sexual urge out of all proportion to its biological usefulness. It seems that society rashly stimulates an urge—for commercial reasons—that can only lead to a rise in the rate of sex crime.

The third major theme was the decline of religion and the

rise of rationalistic materialism. My chief *bête noir* was Bertrand Russell.

All these themes were pulling in different directions, fragmenting the novel. The problem was to find a plot that would unite them. Once I understood this, things began to fall into place. The hero could not be the murderer, as in earlier versions; he had to be the Jamesian observer. This meant the murderer had to be the second major character, an 'outsider' whose frustrations would express themselves in physical violence—like the dancer Nijinsky. There had to be a close relation between the hero and the murderer. The hero, himself 'highly sexed', is preoccupied with the paradox of the sexual impulse, so that when he begins to wonder whether his friend is a sexual killer, he tends to be sympathetic, wondering whether he himself would not do the same if he had more courage.

The next problem was to find 'objective correlatives' for some of these ideas. I was particularly pleased with an episode in which the hero—Gerard Sorme—has been making love to his girlfriend all afternoon, and feels sexually drained. He goes to the door of his basement flat to bring in a bottle of milk, and catches a glimpse up the skirt of a girl who is walking past; instantly, he again experiences violent desire. The sexual impulse goes deeper than any 'normal' satisfaction. I also had in the novel a painter (based loosely on Van Gogh) who is obsessed by a ten-year-old girl who models for him; the desire is partly sexual, but he is horrified at the thought of a sexual relationship. Again, it caught this element of paradox, of 'cross purposes', inherent in sexual desire.

One day, discussing the novel with a friend, I found myself explaining that the hero, the murderer and the painter were the three basic types of Outsider. The hero has intellectual discipline, but lacks discipline of the body and emotions. The painter has emotional discipline—but not of the body or intellect. The murderer has physical discipline, but not of the intellect or emotions. And all, like Nietzsche, Van Gogh, Nijinsky, are in danger of mental breakdown. . . .

Towards Christmas of 1954, spending the season alone in a room in New Cross, it struck me that the novel had far too much intellectual ballast—too many symbols and cross-references in the manner of *The Waste Land*. It suddenly struck me that it would be sensible to throw them all out, and write *another* book about them. I sketched out *The Outsider* on a few pages of my journal, and began to write it as soon as the British Museum opened after Christmas. A few months later, I sent a few pages to a publisher, Victor Gollancz. To my amazement, he replied within a few days, saying he was interested, and would probably like to publish the book. It appeared a year later, a few weeks before my twenty-fifth birthday, and achieved an immediate success that left me dazed. (It left the publisher dazed too; the first edition sold out within a couple of days, and it was some weeks before the second reached the shops.)

I returned to the writing of *Ritual in the Dark*—working at the same time to a sequel to *The Outsider*, on religious mysticism. I discovered that an interesting thing had happened. A great deal of the original violence had evaporated. Dr Johnson once said he had always wanted to be a philosopher, but cheerfulness kept breaking in. I found the same with *Ritual*. Gollancz had turned down an earlier version on the grounds that it was too depressing and nauseating. Now, after so many re-writings (the various manuscripts add up to well over a million words), I was becoming preoccupied with the expression of ideas rather than emotions. I began a new version in Hamburg in the winter of 1957, and finished it two years later. The chief problem in this final version was the ending. The hero's progress is internal—it is basically a *bildungsroman*—so it is difficult to *state* precisely what he has gained. I tried to end the book with a kind of mystical experience. Gollancz sensibly told me to throw away the last ten pages, which were out of key with the rest; he himself chose an arbitrary point to end the book. I realise he was right. Ever since then I have made a practice of concluding a novel whenever it seemed natural, without bothering too much about loose ends.

Ritual in the Dark had been closely connected to *The Outsider*, and I now found it natural to write a novel and a 'philosophical book' at about the same time. Ideas tended to shape themselves into characters and events. *Origins of the Sexual Impulse* was followed immediately by the novel *The Man Without a Shadow* (called in America *The Sex Diary of Gerard Sorme*). *The Mind Parasites* sprang from a paragraph in *Introduction to the New Existentialism*. *Beyond the Outsider* led me to an attempt at a reworking of the basic themes of *Ritual*, in an attempt to create a clearer contrast between the psychology of the criminal and the mystic; this appeared as *The Glass Cage*.

In retrospect, it seems that my most important decision as a novelist was to turn *Ritual* into a *roman policier*. I was consciously following the example of Dostoevsky and Graham Greene. (I admired Greene theoretically, but found his pessimism unbearable.) It seemed clear to me that the novel, like the drama, is intended to be entertainment. Provided it can hold an audience, purely as entertainment, the writer is at liberty to fill it with his obsessions. But if the obsessions come to outweigh the entertainment, he has no right to demand an audience on the grounds that he is a 'serious artist'. In so far as he ceases to be a good entertainer, he also ceases to be a serious artist. An artist's seriousness is not gauged simply by his capacity for strong feeling, but also by the depth of his interest in the objective world, and the attempt to reflect this in his work. A novel that is pure fact and observation may be absorbing, even if it could never be a masterpiece; a novel that is pure subjective feeling will almost certainly be unreadable.

My second novel, *Adrift in Soho*, was intended to be an English 'beat' novel. But I found that formlessness did not come naturally to me; after a couple of hundred pages, I could not see how to continue. Again, Victor Gollancz solved the problem by telling me not to bother, and printing it as it stood. No one has ever complained that it lacks an ending, so he was obviously right. The third novel was to be about commitment; the hero was a mathematician who finds himself torn between the pure world of abstraction and the violent world of social reality. I have always regarded it as one of my best books; but I think that the uncompromising 'intellectualism' of the theme may explain why it was largely ignored. It served to remind me that a novel should have some other aim besides exploring the writer's own ideas and convictions. For example, science-fiction and fantasy are intended to produce wonder or amaze-ment ('astounding stories', etc.). The detective story and the spy story aim at suspense. The adventure story aims at excite-ment. Pornography aims at sexual stimulation. And so on. These may not be their author's primary aim; but they are his excuse for demanding the reader's attention.

This is not to say that the reader should be regarded as an idiot, whose pills have to be carefully disguised to look like candy. The 'entertainment value' of a work is a *convention* between the reader and the writer, designed to establish a relation and a state of mind—as the words 'Once upon a time . . .' cause a child to curl up and put his thumb in his mouth. Ian Fleming turned the James Bond novels into a kind of charade, full of deliberate absurdities, without losing the reader's attention. And it was the Italian Commedia dell'Arte that first recognised the 'Once upon a time' principle with respect to the drama. John Gay utilised it at the end of *The Beggar's Opera* where, as Macheath is about to be hanged, the 'storyteller' intervenes and demands a happy ending; so Macheath is granted a last-minute pardon.

In the early 1920s the dramatist, Bertold Brecht, found him-self encountering problems that were in many ways similar to those of the post-war novel. Naturalism had reached the theatre somewhat later than it reached the novel; its great pioneer was Henrik Ibsen, who played roughly the same role in the drama that Flaubert had played in the novel. When Ibsen came along, the nineteenth-century drama had de-generated into melodrama, spectacle and farce. In the late 1870s, Ibsen began writing his series of social dramas dealing with real-life problems—social hypocrisy, illegitimacy, even syphilis. He was denounced as a muck-raker, but most of the younger dramatists responded with enthusiasm to this new seriousness. Strindberg, Hauptmann, Sudermann, Brieux, Granville-Barker, Bernard Shaw, Chekhov, all brought a new social realism into the theatre. But anyone who is familiar with Ibsen will be aware that most of his dramas seem unnecessarily gloomy; his characters are prone to commit suicide without sufficient provocation. The reason is obvious enough. In order to demonstrate the appalling consequences of the evils he was denouncing it was necessary to show them leading to disaster. (The famous temperance plays of the same period have a similar tendency; the drunkard dies of delirium tremens, and his family go into the workhouse in the snow.) Most of the great social dramas that were written after Ibsen—Tolstoy's *Power of Darkness*, Strindberg's *The Father*, Gorky's *The Lower Depths*, Hauptmann's *The Weavers*, Sudermann's *Sodom's End*—stick to the familiar ingredients: murder, suicide, violence, incest, infanticide and insanity. In its attempt at naturalism, the drama was ceasing to be entertainment, and becoming something more like a hellfire sermon.

Brecht was a socialist revolutionary; he *wanted* to use the drama for propaganda purposes; but he recognised that social-drama is a singularly dull and inflexible vehicle. His early plays attempt to escape from the straitjacket by utilising elements of 'expressionism'—a kind of dream-technique developed by Strindberg and Wedekind—but it was not until he started to adapt Gay's *Beggar's Opera* (as *The Threepenny Opera*) that he saw the logical solution. The drama had to stop these clumsy attempts at absolute realism, and admit that it was *not* real. It had to become a kind of pantomime. Gay had stumbled on the 'alienation effect'. (Bernard Shaw re-discovered it in *Androcles and the Lion*, where the action alternates between serious social drama and pantomime farce.) Now Brecht erected it into a dramatic principle. The audience is told: 'This is a play, an entertainment. It is not supposed to be real.' After that, the author can do what he likes: introduce songs or dances, acrobatics, political lectures, even fragments of documentary film. By establishing a complicity between himself and the audience, he achieves a flexibility that would be impossible for a naturalistic dramatist.

After I had written *Necessary Doubt* and *The Glass Cage* (both detective stories), *The Mind Parasites* (science-fiction) and *The Black Room* (a spy story), it struck me that I was instinctively making use of Brecht's alienation principle, and that it worked as well for the novel as for the drama. And the number of possible 'forms' was still immense. (We could list, for example, the adventure story, the war story, the love story, the horror story, the ghost story, the sporting story, the western, the picaresque novel, the historical novel, the comic novel—and probably a dozen more. One of my books—*The God of the Labyrinth*—even experiments with the conventions of the pornographic novel.)

I am *not* suggesting that the future of the novel lies in parody. Serious novels have been written in most of the forms listed above—including the western. But the problem is that the novel has become bogged-down in its own seriousness. The solution is not to become more 'serious' (i.e. neurotic and obscure), but simply to recognise that serious intentions and a certain casual looseness of form are not incompatible. Once the writer has signalled to the reader that he is about to tell a spy story or a science-fiction story, he is free to be as serious as he likes within that convention. The form is as flimsy as a soap bubble or a dream; but provided he takes care not to break it, he has remarkable freedom of movement.

Besides, it is hardly a question of parody. When Joyce was a third of the way through *Ulysses*, he recognised that a whole book written with 'photographic realism' would be as dull as a whole house painted in grey. The narrow-angle lens was becoming monotonous. It was all 'near', with no 'far'. He solved the problem by introducing parodies of other styles. By the end of *Ulysses*, he had recognised that the problem is to be universal as well as particular, and *Finnegan's Wake* is an attempt to be as universal as possible, even at the expense of becoming unreadable. It could be described as an attempt to combine the conventions of every type of novel that exists. Parody had turned into mythic fantasy.

Since then, many novelists have attempted to achieve the 'wide-angle' effect by similar means. We have already observed how Mervyn Peake and J. R. R. Tolkien used the form of the children's story to write novels for adults. In *The Tin Drum*, Gunther Grass parodied the Rabelaisian epic. Robbe-Grillet, France's leading exponent of experimentalism, has parodied the detective story and the thriller. William

Burroughs has parodied science-fiction. The American John Barth has parodied the picaresque novel. In *The French Lieutenant's Woman*, John Fowles parodied the Victorian novel. But in all these cases, the aim went beyond parody; it was an attempt to move away from the particular towards the universal. The *aim* had been instinctively recognised, but not necessarily its implications for the novel as a whole.

In the early 1930s, at about the same time that Yeats was writing his lines about the 'Shakespearian fish', H. G. Wells had begun to write his *Experiment in Autobiography*. On the third page, he has an image that is strikingly similar to Yeats's. 'We are like early amphibians, so to speak, struggling out of the waters that have hitherto covered our kind, into the air, seeking to breathe in a new fashion and emancipate ourselves from long accepted and long unquestioned necessities.' Wells argues that human life has always been driven by physical necessity: the struggle for food, security, sexual fulfilment. And now, at last, an increasing number of human beings experience another compulsion—to creative activity: to what Wells called 'my distinctive business in the world'. The old struggle for the basic necessities of life becomes increasingly boring for such people, for they want to spend more time in the realm of the imagination, exploring history, philosophy, the laws of consciousness. 'At last it has become for us a case of air or nothing. But the new land has not yet definitely emerged from the waters and we swim distressfully in an element we wish to abandon.' Worst still, this new realm of the mind is more fatiguing than the sea—which at least sustained us. We twist and turn miserably on the sand, labouring to breathe, and striving to grow legs.

And that has become the central necessity: to grow legs, or at least, to become relatively mobile on the sand. I have tried to show that it was the novel that produced in European man that new compulsion to 'creative activity', the desire for 'air or nothing'. He learned that the world of imagination could offer a freedom whose existence he had never suspected. The romantics dreamed that one day man would become a god. Then came the great disillusionment. In effect the dreamers discovered that the land is a far more exhausting medium than the sea. It will not support the weight as the water does. The new sense of freedom turned into bewilderment, fear, suicidal pessimism. The age of romanticism became the age of defeat. And the defeated-intelligent man became the new hero. The implication was that if you wanted to survive in the everyday world, your best chance was to be stupid and ruthless. *The Outsider* dealt with this paradox: that although so far intelligence has been man's chief instrument of survival, a point has come where the intelligent man no longer feels 'at home' in everyday life; he feels he is looking at it from outside, like a Martian peering at the earth through a telescope.

Yet the chief feature of an amphibian is that it is equally at home in the sea *or* on land. Yeats assumed that the strand was the worst possible place for his Shakespearian fish. Wells recognised that the land is not a trap, but the inevitable next step in our evolution. Man must finally learn to become an inhabitant of both worlds. It is possible that the novel may never again play such an important part in human development as it played two centuries ago. Yet there is no reason why it shouldn't. All that is necessary is that the novelist should recognise his true purpose: not merely to reflect the 'immense panorama of futility and anarchy which is contemporary history', but to liberate the human imagination and to give man a glimpse of what he *could* become. He must learn to understand what Shaw meant when he said that a work of art is a magic mirror in which man is able to see his own soul. And when he has grasped that, he will discover that his magic mirror has an even more useful function: to reveal the future direction of human evolution.

BIBLIOGRAPHY

Allen, Walter, *The English Novel*, Penguin Books, London 1958

Berlin, Isaiah, *The Hedgehog and the Fox*, A Mentor Book published by The New American Library, N.Y. 1957

Braine, John, *Writing a Novel*, Eyre Methuen, London 1974

Brebner, John A., *The Demon Within*, Macdonald, London 1973

Burgess, Anthony, *Re Joyce*, Ballantine Books, New York 1966

Cecil, David, *Early Victorian Novelists*, Penguin Books, London 1948

Eaves, T. C. Duncan and Kimpel, Ben D., *Samuel Richardson*, Clarendon Press, Oxford 1971

Forster, E. M., *Aspects of the Novel*, Edward Arnold & Co., London 1945

Grossman, Leonid, *Dostoevsky*, Allen Lane, London 1974

Hoggart, Richard, *The Uses of Literacy*, Penguin Books, London 1958

James, Henry, *The Future of the Novel*, edited by Leon Edel, Vintage Books, New York 1956

James, Henry, *The Art of the Novel*, Charles Scribner's Sons, New York 1934

Kettle, Arnold, *An Introduction to the English Novel*, Volumes 1 & 2, Hutchinson & Co. Ltd., London 1951

Knight, G. Wilson, *The Saturnian Quest*, Methuen & Co. Ltd., London 1964

Kronenberger, Louis (editor), *Novelists on Novelists*, Doubleday & Co., New York 1962

Leavis, F. R., *The Great Tradition*, Penguin Books; first published by Chatto and Windus Ltd., London 1948

Levin, Harry, *James Joyce*, New Directions, New York 1960

Lubbock, Percy, *The Craft of Fiction*, Jonathan Cape, London 1926

Lukacs, Georg, *The Historical Novel*, Penguin Books, London 1962

Martin, Jay, *Nathaniel West: The Art of his Life*, Secker & Warburg, London 1971

Matthiessen, F. O. and Murdock, Kenneth B. (editors), *The Notebooks of Henry James*, Oxford University Press, New York 1961

McBurney, William H. (editor), *Four Before Richardson*, University of Nebraska Press 1963

Montague, C. E., *A Writer's Notes on His Trade*, Phoenix Library, London 1931

Muir, Edwin, *The Structure of the Novel*, The Hogarth Press, London 1967

Praz, Mario, *The Romantic Agony*, Oxford University Press, London 1933

Priestley, J. B., *Literature and Western Man*, Heinemann, London 1960

Pritchett, V. S., *The Living Novel*, London 1946

Putt, S. Gorley, *Scholars of the Heart*, Faber and Faber, London 1962

Savage, D. S., *The Withered Branch*, Eyre & Spottiswoode, London 1950

Schenk, H. G., *The Mind of the European Romantics*, Constable, London 1966

Scholes, Robert and Kain, Richard M. (editors), *The Workshop of Daedalus*, Northwestern University Press, Illinois 1965

Starkie, Enid, *Flaubert*, Penguin Books, London 1971

Trilling, Lionel, *The Opposing Self*, The Viking Press, New York 1955

Turnell, Martin, *The Novel in France*, Penguin Books, London 1958

Watt, Ian, *The Rise of the Novel*, Penguin Books, London 1957

Wellek, Rene and Warren, Austin, *Theory of Literature*, Penguin Books; first published in Great Britain by Jonathan Cape, London 1949

Wilson, Edmund, *A Window on Russia*, Macmillan, London 1973

Wilson, Edmund, *Axel's Castle*, Charles Scribner's Sons, New York 1931

Wilson, Edmund, *Classics and Commercials*, Vintage Books, New York 1962

Wright, Andrew H., *Jane Austen's Novels*, Penguin Books; first published by Chatto & Windus, London 1953

INDEX